To: Sue

a new project,
A new era,
new prosperity

DATE DUE	3/18
	PRINTED IN U.S.A.

california
MOSAIC

a cookbook celebrating cultures and cuisine

california
MOSAIC

a cookbook celebrating cultures and cuisine

The Junior League of Pasadena, Inc.

california MOSAIC

a cookbook celebrating cultures and cuisines

Published by The Junior League of Pasadena, Inc.
149 South Madison Avenue
Pasadena, California 91101
626.796.0244
www.jrleaguepasadena.org
email: JLPI@earthlink.net

Library of Congress Control Number: 2007922575
ISBN: 978-0-9632089-5-8

Edited, Designed, and Manufactured by
Favorite Recipes® Press
An imprint of

FRP®

P.O. Box 305142
Nashville, Tennessee 37230
800.358.0560

Art Director: Steve Newman
Book Design: Starletta Polster
Project Manager and Editor: Debbie Van Mol

Manufactured in China
First Printing 2008   20,000 copies

mission

The Junior League of Pasadena, Inc., is an organization of

women committed to promoting voluntarism, developing

the potential of women, and improving communities

through the effective action and leadership of trained

volunteers. Its purpose is exclusively educational

and charitable. The mission of The Junior League of Pasadena, Inc.,

is to nurture children through family support.

Since 1926, volunteers have contributed thousands upon

thousands of hours and raised millions of dollars for

community projects that support the arts, education, health,

parenting, children's welfare, and most recently, the issues

faced by middle-school-aged girls. One hundred percent

of the net proceeds from the sale of cookbooks support

unique programs for families and children in the community.

introduction

California Mosaic is a celebration of the many pieces that make up the mosaic of life in California. If the United States is considered the melting pot of the world, then California with its many different cultures must certainly be considered the roux—the base which binds this diversity that influences our life and cuisine. Food is an integral part of this mosaic, not only because it is required for one to live, but because food brings people together and is an important part of our life. It can be a source of comfort, familiarity, and cultural heritage, or it can be a means of expression, individuality, and creativity. California, particularly southern California, has one of the most culturally diverse populations in the world, and because of this we have great exposure to the different foods of the world. With the Pacific Ocean as a border, agriculture as our dominant industry, and our diverse terrain and climate that allows an enormous variety of plants to be grown in our state, Californians have access to almost every type of food imaginable. However, to truly understand our mosaic, one needs to understand how incredibly unique California is, not only culturally but also geographically and economically as well, and it is because of this diversity that our mosaic has developed its own unique flair.

California Mosaic uses beautiful mosaic artworks at the opening of each chapter to illustrate the beauty and color of this area, and it explores our uniqueness in sidebars and chapter openings. California has a wild and oftentimes dramatic history that has seen great periods of population explosion and economic growth. *California Mosaic* shows how this history and the many different cultures that have settled here continue to impact our world with a variety of festivals, museums, and traditions. It is the people, with their bright and vivid colors, that have contributed to this masterpiece of cultural exchange that remains unique in the world. However, California's diverse geography and rare Mediterranean climate, where the majority of rainfall occurs in winter followed by hot, dry summers, also contribute greatly to our mosaic, making our state ideal for both recreation and industry, particularly agriculture.

Just as a recipe is a mosaic of ingredients, a meal is a mosaic of recipes; a dinner is a mosaic of the meal, the decorations, the ambience, and the people. However, the mosaic image can be expanded to describe a life whose varied elements include everyday routines and special occasions; work and play; individuals and families; diverse cultures and communities in regions that are themselves mosaics of geography. The combinations are endless, and few places in the world have as magnificent a mosaic as California.

contents

vegetables & side dishes
142

desserts
164

party menus
204

california MOSAIC

Clockwise from left to right: Shrimp Cakes with Grilled Pineapple Salsa (page 32), Greek Salsa with Toasted Pita Wedges (page 19), Slow-Roasted Tomatoes with Chèvre and Arugula (page 27)

appetizers

Untitled
Millard Sheets, 1970
(Families enjoying recreational activities at a local beach)

California Surf Culture and Beaches

With one thousand miles of coastline available for recreation, Californians haven't simply settled in to watch the sunset. On the contrary, our beaches are a haven for whale watchers, people watchers, sun worshippers, families, artists, campers, athletes, and California's icon sport—surfing! Yes, we can hang ten as well as hang out with the best that the sport has to offer. Surfing emerged in Southern California as early as 1910, when H. E. Huntington, then Mayor of Huntington Beach, hired an experienced Hawaiian surfer to demonstrate this ancient Polynesian sport on the beach of his fair city. But it wasn't until the 1950s and 1960s, through the exposure of the *Beach Party* movies and beach music, that surfing ripped and curled its way to the popularity that continues to swell today. Even if you don't surf, the surf and beach culture of California has infiltrated other areas of daily life, from clothing styles, to hairstyles, home décor, and music. Surfing is an intensely exciting sport that requires a great deal of practice and athleticism. However, no formal training is required, and all who wish to try it need do nothing more than practice. California hosts a large number of surfing competitions, drawing some of the best surfers from around the world. Whether you live in Southern California or surf the icy waters of Northern California, surfing has become as much a part of our culture as convertible cars. A spin-off of surfing, called kite surfing, is gaining popularity and puts a whole new twist on riding a board. Simply add a kite, some wind, a few good swells, and hold on tight for an aerobic thrill like no other.

California beaches offer almost every kind of activity, which appeal to a variety of interests. For the artist, photographer, or rock climber, there are jagged, windblown cliffs overlooking the vast and endless Pacific Ocean with views to the west of our island jewels. Tide pools in secluded coves, as well as miles of endless sand, entice the shell seeker, pedestrian, or runner. A network of biking paths, volleyball nets, restaurants, and boutiques dots the eclectic and unique beach cities to the South, and the majestic rise of redwood and pine forests feather the coastal cities to the North. Surfside campsites accommodating everything from basic tents, RVs, and permanent cabins allow the visitor to not only play in the waves but also enjoy on foot, bike, or horseback the myriad mountain trails adjacent to the coast. No matter where, North, Central, or South, the draw of the Pacific is one of the treasures that almost no one misses on a visit to our state.

Environmentally, California has become proactive regarding the many resources that lie just off our coast. From our wildlife species to our water-based industries such as fishing and oil production, California has stepped to the forefront in maintaining the delicate balance required to safeguard our waters and protect for future generations what is an amazing and precious gift of nature.

Chapter photography sponsored by Mary and John Snider

sun-dried tomato pesto

[makes 1 1/3 cups]

Pesto is a versatile sauce originally attributed to the Ligurian region of Northern Italy. Basic pesto contains basil, garlic, cheese, pine nuts, and olive oil. Pesto is very easy to modify with other herbs, vegetables, and nuts, such as sun-dried tomatoes, cilantro, artichokes, and roasted red peppers. The possibilities are endless.

To prepare Traditional Pesto, add 3 large garlic cloves to a food processor with the motor running and process until finely chopped; turn the motor off. Add 3 cups loosely packed fresh basil, 1/2 cup toasted pine nuts, 2 ounces (2/3 cup) coarsely grated Parmigiano-Reggiano cheese, 1 teaspoon salt and 1/2 teaspoon pepper and process until finely chopped. Add 2/3 cup extra-virgin olive oil gradually, processing constantly until incorporated. To store pesto, pour a thin layer of olive oil over the top to prevent discoloration.

1 cup drained oil-pack sun-dried tomatoes (about 6 ounces)
1 cup packed fresh basil leaves
1/4 cup pine nuts, toasted
1 1/2 tablespoons olive oil

1 tablespoon balsamic vinegar
2 large garlic cloves
1 1/2 teaspoons packed grated lemon zest
Salt and pepper to taste

Process the sun-dried tomatoes, basil, pine nuts, olive oil, vinegar, garlic and lemon zest in a food processor until the consistency of a coarse paste. Season with salt and pepper. Spread on breads, toss with pasta, serve as an accompaniment to chicken, or use to flavor mayonnaise.

cook's note ▦ For a creamier version, add 8 ounces softened cream cheese.

caprese skewers

[serves 10 to 12]

Colorful, easy, and very healthy.

1 pound bocconcini (bite-size balls of fresh mozzarella cheese)
24 fresh basil leaves
1 pint grape or cherry tomatoes

Juice of 1 lemon
Extra-virgin olive oil for drizzling
Salt and pepper to taste

Wrap each bocconcini with a basil leaf. Thread bamboo skewers or wooden picks with 1 tomato, 1 wrapped bocconcini and 1 tomato. Arrange the skewers on a platter and drizzle with the lemon juice and olive oil. Season with salt and pepper. You may prepare in advance and store, covered, in the refrigerator. Drizzle with the lemon juice and olive oil just before serving.

cook's note ▦ If bocconcini is not available, cut a large ball of fresh mozzarella into bite-size pieces.

goat cheese and dried apricots

sweet and spicy walnuts

1/4 cup sugar
24 walnut halves
Dash of cayenne pepper

cheese topping and assembly

8 ounces chèvre, softened
2 tablespoons whipping cream
24 dried apricots
Honey for drizzling

To prepare the walnuts, heat the sugar in a skillet over medium heat just until the sugar begins to melt, stirring constantly. Stir in the walnuts and cook until the walnuts are coated and toasted; watch carefully to prevent burning. Remove from the heat and spread the walnuts on a baking sheet lined with foil. Immediately sprinkle with the cayenne pepper. Let stand until cool.

To prepare the topping, mix the cheese and cream in a bowl until smooth. Place a dollop of the cheese topping and a walnut on each apricot and drizzle with honey. Pass on a platter or arrange on a cheese tray.

Dates Wrapped in Bacon make a great appetizer for almost any occasion. Remove the pits from 24 dates. Cut 12 slices of bacon into halves. Stuff the dates evenly with 4 ounces boursin or garlic and herb cheese. Wrap each stuffed date with bacon and secure with wooden picks. Arrange the wrapped dates on a baking sheet and broil until the bacon is crisp, turning once. For a variation, try stuffing figs with Gorgonzola cheese and wrapping in prosciutto. Other dried fruits stuffed with any soft cheese can easily be substituted.

greek tartlets

Great to pass at parties.

Olive Tapenade is a Mediterranean olive paste used as a spread on bread or as an accompaniment to meats. Combine 1½ cups drained pitted kalamata olives, 2 tablespoons capers, 3 garlic cloves, 2 anchovy fillets, 1 tablespoon chopped Italian parsley, 1 tablespoon olive oil, 1 tablespoon butter and a splash of Cognac in a food processor and pulse to the desired consistency.

olive topping

1/3 cup chopped pitted
    kalamata olives
1/2 teaspoon oregano, pressed
1/2 teaspoon olive oil
1/4 teaspoon balsamic vinegar
1 garlic clove, pressed
Dash of ground cumin
Dash of red pepper flakes

tartlets

4 ounces feta cheese, crumbled
3 ounces cream cheese, softened
1 egg, lightly beaten
2 teaspoons lemon juice
1 teaspoon all-purpose flour
30 miniature phyllo shells
Snipped fresh parsley for garnish
Snipped fresh oregano for garnish

To prepare the topping, mix the olives, oregano, olive oil, vinegar, garlic, cumin and red pepper flakes in a bowl.

To prepare the tartlets, preheat the oven to 350 degrees. Combine the feta cheese, cream cheese, egg, lemon juice and flour in a bowl and mix well. Fill each phyllo shell with about 2 teaspoons of the cheese filling and arrange the shells on a baking sheet. Bake for 15 to 20 minutes or until light brown. Top each tartlet with some of the olive topping and sprinkle with parsley and oregano.

cook's note ▥ The tartlets may be baked in advance and topped with the olive tapenade just before serving. If phyllo shells are not available, substitute with 4 phyllo sheets, buttered, stacked, and cut into rounds. Pat the rounds into miniature muffin cups. Puff pastry, pie pastry, or white bread cut into rounds and buttered may also be substituted but must be baked at 375 degrees for 6 to 8 minutes or until light brown before adding the cheese filling.

smoked trout in endive

[makes 2 dozen]

The endive makes this a simple but elegant appetizer.

$1^1/_2$ cups flaked smoked trout
6 green onions, thinly sliced
2 garlic cloves, minced
$^1/_4$ teaspoon paprika
$^1/_8$ teaspoon cayenne pepper
$^1/_8$ teaspoon white pepper

$^1/_4$ cup mayonnaise
$1^1/_2$ teaspoons lemon juice
Salt and black pepper to taste
4 heads Belgium endive, separated
      into spears

Combine the trout, green onions, garlic, paprika, cayenne pepper and white pepper in a bowl and mix well. Add the mayonnaise and lemon juice and stir until combined. Season with salt and black pepper and chill, covered, in the refrigerator. Spoon the trout mixture onto the endive spears and arrange on a serving platter.

cook's note ▥ Serve on toast points or crackers if desired. Any cooked or smoked seafood may be substituted for the trout.

lox pizza olé

[makes 6 pizzas]

Fun and easy.

6 (taco-size) soft flour tortillas
8 ounces cream cheese, softened
8 ounces lox, salami or prosciutto,
      cut into thin strips

$^1/_2$ cup finely chopped red onion
Capers for garnish
Chopped fresh dill weed for garnish

Preheat the oven to 350 degrees. Arrange the tortillas on a baking sheet and toast for 5 minutes or just until the tortillas begin to crisp. Spread each tortilla with some of the cream cheese and layer evenly with the lox and onion. Garnish with capers and dill weed. Cut each pizza into wedges using a pizza cutter.

shrimp angel toasts

$2/3$ cup grated Parmesan cheese
$1/2$ cup chopped cooked shrimp and/or crab meat
$1/4$ cup chopped green onions
$1/4$ cup finely chopped celery
$1/2$ cup mayonnaise
1 loaf cocktail pumpernickel bread, or sliced baguette

Combine the cheese, shrimp, green onions and celery in a bowl and mix well. Add the mayonnaise and stir until combined.

Preheat the broiler. Generously spread the shrimp mixture on the bread slices, covering the edges. Arrange on a baking sheet and broil for 4 minutes or until golden brown and bubbly. Serve immediately. You may prepare the shrimp mixture up to one day in advance and store, covered, in the refrigerator.

cucumber dip

A healthy, light, and refreshing dip.

1 English or hothouse cucumber, grated
8 ounces cream cheese or Neufchâtel cheese,
    softened
$1/4$ cup chopped red onion
Dash of Tabasco sauce
Salt and pepper to taste

Drain the cucumber in a colander for 5 minutes. Cover the cucumber with a paper towel and press gently to remove any remaining moisture. Combine the cucumber, cream cheese, onion, Tabasco sauce, salt and pepper in a bowl and mix well. Serve with fresh vegetables and/or assorted party crackers.

cook's note ▦ If using other varieties of cucumbers, peel and seed before grating.

shrimp dip

Very easy—like your favorite shrimp cocktail on crackers. My German great-grandmother always served this dip at her traditional Christmas Eve smorgasbord.

16 ounces cream cheese, softened
1/2 onion, grated
2 tablespoons lemon juice
1 teaspoon lemon pepper
1 teaspoon prepared horseradish
6 shakes of Tabasco sauce, or
    to taste

2 to 3 shakes of Worcestershire
    sauce, or to taste
Salt to taste
1 pound frozen shelled cooked
    shrimp, thawed and chopped
Cocktail sauce for garnish
Chopped fresh parsley for garnish

Combine the cream cheese, onion, lemon juice, lemon pepper, prepared horseradish, Tabasco sauce, Worcestershire sauce and salt in a bowl and mix well. Fold in the shrimp and spoon the dip into a serving bowl.

Chill, covered, for 2 hours or longer. Garnish with cocktail sauce and parsley and serve with fresh vegetable chunks, assorted party crackers and/or chips.

My parents met in a border town when my mother was sixteen and my father was nineteen. My mother knew my father's sister and, once they met, they fell in love. My father, being an orphan and with no prospects, moved to Los Angeles to find a better life. Before my parents wed, my father worked as a cook and, having no money, slept at MacArthur Park in downtown. Once my parents married, they settled in Los Angeles and raised three children. All three children eventually earned master's degrees.

(My parents were married in 1963.)

feta and oregano dip

1 pound Greek feta cheese, crumbled
1/3 cup plain yogurt
1 to 2 ounces blue cheese, crumbled
2 tablespoons fresh oregano, chopped
1 tablespoon olive oil
1 teaspoon dried oregano
2 shakes of red chile flakes

Combine the feta cheese, yogurt, blue cheese, fresh oregano, olive oil, dried oregano and chile flakes in a bowl and mix well. Serve with toasted pita chips, assorted party crackers and/or fresh vegetables.

cook's note ▥ Serve as an accompaniment to lamb or steaks, as a topping for baked potatoes, or tossed with hot pasta.

spanish olive and pecan dip

[makes 2 cups]

The unusual combination of olives and pecans makes this a hit no matter the occasion.

8 ounces cream cheese, softened
3/4 cup pimento-stuffed Spanish (manzanilla)
    olives, chopped
1/2 cup pecans, chopped
1/2 cup mayonnaise

Combine the cream cheese, olives, pecans and mayonnaise in a food processor and process until smooth. Serve with thin wheat crackers and/or fresh vegetables. Also may be used as a spread for finger sandwiches.

greek salsa with toasted pita wedges

[serves 6 to 8]

A Mediterranean spin on a classic salsa.

8 ounces feta cheese, crumbled
1 large tomato, seeded and chopped
1/2 cup kalamata olives, pitted and
    coarsely chopped
1/4 cup minced fresh flat-leaf parsley
3 green onions, thinly sliced and
    coarsely chopped

2 tablespoons minced fresh oregano
2 tablespoons snipped fresh
    dill weed
Juice of 1/2 lemon
Salt and pepper to taste
Pita bread, split and cut into wedges

Combine the feta cheese, tomato, olives, parsley, green onions, oregano, dill weed and lemon juice in a bowl and mix gently. Season with salt and pepper. Chill, covered, for 2 to 24 hours.

Preheat the oven to 300 degrees. Arrange the pita wedges in a single layer on a baking sheet and toast until light brown and crisp. Remove to a wire rack to cool. Serve with the salsa.

cook's note ▥ Toss the salsa with hot cooked pasta for a quick and easy meal.

Photograph for this recipe on page 8.

central american salsa

[serves 8 to 10]

4 or 5 large vine-ripened tomatoes,
    peeled and cut into quarters
1 small sweet onion,
    cut into quarters
1 large jalapeño chile, seeded, or
    to taste

1 large bunch cilantro, trimmed
Juice of 1 lime
1 tablespoon dried oregano
Kosher salt and freshly cracked
    pepper to taste

Combine the tomatoes, onion, jalapeño chile, cilantro, lime juice and oregano in a blender or food processor. Process to the desired consistency and season with salt and pepper. Serve with chips.

Salsa is the Spanish and Italian word for sauce, but most people in America think Mexican food when they think of salsa. Salsa is typically made from such fruits as tomatoes and tomatillos, but other fruits such as mangoes, pineapple, peaches, and so forth have gained much popularity. The fruit is mixed with jalapeño chiles, fresh cilantro, chopped onion, and either lemon juice, lime juice, or vinegar. It can be puréed or chunky like pico de gallo. The varieties are restricted only by imagination.

garlic pesto goat cheese spread

Using commercially prepared pesto makes this an instant appetizer.

2 ounces cream cheese, softened
3 garlic cloves, pressed
4 ounces mild goat cheese, softened
1/4 cup pesto

Salt to taste
1 baguette, thinly sliced
Olive oil for brushing

Mix the cream cheese and garlic in a bowl. Stir in the goat cheese and pesto. Add salt and stir until of a creamy consistency.

Preheat the oven to 250 degrees. Arrange the baguette slices in a single layer on a baking sheet and brush with olive oil. Toast for 10 minutes or just until crisp. Serve with the goat cheese spread. The spread may be prepared up to one day in advance and stored, covered, in the refrigerator.

cook's note ▥ To serve hot, spread the goat cheese mixture on the toasts, sprinkle with shredded Parmesan cheese, and broil for 1 to 2 minutes or until bubbly; watch carefully to prevent burning. For variety, serve the goat cheese mixture as a dip with fresh vegetables or spoon into mushroom caps that have been lightly sautéed in butter and lemon juice.

white bean and basil spread

Good alternative to traditional hummus. Great for picnics.

2 cups (15 ounces) cannellini or
    small white beans, drained
1 cup packed fresh basil leaves
1 to 3 garlic cloves, minced
2 tablespoons red wine vinegar

1 tablespoon olive oil
Salt and pepper to taste
Lemon juice to taste
Grated lemon zest to taste

Mash the beans in a bowl and stir in the basil, garlic, vinegar, olive oil, salt, pepper, lemon juice and lemon zest. Chill, covered, for up to one week. Serve with toasted Italian or whole wheat bread, toasted pita bread and/or assorted party crackers.

cook's note ▥ The spread is much easier to make in a food processor but the end result is brownish in color. If processed in a blender, the end result is greenish in color.

cranberry brie

[serves 12]

*The colorful contrast of the warm Brie and bright red cranberries will be
a welcome addition to any holiday gathering.*

1 cup fresh cranberries, chopped	2 teaspoons lemon juice
1/2 cup chopped peeled pear	1/8 teaspoon ground nutmeg
1/2 cup chopped peeled apple	1/8 teaspoon ground cloves
3 tablespoons cranberry juice	1/8 teaspoon mace
2 tablespoons red wine vinegar	1 (15-ounce) round fully ripened
2 tablespoons honey	Brie cheese
1 tablespoon dried cranberries	

Bring the fresh cranberries, pear, apple, cranberry juice, vinegar, honey, dried
cranberries, lemon juice, nutmeg, cloves and mace to a boil in a heavy saucepan
over medium-high heat. Reduce the heat to low and simmer, covered, for 30 minutes,
stirring frequently. Remove the cover and simmer for 5 minutes longer or until
thickened, stirring frequently. Cool to room temperature.

Preheat the oven to 350 degrees. Cut a circle in the top rind of the Brie round to within
1/4 inch of the edge. Carefully remove the center circle, leaving the border intact.
Arrange the round on an ovenproof serving platter and spread the cranberry mixture over
the top. Bake for 12 to 15 minutes or until the Brie is bubbly. Serve immediately
with melba rounds and/or sliced apples and sliced pears.

*Fresh cranberries
are easy to freeze.
Purchase extra bags
of cranberries when
available and freeze
in the bags for use
year round. Frozen
cranberries can be
used directly from the
freezer, without thawing,
in any recipe that calls
for cranberries.*

elegant caviar romanoff

Treat your guests as royalty with this easy but refined appetizer.

*California has one of
the widest varieties
of terrain of any state.
The lowest point in
the continental United
States, Badwater Basin,
Death Valley, is 282
feet below sea level.
It is located on the
northern edge of the
Mojave Desert and
on the eastern side of
the state. It is only
eighty miles from the
highest point in the
continental United
States, Mt. Whitney.
On the western side of
the Sierras is the Great
Central Valley that
runs up the middle of
the state. It is the heart
of our agricultural
industry and is bordered
on the west by the lower
coastal mountain ranges
that run the length of
the state and house our
giant redwoods. Many of
these ranges plummet
dramatically into the
Pacific Ocean. However,
in some areas the
mountains gently fall
away to great basins,
as in the case of Los
Angeles, that lead to
the ocean and create
long sandy beaches
and natural and man-
made harbors.*

6 eggs

$1/4$ cup ($1/2$ stick) butter, softened

1 teaspoon vinegar

1 teaspoon Dijon mustard

$1/4$ teaspoon salt

$1/8$ teaspoon pepper

1 cup chopped green onions

1 cup sour cream

3 ounces cream cheese, softened

1 (3-ounce) jar caviar

Hard-cook the eggs in boiling water in a saucepan; drain. Peel the eggs and cut into quarters when cool enough to handle comfortably.

Combine the warm egg quarters, butter, vinegar, Dijon mustard, salt and pepper in a blender or food processor and process for 15 to 20 seconds or until smooth. Spread the egg mixture over the bottom of an 8-inch springform pan. Sprinkle with the green onions. Chill for 1 to 10 hours.

Process the sour cream and cream cheese in a food processor until blended and spread over the chilled layer. Chill for 1 hour or longer. Gently spoon the caviar over the prepared layers. Remove the side of the pan and serve with toast points, assorted party crackers and/or crudités.

cook's note ▦ Must be prepared at least 2 hours in advance to allow time to properly set. Using paddlefish caviar makes this recipe more affordable.

layered cheese torta

Three great spreads come together in one decadent combination.

cheddar layer

4 cups (16 ounces) shredded sharp
    Cheddar cheese
1 cup pecans, chopped into
    small pieces
1/2 cup finely chopped or
    grated onion
1 garlic clove, pressed
Dash of Tabasco sauce, or to taste
1 cup mayonnaise

chutney layer

8 ounces cream cheese, softened
1/4 cup chutney

1/4 teaspoon curry powder, or
    to taste

spinach layer and assembly

1 (10-ounce) package chopped
    spinach, cooked and drained
8 ounces cream cheese, softened
1/2 teaspoon (heaping) Creole
    seasoning, or to taste
Chopped pecans (optional)
Chutney (optional)
1/2 cup pecans, chopped for garnish

To prepare the cheddar layer, combine the cheese, pecans, onion, garlic and Tabasco sauce in a bowl and mix well. Add the mayonnaise and stir until combined.

To prepare the chutney layer, mix the cream cheese, chutney and curry powder in a bowl until combined.

To prepare the spinach layer, press the excess moisture from the spinach. Combine the spinach, cream cheese and Creole seasoning in a bowl and mix well. Grease a 2 1/2-quart baking dish or bundt pan and line with plastic wrap. Sprinkle the bottom of the dish with chopped pecans and/or spread with chutney. Spread half the Cheddar mixture over the bottom of the prepared dish. Layer with the chutney mixture, spinach mixture and remaining cheese mixture in the order listed. Chill, covered, for up to 10 hours for optimal flavor or until set.

Invert the torta onto a platter and garnish with 1/2 cup pecans. Serve with thin wheat crackers and/or cocktail bread. If desired, spread additional chutney or berry preserves over the top or fill the center if using a bundt pan. Freeze for future use if desired.

cook's note ▦ Each layer can be served individually. Shape the Cheddar layer into a ring and fill the center with chutney, raspberry preserves, or strawberry preserves. Transform the chutney layer into a Chicken Chutney Spread by increasing the chutney to 1/2 cup and the curry powder to 1/2 teaspoon. Add 1 cup shredded cooked chicken (canned is acceptable), 3/4 teaspoon dried minced onion, 3/4 teaspoon Worcestershire sauce, 1/2 teaspoon Dijon mustard, 1 teaspoon prepared horseradish, and 2 tablespoons chopped toasted almonds. Enhance the spinach layer by increasing the spinach to 2 packages, substituting 2 tablespoons Beau Monde seasoning for the Creole seasoning and adding 1 cup mayonnaise, 1 cup sour cream, and 2 tablespoons minced onion.

salmon and pesto pâté

Beautiful and very colorful.

salmon pâté

1 white onion, chopped
2 tablespoons butter
12 ounces uncooked salmon
8 ounces cream cheese
2 tablespoons lemon juice, or
    to taste
1 tablespoon dill weed
1 teaspoon garlic salt
Salt and pepper to taste

sun-dried tomato basil pesto and assembly

2 garlic cloves
1 cup pine nuts
3 tablespoons grated
    Romano cheese
2 cups fresh basil
$1/2$ cup sun-dried tomatoes
3 tablespoons olive oil

To prepare the pâté, sauté the onion in the butter in a small skillet until golden brown. Process the sautéed onion, salmon, cream cheese, lemon juice, dill weed, garlic salt, salt and pepper in a food processor until puréed.

To prepare the pesto, process the garlic in a food processor until minced. Add the pine nuts and process until mixed. Add the cheese and process until mixed. Add the basil and sun-dried tomatoes and pulse until chopped. Add the olive oil gradually, processing constantly until of a smooth consistency.

Line a 4×8-inch loaf pan, medium soufflé dish or small bundt pan with plastic wrap, allowing enough overhang to cover the pâté. Layer half the salmon pâté, the pesto and the remaining salmon pâté in the prepared pan and cover with the plastic wrap. Chill for 1 hour or until set. Invert onto a serving platter and discard the plastic wrap. Serve with assorted party crackers and/or party bread.

cook's note ▦ May be prepared up to 1 day in advance. Serve each layer as a separate spread if desired.

falafel with tahini dip

A traditional Middle Eastern favorite.

falafel

2 pounds dried garbanzo beans, or
    2 (15-ounce) cans garbanzo
    beans, drained
2 cups chopped fresh parsley
1 cup chopped fresh cilantro
1 white onion, cut into quarters
10 garlic cloves
1/2 teaspoon salt
1/2 teaspoon pepper
1/2 teaspoon ground cumin

1/2 teaspoon dried cilantro
1/2 teaspoon ground nutmeg
1 egg white
1 tablespoon baking powder
Vegetable oil for frying

tahini dip

1/4 cup tahini (sesame seed paste)
1/4 cup water
1/4 cup lemon juice
1 garlic clove, minced

To prepare the falafel, soak the dried beans in a generous amount of water in a bowl for 8 to 10 hours; drain. Process the beans, parsley, fresh cilantro, onion, garlic, salt, pepper, cumin, dried cilantro and nutmeg in a food processor until the consistency of a coarse purée. Add the egg white and baking powder and process until combined. Shape the bean mixture into small balls and deep-fry in hot oil in a skillet until brown on all sides. Drain on paper towels.

To prepare the dip, combine the tahini, water, lemon juice and garlic in a bowl. Serve with the falafel along with pita bread.

cook's note ▦ White Bean and Basil Spread on page 20 or traditional hummus, either commercially prepared or homemade, can be substituted for the Tahini Dip. Tahini is located in the ethnic food section of most grocery stores. Hummus is a traditional dip made with garbanzo beans puréed with tahini, garlic, lemon juice, and olive oil. There is a delicious version called Moroccan Dip in The Junior League of Pasadena's cookbook **California Heritage Continues**. This recipe is published here with permission from the New Horizon School PTO.

ham and cheese crisps

1 (17-ounce) package frozen
    puff pastry
2 tablespoons honey
2 tablespoons Dijon mustard

1/4 cup (1 ounce) grated Romano or
    Parmesan cheese
6 ounces cooked ham, thinly sliced
1 egg
2 teaspoons water

Thaw the puff pastry at room temperature for 20 minutes. Line a baking sheet with baking parchment. Mix the honey and Dijon mustard in a bowl.

Preheat the oven to 400 degrees. Unfold one of the puff pastry sheets on a lightly floured surface. Spread with half the honey mixture, sprinkle with half the cheese and top with half the ham. Starting at the long edge, roll as for a jelly roll halfway to enclose the filling. Repeat the process from the opposite edge, forming two rolls that meet in the center. Cut the roll crosswise into 1/2-inch slices. If the roll is too soft to slice, chill in the refrigerator for several minutes.

Arrange the slices 2 inches apart on the prepared baking sheet. Repeat the process with the remaining puff pastry, remaining honey mixture, remaining cheese and remaining ham. The slices can be frozen at this point for future use. Whisk the egg and water in a bowl until combined and brush the egg wash over the slices. Bake fresh or frozen pastry slices for 15 to 18 minutes or until golden brown. Remove to a wire rack. Serve warm or at room temperature.

cook's note ▥ Any combination of meat and cheese will work in this recipe. Try prosciutto with provolone cheese, salami with Gruyère cheese, or smoked turkey with Cheddar cheese.

broiled prosciutto-wrapped asparagus

Broiling gives a crisp texture to an old favorite.

24 asparagus spears
4 ounces boursin
8 ounces prosciutto, cut into
    24 slices

Juice of 1 lemon
1 tablespoon extra-virgin olive oil
1 tablespoon drained capers
Freshly ground pepper

Snap off the thick woody ends of the asparagus spears and discard. Blanch the asparagus spears in boiling water in a saucepan. Drain and immediately plunge the spears into a bowl of ice water to stop the cooking process. Drain again and pat dry with paper towels.

Spread a small amount of the cheese on each slice of the prosciutto. Wrap one slice of the prosciutto cheese side in around each asparagus spear. You may prepare to this point up to one day in advance and store, covered, in the refrigerator. Preheat the broiler. Arrange the wrapped asparagus spears on a baking sheet and broil until light brown, turning once. Remove to a serving platter. Mix the lemon juice, olive oil and capers in a bowl and drizzle over the asparagus. Sprinkle with freshly ground pepper.

cook's note ▥ Delicious as a first course served on a bed of salad greens.

slow-roasted tomatoes with chèvre and arugula

These tomatoes are amazing and very versatile.

1 head garlic, minced
1 to 2 teaspoons sea salt or
    kosher salt
1 cup olive oil (extra-virgin preferred)
10 to 20 plum tomatoes or
    Roma tomatoes

Salt and pepper to taste
Bagel toast, melba toast or toasted
    sliced French bread
Chèvre
Arugula or other strong leaf lettuce
Balsamic vinegar (optional)

Preheat the oven to 225 degrees. Mix the garlic and 1 to 2 teaspoons salt in a bowl and stir in the olive oil. Cut the tomatoes lengthwise into halves and remove the pulp. Cut away the stems, leaving just the outer shells. Or, cut the shells into quarters if desired for bite-size pieces.

Coat the tomatoes with the oil mixture and arrange in a single layer in two 9×13-inch baking dishes; the sides of the tomatoes can touch and can face either cut side up or cut side down. Drizzle with any remaining oil mixture and season generously with salt and pepper to taste. Roast for 4 hours.

Layer 1 slice of chèvre and 1 roasted tomato half on each bagel toast, melba toast or toasted French bread slice and top with arugula. Drizzle with balsamic vinegar. Or, line a serving platter with arugula and place the chèvre in the middle of the platter. Surround the chèvre with the roasted tomatoes. For variety, serve warm or cold as a side dish with grilled meats.

cook's note ▥ To store, layer the tomatoes in a jar and cover completely with the oil. Store in the refrigerator for up to one month. The tomatoes can be tossed with pasta, layered on pizzas, or tossed in a salad. Substitute the Slow-Roasted Tomatoes for the sun-dried tomatoes in Balsamic-Marinated Lamb with Tomatoes and Feta Cheese on page 47. Use any excess oil in homemade salad dressings. For a nice hostess gift, layer the tomatoes in a jar, tie with a pretty ribbon, and then place in a basket with chèvre and a loaf of bread.

Photograph for this recipe on page 9.

swedish meatballs

A traditional smorgasbord favorite.

Italian Wedding Soup Meatball
   recipe (page 86)
1/2 cup (1 stick) butter
1 small onion, minced
1/4 cup all-purpose flour

2 1/4 cups beef broth
1 cup sour cream
1/2 teaspoon dill weed
Salt and pepper to taste

Double the recipe for the meatballs, omitting the basil. Pan-fry the meatballs in a nonstick skillet or bake on a baking sheet at 375 degrees for 10 minutes or until cooked through; drain.

Melt the butter in a heavy saucepan and add the onion. Cook until the onion is tender and stir in the flour. Cook until bubbly, stirring constantly. Add the broth gradually and cook until the sauce thickens, stirring constantly. Decrease the heat to low and stir in the sour cream, dill weed, salt and pepper; do not allow the sauce to boil. Mix in the meatballs. Spoon the meatballs and sauce into a chafing dish if desired, keeping the flame low to prevent the sauce from boiling. Or, serve over hot cooked rice or egg noodles for an entrée.

cook's note ▦ Substitute your favorite homemade meatball recipe for the Italian Wedding Soup Meatball recipe or use frozen meatballs. Ground veal and/or ground pork can be added for additional flavor.

rosemary and lemon lamb rib chops

2 tablespoons olive oil
Juice of 2 lemons
4 to 6 garlic cloves, pressed
3 or 4 sprigs of rosemary

2 teaspoons coarse sea salt
1 teaspoon coarsely ground pepper
2 racks of lamb

Mix the olive oil, lemon juice, garlic, rosemary, salt and pepper in a bowl. Arrange the lamb in a shallow dish and pour the oil mixture over the lamb, turning to coat. Marinate, covered, in the refrigerator for 1 to 10 hours, turning occasionally.

Preheat the grill. Grill the lamb to medium-rare, turning occasionally. Cut between the chops to serve.

cook's note ▦ Substitute butterflied boneless leg of lamb or thick lamb chops for an entrée. Delicious served with Sweet-and-Sour Peach Sauce on page 33.

asian pork lettuce wraps [serves 4]

1 Japanese eggplant
1 pound ground pork
1 teaspoon vegetable oil
1 zucchini, thinly sliced
1/4 cup spicy garlic sauce
1/4 cup hoisin sauce

1 head butter lettuce, trimmed and
    separated into leaves
Japanese Miso Salad Dressing
    (page 77)
Sweet-and-Sour Peach Sauce
    (page 33)

Cut the eggplant diagonally into small slices. Combine the eggplant with enough water to cover in a saucepan and bring to a boil. Boil for 3 to 4 minutes or until tender-crisp; drain.

Brown the ground pork in the oil in a skillet for about 5 minutes; drain. Add the zucchini, 1/4 cup spicy garlic sauce and 1/4 cup hoisin sauce to the ground pork and cook for 5 minutes, stirring occasionally. Stir in the eggplant and cook for 2 minutes. Taste and add additional spicy garlic sauce and/or hoisin sauce if desired. Serve in lettuce leaves with Japanese Miso Salad Dressing and/or Sweet-and-Sour Peach Sauce.

cook's note ▦ Substitute ground turkey or any ground meat for the ground pork. Serve as an entrée with hot cooked white rice and lettuce on the side.

italian chicken bites [serves 6 to 8]

1/2 cup fine bread crumbs
1/3 cup grated Parmesan cheese
1 teaspoon dried thyme
1 teaspoon dried basil

1/2 teaspoon salt
2 pounds chicken tenders
    or drumettes
1/2 cup (1 stick) butter, melted

Preheat the oven to 400 degrees. Combine the bread crumbs, cheese, thyme, basil and salt in a bowl and mix well. Dip the chicken tenders in the butter and coat with the bread crumb mixture.

Arrange the coated chicken tenders in a single layer on a baking sheet and bake for 8 to 10 minutes or until cooked through and brown. You may bread the chicken tenders in advance and store, covered, in the refrigerator. Bake just before serving.

cook's note ▦ Delicious served with Orange Miso Sauce on page 30. Serve as an entrée with hot cooked rice or orzo. Substitute ranch salad dressing for the butter for a different twist.

sesame salmon with orange miso sauce

Sophisticated but easy to prepare.

Miso paste is a rich, salty condiment that embodies Japanese cooking and is used especially in soups and sauces. It is made from soybeans and sometimes a grain such as rice, salt, and a mold culture. Adding different ingredients and varying the aging process produces different types of miso that have different flavors and aromas. The types most commonly found in the United States are yellow, red, and white. Use as a substitute for salt, soy sauce, or anchovy paste. Miso paste is usually located close to the tofu in the refrigerator section of some grocery stores, natural food stores, or Asian markets.

orange miso sauce

1 cup mayonnaise
2 tablespoons frozen orange juice
    concentrate, thawed
1 tablespoon yellow miso
1 tablespoon grated fresh ginger
1/2 teaspoon grated orange zest
Salt and pepper to taste

salmon

1 (1 1/2-pound) salmon fillet,
    cut into 3/4-inch pieces
2 tablespoons vegetable oil
Salt and pepper to taste
2 1/2 tablespoons white
    sesame seeds
2 1/2 tablespoons black sesame seeds

To prepare the sauce, whisk the mayonnaise, orange juice concentrate, miso, ginger and orange zest in a bowl until combined. Season with salt and pepper. Store, covered, in the refrigerator up to one day in advance. Bring to room temperature before serving.

To prepare the salmon, preheat the oven to 400 degrees. Toss the salmon with the oil in a bowl. Or, spray the salmon with olive oil nonstick cooking spray. Season with salt and pepper.

Mix the sesame seeds in a shallow dish. Coat the salmon with the sesame seeds and arrange in a single layer on a foil-lined baking sheet. Bake for 5 minutes or just until cooked through. Skewer each salmon piece with a wooden pick and serve warm with the sauce.

cook's note ▦ The white and black sesame seeds provide a beautiful color contrast, but may not be available. Substitute with the easily found grayish-ivory sesame seeds. The Orange Miso Sauce will become a favorite and has many uses. Try it with Italian Chicken Bites on page 29 and Halibut with Shiitake Mushrooms on page 129.

thai curried clams

This delicate clam dish is special enough for company.

1 teaspoon minced fresh ginger
1 teaspoon minced garlic
1 tablespoon butter
3 dozen Manila or cockle clams
    in shells, scrubbed
1 (12-ounce) bottle beer
1 teaspoon red curry paste, or
    to taste

1 (10-ounce) can coconut milk
1 small bunch cilantro, trimmed and
    finely chopped
1 small tomato, chopped
3 green onions, finely chopped
Salt and pepper to taste

Sauté the ginger and garlic in the butter in a large skillet over high heat for about 1 minute. Add the clams, beer and curry paste and mix well. Steam, covered, for about 5 minutes or until the clam shells open.

Add the coconut milk, cilantro, tomato and green onions to the clam mixture and bring to a boil. Season with salt and pepper. Serve in individual bowls with French bread for dipping.

cook's note ▥ Substitute Oriental curry powder for the red curry paste if desired.

sea scallops

1 pound large sea scallops
1/2 cup (1 stick) butter, melted
1 tablespoon lemon juice

Salt and pepper to taste
Sliced bacon
Sesame seeds for coating

Arrange the scallops in a single layer in a large shallow dish. Mix the butter, lemon juice, salt and pepper in a bowl and pour over the scallops, turning to coat. Marinate while the bacon cooks. Partially cook the bacon in a skillet and drain.

Preheat the broiler. Wrap each scallop with 1 slice of bacon and secure with wooden picks. Coat with sesame seeds and arrange the bacon-wrapped scallops on a broiler rack in a broiler pan. Broil until the scallops are tender and the bacon is crisp; watch carefully to prevent burning. Serve immediately.

shrimp cakes with
grilled pineapple salsa

grilled pineapple salsa

1/2 cup grilled pineapple, cut
    into 1/4-inch pieces
    (see cook's note)
1/4 cup minced red bell pepper
2 tablespoons minced red onion
2 tablespoons fresh cilantro,
    finely chopped
1 tablespoon fresh mint leaves,
    finely chopped
1 tablespoon seasoned rice vinegar
1 tablespoon extra-virgin olive oil
1/4 teaspoon salt
1/4 teaspoon freshly ground pepper

shrimp cakes

1 pound large shrimp, peeled
    and deveined
1 egg
1 green onion, chopped
2 tablespoons lemon juice
1 tablespoon Dijon mustard
1 tablespoon fresh cilantro, minced
1/2 teaspoon hot red pepper sauce
1/2 teaspoon salt
Pinch of freshly ground pepper
2 cups panko (see page 158)
2 tablespoons (or more) peanut oil

To prepare the salsa, gently mix the pineapple, bell pepper, onion, cilantro and mint in a bowl. Add the vinegar, olive oil, salt and pepper and toss gently until coated.

To prepare the shrimp cakes, process the shrimp in a food processor until coarsely chopped. Add the egg, green onion, lemon juice, Dijon mustard, cilantro, hot sauce, salt and pepper and pulse just until combined. Add 1 cup of the bread crumbs and pulse until combined.

Shape the shrimp mixture into twelve 3-inch cakes and coat the cakes with the remaining 1 cup bread crumbs. Arrange the cakes on a baking sheet lined with waxed paper. Chill, covered, for 10 minutes to 4 hours.

Heat the peanut oil in a large heavy skillet over medium-high heat. Fry the shrimp cakes in batches in the hot oil for about 6 minutes or until cooked through and golden brown on both sides, adding additional peanut oil as needed. Drain and serve with the salsa.

cook's note ▦ For Grilled Pineapple, peel 1 pineapple and cut into 1/4-inch slices. Grill the slices over hot coals or sear in a small amount of olive oil in a skillet for 1 minute per side. Let stand until cool and chop into 1/4-inch pieces.

Photograph for this recipe on page 8.

shrimp egg rolls with
sweet-and-sour peach sauce

[makes 80 to 85 egg rolls]

sweet-and-sour
peach sauce
3/4 cup peach preserves
3 tablespoons cider vinegar
1 1/2 teaspoons pimento,
    finely chopped

egg rolls
5 cups bean sprouts
1 pound peeled cooked shrimp

1 cup peanuts, chopped
3/4 cup peanut butter
1/2 cup water chestnuts, chopped
1/2 cup thinly sliced green onions
1/4 cup soy sauce
3/4 teaspoon ground ginger
1 small garlic clove, minced
2 packages won ton wrappers
Vegetable oil for deep-frying

To prepare the sauce, process the preserves in a blender or food processor until of a smooth consistency if needed. Combine the preserves, vinegar and pimento in a bowl and mix well.

To prepare the egg rolls, pour enough boiling water over the bean sprouts in a heatproof bowl to cover. Let stand for 15 minutes and drain. Squeeze the bean sprouts until all the excess moisture is removed. Combine the bean sprouts, shrimp, peanuts, peanut butter, water chestnuts, green onions, soy sauce, ginger and garlic in a food processor and process just until chopped; do not overprocess.

Spoon approximately 1 tablespoon of the shrimp filling slightly below the center of each won ton wrapper. Moisten the edges of the wrappers with water and fold the bottoms over to enclose the filling. Fold the sides over and roll tightly to ensure the filling is securely enclosed and air bubbles are not present.

Preheat oil in a deep skillet to 350 degrees. Deep-fry the egg rolls in batches in the hot oil for 3 to 4 minutes or until golden brown on all sides. Drain on paper towels and serve with the sauce.

cook's note ▓ The Sweet-and-Sour Peach Sauce can be served with a variety of recipes, such as Rosemary and Lemon Lamb Rib Chops on page 28, Asian Pork Lettuce Wraps on page 29, or Italian Chicken Bites on page 29.

lemon rosemary crackers

1³/4 cups all-purpose flour
1¹/4 cups (5 ounces) three-cheese
    blend (or any combination of
    Parmesan cheese, pecorino
    cheese, Romano cheese and/or
    asiago cheese)
1 tablespoon sugar
2¹/2 to 3 teaspoons fresh rosemary,
    finely chopped

1 teaspoon salt (optional)
Pinch of freshly ground nutmeg
1 cup (2 sticks) butter, softened
1¹/2 teaspoons finely grated
    lemon zest
6 tablespoons heavy cream,
    at room temperature
1 egg yolk, at room temperature

Mix the flour, cheese, sugar, rosemary, salt and nutmeg in a bowl. Beat the butter and lemon zest in a mixing bowl at medium speed until creamy. Decrease the mixer speed to low and add the cream and egg yolk, beating constantly until blended. Add the flour mixture gradually, beating constantly until combined. Scrape the side of the bowl, increase the mixer speed to medium and beat until a well-blended dough forms.

Preheat the oven to 325 degrees. Divide the dough into several portions and roll each portion ¹/4 inch thick on a lightly floured surface. Cut into rounds using a 1-inch cookie cutter. Or, shape the dough into four rolls and slice into rounds.

Arrange the rounds on an ungreased baking sheet and bake for about 20 minutes or until the crackers emit a nutty aroma and the bottoms are brown. Cool briefly on the baking sheet and remove to a wire rack to cool completely. Store in an airtight container for up to one month. Freeze baked or unbaked for future use. Bake frozen crackers for about 25 minutes.

cook's note ▦ For a saltier cracker, sprinkle a small amount of salt on the top of the rounds before baking.

ultimate quick and easy munchies

These no-bake goodies are addictive and always a hit.

¹/2 cup vegetable oil
1 envelope ranch salad dressing mix
2 teaspoons lemon pepper
1 teaspoon dill weed
1 teaspoon garlic salt

1 teaspoon garlic powder
1 (16-ounce) package Quaker
    Oatmeal Squares cereal with
    brown sugar

Mix the oil, dressing mix, lemon pepper, dill weed, garlic salt and garlic powder in a bowl. Pour the oil mixture over the cereal in a large bowl and mix well. Store in a 1-gallon sealable plastic bag or in an airtight container. The flavor is enhanced if prepared in advance to allow the flavors to blend, but they can be served immediately.

christmas pepper jelly   [makes 7 (1/2-pint) jars]

This festive dark green jelly speckled with red is always a treat served over cream cheese or Brie cheese. A perfect hostess gift because it makes a quick appetizer, travels well, and keeps indefinitely.

1 cup chopped green bell pepper
1/2 to 3/4 cup seeded canned
    jalapeño chiles, drained
    and rinsed
1 1/4 cups apple cider vinegar

6 cups sugar
1/2 cup finely chopped red
    bell pepper
2 (3-ounce) packets liquid fruit pectin
8 or 9 drops of green food coloring

Process the green bell pepper, jalapeño chiles and 1/2 cup of the vinegar in a blender until smooth and pour the mixture into a 4-quart saucepan. Rinse the blender container with the remaining 3/4 cup vinegar and add to the saucepan. Stir in the sugar and red bell pepper. Bring to a hard boil that cannot be stirred down. Remove from the heat and let stand for 5 minutes.

Skim the foam carefully off the top, leaving as many of the red bell pepper pieces as possible on the surface. Add the fruit pectin and food coloring and stir until combined. Immediately ladle the jelly into seven sterilized 1/2-pint jars, leaving a 1/2-inch headspace. Seal with two-piece lids.

To prepare in advance, cover the jelly with plastic wrap and store indefinitely in the refrigerator. If vacuum-sealed, store in a cool, dark environment for up to six months. If sealed with paraffin, store in a cool, dark environment for up to two months. Store in the refrigerator after opening.

cook's note ▦ Wear gloves to protect hands when handling jalapeño chiles. The jelly looks beautiful presented in soufflé dishes and tied with green and red plaid ribbon. Also delicious served as an accompaniment to meats.

Clockwise from left to right: Baked Strawberry-Stuffed French Toast (page 49), Harvest Muffins (page 55), Rolls as You Like Them (page 56), Prosciutto Pesto Strata (page 42)

breakfast, brunch & breads

Los Angeles Child Guidance Mosaic
June Edmonds, 2005

Los Angeles Child Guidance Clinic

"Hold my hand"—whether prompted by a child or an adult, implies help, security, and encourage–ment. The Los Angeles Child Guidance Clinic has provided families in the Central and South Los Angeles communities with a long-standing commitment toward ensuring that mental health services and early intervention are a reality to families in need.

The Los Angeles Child Guidance Clinic was established in 1924 to create access to mental health services for emotionally disturbed children. Today, the Clinic is a consumer-centered, family-focused provider of mental health services for children from birth to twenty-five. The Clinic is noted for its expertise in treating seriously disturbed children whose level of impairment places them at risk for out-of-home placement, school failure, utilization of high-end mental health services, and involvement in the criminal justice system. Culturally sensitive services are offered in both English and Spanish and are offered at three community-based sites, in schools, and in client homes.

Each year, approximately five thousand individuals benefit from services that include outpatient mental health treatment; a no-fee, no-appointment Walk-In Clinic; intensive day treatment for children beginning at age two and one-half; early intervention program services; in-home and school-based services; parent education; pre-employment and job placement services; and psychiatric services. In order to best address and meet the needs of children, we have long-standing collaborative relationships with the Los Angeles Unified School District, as well as many local Head Start programs. In addition, through a long-standing affiliation with the USC Keck School of Medicine, the Clinic provides on-site psychiatric training for resident child psychiatrists.

The various programs and services offered by the Los Angeles Child Guidance Clinic provide the opportunity for a brighter future to those in need in our community and the community as a whole—one hand at a time.

Food photography sponsored by Theresa and Kashif Sheikh
Mosaic photography sponsored by Bill and Claire Bogaard

eggs jean lafitte

[serves 6]

Named for the famous French pirate who helped the United States in the Battle of New Orleans. Delicious served with fruit and mimosas.

6 frozen puff pastry shells
1/4 cup (or more) all-purpose flour
Salt and pepper to taste
8 ounces chicken livers

2 tablespoons butter
2 tablespoons vegetable oil
12 eggs, poached
Béarnaise sauce

Bake the pastry shells using the package directions and remove the tops. Mix the flour, salt and pepper in a bowl. Lightly coat the livers with the flour mixture. Heat the butter and oil in a skillet until the butter melts. Sauté the livers in the hot butter mixture until cooked through.

Place 1 pastry shell on each of six plates. Top each pastry shell with 2 poached eggs and drizzle with the desired amount of sauce. Arrange the livers evenly around the pastry shells and serve immediately.

cook's note ■ Béarnaise sauce is similar to hollandaise sauce with the addition of tarragon, shallots, and vinegar. Packaged mixes are available in most grocery stores, and there is an excellent version of the sauce in The Junior League of Pasadena's **The California Heritage Cookbook**. Chicken liver pâté may be substituted for the sautéed chicken livers. Spread the pâté on the pastry shells and top with the poached eggs and Béarnaise sauce.

huevos jorge

[serves 6]

George, my father-in-law, adapted this recipe from an old standby. He is known as "Jorge" to his grandchildren, hence the name. The chili sauce or salsa makes it delicious and unique.

12 slices bacon, partially cooked
1/4 cup (12 teaspoons) chili sauce
    or salsa
12 eggs
Salt to taste

Paprika to taste
6 English muffins, split
Butter for brushing
Chopped fresh parsley for garnish

Preheat the oven to 375 degrees. Grease the bottoms of twelve muffin cups. Line the side of each muffin cup with 1 slice of the bacon; the bacon forms a ring. Spoon 1 teaspoon of the chili sauce into each muffin cup. Add 1 egg to each cup, being careful not to break the yolks. Sprinkle with salt and paprika and bake for 10 to 12 minutes or until the eggs are set. Run a sharp knife or spoon around the edges of the muffin cups to loosen.

Toast the muffins and brush with butter. Arrange 2 muffin halves on each of six plates and top each muffin half with 1 egg cup. Garnish with parsley and serve immediately.

cook's note ■ For a twist, serve the egg cups on drained pineapple slices.

sausage and vegetable frittata

1 pound sweet Italian sausage,
  casings removed
3/4 cup shredded zucchini
3/4 cup shredded carrots
3/4 cup mushrooms, sliced
3/4 cup chopped red bell pepper
3/4 cup chopped onion
1 garlic clove, pressed

2 tablespoons fresh basil, chopped
1/2 teaspoon salt
1/8 teaspoon pepper
8 eggs
1 cup ricotta cheese
1 pound mozzarella
  cheese, shredded

Preheat the oven to 375 degrees. Cook the sausage in an ovenproof skillet for about 10 minutes or until brown and crumbly, stirring frequently; drain. Add the zucchini, carrots, mushrooms, bell pepper, onion, garlic, basil, salt and pepper to the skillet and sauté until the vegetables are tender.

Whisk the eggs in a bowl until blended and stir in the ricotta cheese and mozzarella cheese. Pour the egg mixture evenly over the sausage mixture and bake for 30 to 40 minutes or until the eggs are set. Let rest for 5 minutes before serving.

cook's note ■ For a vegetarian entrée, omit the sausage and sauté the vegetables and spices in margarine.

pancetta spinach tart

8 ounces pancetta, chopped
1/2 cup sliced onion
1/2 cup chopped leeks
6 ounces spinach, chopped, cooked
  and drained
1 3/4 cups heavy whipping cream

3 eggs, lightly beaten
1 cup crumbled goat cheese
Pinch of nutmeg
Freshly ground pepper to taste
1 baked (9-inch) pie shell

Preheat the oven to 350 degrees. Sauté the pancetta, onion and leeks in a skillet until the onion is tender and the bacon is partially cooked but not crisp. Add the spinach and stir just until combined.

Scald the cream in a heavy saucepan. Remove from the heat and whisk a small amount of the hot cream into the eggs. Gradually whisk the eggs into the hot cream. Stir in the cheese, nutmeg and pepper.

Spoon the pancetta mixture into the pie shell and pour the egg mixture over the top. Bake for 30 to 40 minutes or until a knife inserted in the center comes out clean. Let rest for 10 to 15 minutes before serving.

asparagus and ham quiche

[serves 6 to 8]

A classic French quiche.

1/2 cup (2 ounces) shredded
    Gruyère cheese
1 baked tart shell
1/2 cup (1/4- to 3/8-inch) cubes
    cooked ham

1/2 cup (1-inch) pieces trimmed
    fresh asparagus
3 eggs
Milk or half-and-half
1/2 teaspoon salt

Preheat the oven to 375 degrees. Sprinkle the cheese over the bottom of the tart shell. Layer with the ham and asparagus.

Whisk the eggs in a bowl until blended. Combine the eggs with enough milk to measure 1 1/2 cups. Stir in the salt and pour the egg mixture over the prepared layers. Bake for 35 to 40 minutes or until set and light brown.

prosciutto pesto strata

[serves 8]

Works wonderfully on a busy holiday morning.

1 (1- to 1 1/4-pound) loaf country or
    sourdough bread, crusts
    removed if thick
8 ounces cream cheese, cubed
8 ounces fresh or other mozzarella
    cheese, cut into small pieces
    or shredded
3/4 cup prepared pesto (refer to
    Traditional Pesto on page 12)

6 ounces prosciutto, thinly sliced
1 pound ripe red tomatoes, thinly
    sliced (about 3 medium tomatoes)
1 1/2 cups milk
5 eggs
1/2 teaspoon salt
Freshly ground pepper
    to taste

Cut the bread loaf into 1/2-inch slices. Layer the bread, cream cheese, mozzarella cheese, pesto, prosciutto and tomatoes 1/2 or 1/3 at a time in a buttered deep 9- to 10-inch baking dish. Cut or tear the bread slices if needed for a better fit.

Whisk the milk, eggs, salt and pepper in a bowl until blended and pour over the prepared layers. Chill, covered, for 2 to 10 hours. Let stand at room temperature for 20 to 30 minutes before baking.

Preheat the oven to 350 degrees. Bake for 50 to 55 minutes or until puffed, golden brown and lightly set in the center. Serve hot.

cook's note ■ Can be assembled the night before, stored in the refrigerator, and baked just before serving. The strata travels well.

Photograph for this recipe on page 37.

crab soufflé

Butter for coating
1 tablespoon grated
    Parmesan cheese
1/4 cup (1/2 stick) butter
3 tablespoons all-purpose flour
1 cup boiling milk
1/2 teaspoon salt
1/8 teaspoon cayenne pepper

Pinch of nutmeg
4 eggs
1 egg white
Pinch of salt
1/3 cup coarsely grated
    Parmesan cheese
2 to 4 ounces fresh or canned
    crab meat, drained and flaked

Preheat the oven to 400 degrees. Coat a 2 1/2-quart soufflé dish with butter and sprinkle with 1 tablespoon cheese. Melt 1/4 cup butter in a saucepan and stir in the flour with a wooden spoon until blended.

Cook over medium heat for 2 minutes or until bubbly; do not allow to brown. Remove from the heat and let stand until the mixture stops bubbling. Add the boiling milk all at once and whisk vigorously until blended. Whisk in 1/2 teaspoon salt, the cayenne pepper and nutmeg. Bring to a boil over medium-high heat and boil for 1 minute, whisking constantly. The sauce will be very thick. Remove from the heat.

Immediately begin to separate the eggs one at a time. Drop the white into a mixing bowl and the yolk into the center of the hot sauce. Whisk until the egg yolk is blended. Repeat the process in the same manner three more times. Correct the seasonings as desired. You may prepare in advance to this point and store, covered, in the refrigerator. Dot the top of the chilled sauce with additional butter and heat to tepid before continuing with the recipe.

Add 1 egg white to the 4 egg whites along with the pinch of salt and beat until stiff peaks form. Stir about 1/4 (1 large spoonful) of the egg whites into the sauce. Stir all but 1 tablespoon of the 1/3 cup cheese into the sauce. Fold in the remaining egg whites and then the crab meat. Spoon the crab meat mixture into the prepared soufflé dish; the dish should be about 3/4 full. Tap the bottom of the dish lightly on the table and smooth the surface of the soufflé with the flat side of a knife. Sprinkle with the remaining 1 tablespoon cheese.

Arrange the soufflé dish on the middle oven rack and immediately decrease the oven temperature to 375 degrees. Do not open the oven door for 20 minutes or the soufflé will fall. The soufflé will puff about 2 inches over the rim of the dish and the top will be brown in 25 to 30 minutes. Bake for 4 to 5 minutes longer to firm it up and then serve immediately.

greek leeks in phyllo

A nice vegetarian entrée or side dish for any brunch.

$1/2$ cup (1 stick) butter	5 tablespoons Cream of Wheat
5 pounds leeks, chopped into 1-inch pieces	Salt and pepper to taste
	$1/2$ cup (1 stick) butter
8 eggs, lightly beaten	1 (16-ounce) package phyllo pastry sheets, thawed
8 ounces feta cheese, crumbled	

Grease a 9×13-inch baking dish. Melt $1/2$ cup butter in a large skillet and stir in the leeks. Bring to a boil and reduce the heat to low. Simmer for 30 minutes or until the liquid evaporates, stirring occasionally. Remove from the heat and let stand until cool. Stir in the eggs, cheese, Cream of Wheat, salt and pepper.

Preheat the oven to 350 degrees. Melt $1/2$ cup butter in a saucepan. If using 13×17-inch phyllo sheets, cut the stack into halves, making two stacks of $81/2$×13-inch sheets. Keep the phyllo covered with a damp towel to avoid drying out, removing 1 sheet at a time and working quickly.

Layer 10 sheets of the phyllo in the prepared baking dish, brushing each sheet with some of the $1/2$ cup melted butter; do not be concerned if the sheets tear. Spread half the leek mixture over the phyllo stack. Layer with 6 more phyllo sheets, brushing each sheet with some of the remaining melted butter. Spread with the remaining leek mixture and continue layering with 10 more phyllo sheets, brushing each sheet with the remaining melted butter. Bake for 30 to 40 minutes or until golden brown.

cook's note ■ Working with phyllo sounds much more intimidating than it actually is. Just remember to keep the unused pastry stack covered to prevent its drying out. It is important to let it thaw completely in its package before using. This recipe can easily be adapted to other Mediterranean favorites such as the following:

Spinach Pie (Spanakopita): Omit the eggs and Cream of Wheat. Substitute 3 thawed and drained 10-ounce packages of frozen chopped spinach and 8 finely chopped scallions for the leeks. Sauté the spinach and leeks in the butter until the moisture evaporates and stir in $3/4$ cup pine nuts and 16 ounces crumbled feta cheese. Season with salt and pepper and a pinch of nutmeg. Stack half the phyllo, brushing each sheet with some of the melted butter. Spread with the spinach mixture and layer with the remaining phyllo, brushing each sheet with some of the remaining melted butter. Bake as directed above.

Easy Cheese Squares (Armenian Boerag): Mix 8 ounces feta cheese and 1 bunch trimmed and chopped parsley. Stack half the phyllo on a rimmed baking pan, brushing each sheet with melted butter. Spread with the cheese mixture and top with the remaining phyllo, brushing each sheet with melted butter. Cut into squares; you can freeze for future use at this point. Whisk $1/2$ cup milk and 2 eggs until blended and pour over the squares; shake lightly to disperse the liquid. Bake as directed above until golden brown.

hot chicken salad

[serves 6 to 8]

The crunchy texture of the celery and almonds changes this from a typical chicken casserole to a warm luncheon entrée that will receive rave reviews.

3 to 5 pounds cooked
   chicken breasts
3 cups chopped celery
1 cup slivered almonds, toasted
1/2 cup chopped mushrooms
1/3 cup grated onion
1 tablespoon lemon juice

1 1/2 teaspoons salt
1/2 teaspoon tarragon
1 1/2 cups mayonnaise
1/4 cup extra-dry vermouth
3/4 cup bread crumbs
1/2 cup (2 ounces) grated
   Parmesan cheese

Chop the chicken into 3/4-inch pieces (about 4 to 5 cups), discarding the skin and bones. Combine the chicken, celery, almonds, mushrooms, onion, lemon juice, salt and tarragon in a bowl and mix well. Stir in the mayonnaise and vermouth. Chill, covered, for 1 hour or longer.

Preheat the oven to 350 degrees. Spoon the chicken mixture into a buttered 7×11-inch baking dish and sprinkle with the bread crumbs and cheese. Bake for 30 minutes or until heated through.

croque monsieur ring

[serves 8 to 10]

A croque monsieur is a traditional French grilled ham and cheese sandwich. This is the same combination of flavors but is served as a bread ring.

1 cup milk
1/2 cup (1 stick) butter
1 cup all-purpose flour
4 eggs, at room temperature

1 cup (4 ounces) shredded
   Gruyère cheese
4 ounces cooked ham, chopped
1/4 cup chopped red bell pepper
1 egg white, lightly beaten

Preheat the oven to 400 degrees. Grease and lightly flour a baking sheet. Bring the milk and butter to a boil in a heavy saucepan and stir in 1 cup flour. Reduce the heat to low and cook until the mixture is smooth and begins to pull from the side of the pan, stirring frequently. Remove from the heat and cool for 5 minutes. Add the eggs one at a time, beating until blended after each addition. Stir in the cheese, ham and bell pepper.

Using a large spoon, drop the ham mixture by dollops onto the prepared baking sheet in the shape of a ring. Brush the ring with the egg white and bake for 10 minutes. Reduce the oven temperature to 350 degrees and bake for 30 minutes longer. Turn off the oven and let the ring rest in the oven with the door closed for 10 minutes. Remove to a serving platter and cut as desired. Serve warm.

monte cristo sandwiches

An easy home version of the traditional Monte Cristo whose origins date back to Los Angeles restaurants as early as the 1940s. This sandwich is possibly related to the French croque monsieur.

3 eggs
1/3 cup milk
1/2 cup (1 stick) butter, softened
2 teaspoons prepared mustard
12 slices white bread

6 (2-ounce) slices Swiss cheese,
    cut into halves
6 (1-ounce) slices smoked ham
Confectioners' sugar to taste
Preserves or jam of choice for garnish

Whisk the eggs and milk in a shallow dish. Beat the butter and prepared mustard in a bowl until blended. Spread one side of each slice of the bread with the butter mixture. Layer each of the buttered sides of 6 slices of the bread with 1 slice of the cheese, 1 slice of the ham and 1 slice of the cheese. Top with the remaining bread slices buttered side down.

Preheat the oven to 425 degrees. Dip each sandwich in the egg mixture. Brown the sandwiches on both sides on a lightly buttered griddle. You may prepare in advance to this point and store, covered, in the refrigerator until ready to bake.

Arrange the sandwiches on a baking sheet and bake for 8 to 10 minutes. To serve, slice each sandwich diagonally into halves and sprinkle with confectioners' sugar. Garnish with a spoonful of preserves.

cook's note ■ Great for a luncheon or committee meeting.

balsamic-marinated lamb with tomatoes and feta cheese

A lovely open-face sandwich for an intimate group.

1^1/$_2$ tablespoons olive oil

1^1/$_2$ tablespoons balsamic vinegar

Ground pepper to taste

14 to 16 ounces lamb shoulder, blade
   chops or boneless leg of lamb

1 (16-ounce) loaf Italian or French
   bread, cut into eight ^{1}/$_2$- to
   ^{3}/$_4$-inch slices

Olive oil for brushing

^{3}/$_4$ cup Slow-Roasted Tomatoes
   (page 27) or sun-dried tomatoes

3 green onions, chopped

2 ounces green salad leaves

8 ounces feta cheese, crumbled

Whisk 1^1/$_2$ tablespoons olive oil, the vinegar and pepper in a bowl until combined. Arrange the lamb in a shallow glass or ceramic dish and pour half the vinegar mixture over the lamb, turning to coat. Marinate, covered, in the refrigerator for 30 minutes or longer, turning occasionally. Preheat the grill to medium-high. Drain the lamb, discarding the marinade. Grill the lamb for 3 to 4 minutes per side and remove to a platter. Brush both sides of the bread slices with olive oil and grill for approximately 2 minutes per side or until grill marks appear. Toss the tomatoes and green onions in a bowl. Cut the lamb into thin slices. Arrange two grilled bread slices on each of four serving plates and top equally with the salad leaves, feta cheese, lamb and tomato mixture. Drizzle with the remaining vinegar mixture and sprinkle with pepper. Serve immediately.

baked artichoke sandwiches

A versatile dish that is hearty enough to be served as a luncheon entrée or sliced smaller and served on a buffet.

1 (16-ounce) loaf French bread

^{1}/$_2$ cup (1 stick) butter

3 garlic cloves, chopped or pressed

2 cups sour cream

2 cups (8 ounces) shredded
   mozzarella cheese

1 cup (4 ounces) shredded
   Cheddar cheese

1 (12-ounce) can artichoke hearts,
   drained and chopped

Preheat the oven to 325 degrees. Cut the loaf lengthwise into halves. Carefully remove the centers, leaving the shells intact. Tear the center bread into chunks and reserve. Melt the butter in a saucepan and stir in the garlic. Add the reserved bread chunks, sour cream, mozzarella cheese, Cheddar cheese and artichokes and mix well. Spoon the artichoke mixture into the bread shells. At this point the stuffed bread shells may be wrapped in foil for travel or frozen for future use. To serve, arrange the wrapped bread shells on a baking sheet and bake for 20 minutes or until heated through. Slice as desired.

cook's note ■ For a heartier sandwich, arrange a layer of sliced meat, such as turkey or ham, in the bread shells before filling with the cheese mixture.

grilled portobello sandwiches

A yummy grilling alternative for vegetarians.

4 portobello mushrooms,
  stems removed
Salt and pepper to taste
Olive oil for brushing
4 red bell peppers

Olive Tapenade (page 14)
4 ciabatta rolls, split and
  lightly toasted
1 ball buffalo mozzarella cheese,
  cut into 4 equal slices

Preheat the grill. Sprinkle the mushrooms with salt and pepper and brush lightly with olive oil. Arrange the mushrooms on a grill rack and grill for 20 minutes. Lightly salt the mushrooms while warm. Arrange the bell peppers on the grill rack and grill for 10 minutes per side or until soft but not charred, turning occasionally. Let stand until cool. Chop the bell peppers, discarding the seeds and membranes.

Spread the tapenade on the bottom half of each roll. Layer equally with the mozzarella cheese, bell peppers and mushrooms. Top with the remaining bread tops and serve immediately.

cook's note ■ The Olive Tapenade on page 14 works beautifully with this recipe, but commercially prepared tapenade will work as well.

sweet-and-spicy bacon

People rave over this treatment of bacon. Serve anytime you would serve bacon.

3 tablespoons brown sugar
1/2 teaspoon black pepper

1/8 to 1/4 teaspoon cayenne pepper,
  or to taste
1 pound sliced bacon, cut into halves

Preheat the oven to 350 degrees. Mix the brown sugar, black pepper and cayenne pepper in a shallow dish. Coat the bacon with the brown sugar mixture and twist each slice.

Arrange the slices on a broiler rack in a broiler pan and place the pan on the middle oven rack. Bake for 20 to 30 minutes or until the bacon is cooked through; watch carefully. Remove to a sheet of foil to cool.

cook's note ■ Twisting the bacon allows the bacon to cook through without turning. The sugar caramelizes as the bacon cools.

baked strawberry-stuffed french toast

A beautiful asset to any brunch buffet. Remarkably easy and can be prepared in advance. This dish travels well.

strawberry filling

8 ounces cream cheese or low-fat
    cream cheese, softened
1 tablespoon frozen orange
    juice concentrate
1 cup thickly sliced fresh strawberries

french toast

1 (16-ounce) loaf Italian bread
    (about 4 inches wide)
4 eggs
$1/2$ cup whole, low-fat or skim milk
2 teaspoons vanilla extract

strawberry grand marnier sauce

$1/3$ cup sugar
1 tablespoon cornstarch
2 cups thickly sliced
    fresh strawberries
$2/3$ cup water
$1/3$ cup Grand Marnier
3 tablespoons frozen orange
    juice concentrate
1 cup thickly sliced fresh strawberries
1 tablespoon Grand Marnier

To prepare the filling, stir the cream cheese in a bowl until smooth. Mix in the orange juice concentrate and fold in the strawberries; there is no need to completely incorporate.

To prepare the French toast, preheat the oven to 450 degrees. Cut a small diagonal slice off both ends of the bread loaf and discard. Slice the loaf diagonally into 1- to $1^{1}/2$-inch slices. Holding the knife parallel to the counter, cut each bread slice almost in half, leaving one side attached to form a pocket. Divide the filling evenly between the pockets, pressing to seal around the edges. Arrange the stuffed slices on a rimmed baking sheet. Whisk the eggs, milk and vanilla in a bowl until blended. Gradually pour the egg mixture over the slices and turn to coat. At this point the stuffed bread slices may be baked immediately; chilled, covered with plastic wrap, for up to 24 hours; or transferred to sealable plastic bags and stored in the refrigerator.

Arrange the slices 2 inches apart on a baking sheet sprayed with nonstick cooking spray or generously greased. Bake for 6 to 9 minutes or until the bottoms are golden brown. Turn and bake for 6 to 9 minutes longer or until golden brown on the remaining sides.

To prepare the sauce, combine the sugar and cornstarch in a saucepan and mix well. Stir in 2 cups strawberries, the water, $1/3$ cup liqueur and the orange juice concentrate. Bring to a boil over medium to low heat and boil until the sauce is glossy and thickened, stirring frequently. Remove from the heat and let stand until cool. Stir in 1 cup strawberries and 1 tablespoon liqueur. Serve warm or at room temperature drizzled over the French toast or on the side. You may store the sauce in the refrigerator for up to 24 hours. Bring to room temperature or reheat before serving.

cook's note ▪ Garnish with additional fresh strawberry halves if desired. Do not use a cushioned baking sheet as it does not facilitate browning.

Photograph for this recipe on page 36.

french toast soufflé

Assemble the night before so you can wake up and pop the soufflé into the oven and have more time to spend with family and friends. This soufflé also travels well.

10 cups (1-inch) cubes French bread	2 tablespoons granulated sugar
8 ounces cream cheese, softened	1 tablespoon vanilla extract
8 eggs	3/4 teaspoon salt
3 cups milk	2 tablespoons butter
1/2 cup maple syrup	Confectioners' sugar to taste

Grease a 9×13-inch baking dish or spray with nonstick cooking spray. Cover the bottom of the prepared dish with the bread cubes. Beat the cream cheese in a mixing bowl until smooth. Add the eggs one at a time, beating well after each addition. Add the milk, syrup, granulated sugar, vanilla and salt and beat until blended. Pour the milk mixture over the bread cubes. Chill, covered, for 8 to 10 hours.

Preheat the oven to 350 degrees. Dot the top of the soufflé with the butter and bake for 45 to 50 minutes or until puffy and light brown. Dust with confectioners' sugar and serve with additional syrup if desired.

banana pancakes

The bananas add a new dimension to pancakes.

1 cup all-purpose flour	1 egg
1 1/2 teaspoons sugar	2 tablespoons butter or
1 1/4 teaspoons baking powder	margarine, melted
3/4 teaspoon baking soda	1/4 cup shredded coconut (optional)
1/4 teaspoon salt	2 ripe bananas, thinly sliced
1 1/2 cups buttermilk	1/4 cup chopped pecans for garnish

Mix the flour, sugar, baking powder, baking soda and salt in a bowl. Whisk the buttermilk, egg, butter and coconut in a bowl until combined. Add the buttermilk mixture to the dry ingredients and stir until combined.

Ladle the batter 1/4 cup at a time into a lightly buttered skillet or onto a lightly buttered griddle. Top each pancake with 3 to 5 banana slices and cook for 3 to 4 minutes or until the edges of the pancakes appear dry. Turn with a wide spatula and cook for 3 to 4 minutes longer or until brown on the remaining side.

Serve immediately or arrange the pancakes in a single layer on a baking sheet and keep warm in a 200-degree oven. Sprinkle with the pecans just before serving. For a different twist, serve the pancakes topped with a dusting of cinnamon and sugar.

middle eastern pancakes (atayeff)

[serves 6 to 8]

1/2 cup warm water
11/2 teaspoons dry yeast
1/2 teaspoon sugar
1 cup semolina
1 cup all-purpose flour
1/2 teaspoon baking soda (optional)
11/4 cups water

11/4 cups milk
Cinnamon to taste
Chopped nuts to taste
Sugar to taste
Ricotta cheese (optional)
Syrup

Proof the yeast by combining 1/2 cup warm water, the yeast and 1/2 teaspoon sugar in a bowl and stir gently. Mix the semolina, all-purpose flour and baking soda in a mixing bowl. Add the yeast mixture, 11/4 cups water and the milk and beat until blended. Let stand for 1 to 2 hours. The batter should be very thin.

Pour the desired amount of the batter for each pancake onto a hot griddle and cook the pancakes on one side. Remove the pancakes to a platter and sprinkle with cinnamon, nuts and sugar to taste, or fill with ricotta cheese. Fold over to enclose the filling and press the edges to seal. Return the pancakes to the griddle and cook just until brown on both sides. Dip each pancake in syrup before serving.

cook's note ■ These pancakes may be frozen. To reheat, warm in the oven and brush lightly with melted butter to soften.

maple doughnut bites

[serves 6 to 8]

A big hit with kids of all ages.

1/2 cup all-purpose flour
1 tablespoon brown sugar
21/2 teaspoons baking powder
1 cup ricotta cheese

1 egg, lightly beaten
2 tablespoons maple syrup
2 to 3 cups vegetable oil for frying
1 tablespoon confectioners' sugar

Combine the flour, brown sugar and baking powder in a bowl and mix well. Stir in the ricotta cheese, egg and syrup. Chill, covered, for 1 hour.

Heat the oil in a saucepan or deep-fat fryer over medium-high heat until hot but not smoking. Test the oil by dropping a bread cube into the hot oil. The bread should brown in about 1 minute if the oil is the correct temperature.

Working in small batches, drop the batter by rounded teaspoonfuls into the hot oil. Fry for 4 to 5 minutes or until golden brown. Remove to a paper towel to drain. Dust the warm doughnut bites with confectioners' sugar and serve immediately.

dutch apple skillet cake [serves 2 to 3]

Tournament of
Roses Parade®
*In 1890, the Valley
Hunt Club staged
the first Tournament
of Roses Parade® to
showcase the glorious
weather and flowers
Pasadena enjoys
in the dead of winter.
Soon the parade
became a national
spectacle, and the
Tournament of Roses
Association® was
formed to oversee the
event. The parade
includes the Rose
Queen® and her court,
high school marching
bands, horses, and
beautiful floats. Each
float is a work of art
and is made entirely of
plant material such
as flowers, fruits, seeds,
vegetables, grasses,
and so forth. Thousands
of dedicated volunteers
spend countless hours
building floats and
organizing the parade.*

4 tart apples, peeled and sliced
1/3 cup packed dark brown sugar
2 teaspoons ground cinnamon
1 teaspoon cardamom
1/4 cup (1/2 stick) butter
1 cup all-purpose flour
1 teaspoon salt
1 cup whole or low-fat milk
6 eggs, beaten

Preheat the oven to 450 degrees. Combine the apples, brown sugar, cinnamon and cardamom in a bowl and mix well. Melt the butter in a cast-iron or ovenproof skillet, tilting the skillet to coat the side. Add the apple mixture to the hot butter and sauté until the apples are tender.

Mix the flour and salt in a bowl. Add the milk and eggs and whisk until blended. Pour the batter evenly over the apple mixture and bake for 20 minutes. Reduce the oven temperature to 350 degrees and bake for 10 minutes longer or until crisp. Serve with warm syrup, confectioners' sugar and/or cinnamon and sugar.

cook's note ■ Bananas or pears can be substituted for the apples.

pumpkin and blueberry
pecan coffee cake

The unusual combination of pumpkin and blueberry takes this coffee cake to a new level.

brown sugar streusel

1 cup packed brown sugar

1/3 cup butter, softened

2 teaspoons ground cinnamon

1 cup pecans, chopped

coffee cake

2 cups all-purpose flour

1 teaspoon baking powder

1 teaspoon baking soda

3/4 cup sugar

1/2 cup (1 stick) butter, softened

1 teaspoon vanilla extract

3 eggs

1 cup sour cream or crème fraîche

1 egg

1 (15-ounce) can pumpkin purée

1/3 cup sugar

1 cup dried blueberries

1 teaspoon pumpkin pie spice

To prepare the streusel, mix the brown sugar, butter and cinnamon in a bowl until crumbly. Stir in the pecans.

To prepare the coffee cake, preheat the oven to 325 degrees. Mix the flour, baking powder and baking soda in a bowl. Combine 3/4 cup sugar, the butter and vanilla in a mixing bowl and beat until creamy. Add 3 eggs and beat until blended. Add the dry ingredients and sour cream 1/3 at a time, stirring well after each addition. Wipe out the dry ingredient bowl and lightly beat 1 egg. Stir in the pumpkin purée, 1/3 cup sugar, the blueberries and pumpkin pie spice.

Spoon half the batter into a 9×13-inch baking pan, spreading to the corners. Sprinkle with half the streusel and spread with the pumpkin mixture. Carefully spread the remaining batter over the prepared layers and sprinkle with the remaining streusel. Bake for 50 to 60 minutes or until a wooden pick inserted in the center comes out clean. Cut into twelve squares.

cook's note ■ Use moist hands to spread the batter if necessary. Dried mixed berries may be substituted for the dried blueberries.

orangy pumpkin bread

Fills the kitchen with a wonderful aroma.

3$1/3$ cups all-purpose flour
2 teaspoons baking soda
1$1/2$ teaspoons salt
1 teaspoon ground cinnamon
1 teaspoon ground cloves
$1/2$ teaspoon baking powder
2$2/3$ cups sugar

$2/3$ cup shortening
2 cups pumpkin
$2/3$ cup water
4 eggs
1 orange, seeded and ground
$2/3$ cup raisins or chopped dates
$2/3$ cup chopped nuts

Preheat the oven to 350 degrees. Sift the flour, baking soda, salt, cinnamon, cloves and baking powder into a bowl and mix well. Beat the sugar and shortening in a mixing bowl until creamy. Add the pumpkin, water and eggs and beat until blended. Blend in the flour mixture. Mix in the orange and stir in the raisins and nuts.

Spoon the batter into a greased and floured bundt pan and bake for 1 hour. Cool in the pan for 10 minutes and invert onto a wire rack to cool completely.

cook's note ■ Use any dried fruit such as raisins, cranberries, and/or apricots. May also bake as muffins.

rhubarb bread

The earliest records of rhubarb date back to 2700 B.C. in China, where it was used medicinally. Due to its very tart flavor, rhubarb was not used in cooking until sugar became more readily available. Now it is often called the "pie plant" and is very popular in breads, pies, and sauces.

1$1/2$ cups packed brown sugar
$2/3$ cup vegetable oil
1 cup buttermilk
1 egg, lightly beaten
1 teaspoon baking soda
1 teaspoon salt
1 teaspoon vanilla extract

2$1/2$ cups all-purpose flour
1$1/2$ cups chopped fresh or
    frozen rhubarb
$1/2$ cup chopped nuts
$1/2$ cup granulated sugar
1$1/2$ tablespoons grated orange zest
1 tablespoon butter, softened

Preheat the oven to 350 degrees. Combine the brown sugar and oil in a large mixing bowl and beat until blended. Whisk the buttermilk, egg, baking soda, salt and vanilla in a bowl until blended. Add the buttermilk mixture to the brown sugar mixture and mix well. Fold in the flour, rhubarb and nuts. Spoon the batter evenly into two greased and floured 5×9-inch loaf pans.

Combine the granulated sugar, orange zest and butter in a small bowl and mix well with a fork. Sprinkle the sugar mixture evenly over the prepared loaves. Bake for 1 hour or until a wooden pick inserted in the centers comes out clean. Cool in the pans for 10 minutes and remove to a wire rack to cool completely.

harvest muffins

[makes 2 dozen muffins]

A nice, healthy treat when you are on the go.

3 cups whole wheat flour
2 cups all-purpose flour
2 tablespoons pumpkin pie spice
2 1/2 teaspoons baking powder
4 cups granulated sugar
2 cups pumpkin purée

1 cup vegetable oil
4 eggs, lightly beaten
2 cups finely chopped peeled apples
2 cups dried cranberries
1 cup chopped walnuts
1/2 cup packed brown sugar

Preheat the oven to 350 degrees. Spray twenty-four muffin cups with nonstick cooking spray or line with paper liners. Sift the whole wheat flour, all-purpose flour, pumpkin pie spice and baking powder into a bowl and mix well. Combine the granulated sugar, pumpkin purée, oil and eggs in a large bowl and mix well. Add the dry ingredients, apples, cranberries and walnuts and stir just until combined. Spoon equal portions of the batter into the prepared muffin cups and sprinkle about 1 teaspoon of the brown sugar over each muffin. Bake for 30 minutes or until a wooden pick inserted in the centers comes out clean and the tops are brown. Serve warm or at room temperature.

cook's note ■ Make sure the apples are finely chopped or it will be difficult to scoop the batter into the muffin cups. Keep these muffins on hand in the freezer to take when traveling or hiking, or just when you want a healthy snack.

Photograph for this recipe on page 36.

For Cream Cheese Biscuits, preheat the oven to 350 degrees. Mix 1/2 cup softened butter, 8 ounces softened cream cheese and 1 cup all-purpose flour in a bowl. Chill for 30 minutes. Roll the dough 1/4 to 1/2 inch thick on a lightly floured surface and cut into rounds using a biscuit cutter. Arrange the rounds on a baking sheet and chill until ready to bake. Bake for 15 to 20 minutes or until the edges are brown. Serve warm.

cheesy herb popovers

[makes 6 to 9 popovers]

My dad made popovers every holiday when I was growing up. I made them for my children and now my children make them for their families.

2 cups all-purpose flour
1 teaspoon salt
1/2 teaspoon oregano
1/2 teaspoon basil
1/2 teaspoon thyme

2 cups milk
4 eggs, lightly beaten
6 to 9 tablespoons shredded
    Cheddar cheese or Monterey
    Jack cheese

Combine the flour, salt, oregano, basil and thyme in a bowl and mix well. Add the milk and eggs and stir for 2 minutes or less or until the batter is reasonably smooth. Fill six generously greased custard cups or nine muffin cups 2/3 full. Sprinkle each popover with 1 tablespoon of the cheese. Place the custard cups directly on the oven rack in a cold oven. Bake at 400 degrees for 40 minutes or until golden brown and completely puffed. Popovers will fall if undercooked. Serve immediately.

cook's note ■ Serve with butter, jam, and crisp-cooked bacon. Great for lunch with a salad. For traditional popovers, omit the herbs and cheese.

rolls as you like them

These yeast rolls are so wonderful you will want to make them often.

basic dough

2 envelopes dry yeast
1/2 cup warm
     (105- to 115-degree) water
1 teaspoon sugar
1/2 cup shortening
1/2 cup sugar
1 cup hot water
3 eggs, beaten
4 1/2 cups all-purpose flour
2 teaspoons salt

christmas cinnamon rolls

1/2 cup (1 stick) butter, melted
1/2 cup granulated sugar
2 teaspoons (or more)
     ground cinnamon
1/2 cup raisins (optional)
2 tablespoons almonds or pecans,
     toasted and chopped (optional)
2 teaspoons grated lemon
     zest (optional)
3/4 cup confectioners' sugar
1/4 cup lemon juice or orange juice

To prepare the basic dough, mix the yeast, warm water and 1 teaspoon sugar in a bowl and let stand until bubbly. Beat the shortening and 1/2 cup sugar in a large mixing bowl until blended. Add the hot water and beat until combined. Blend in the eggs and stir in the yeast mixture. Mix the flour and salt in a bowl. Add the flour mixture 1 cup at a time to the liquid mixture, mixing well after each addition. Let rise until doubled in bulk. Cover with buttered plastic wrap and a damp tea towel. Chill for 8 to 10 hours or until doubled in bulk.

To prepare the cinnamon rolls, roll the basic dough into a 14×18-inch rectangle on a lightly floured surface and brush with 6 tablespoons of the butter. Sprinkle with a mixture of the granulated sugar and cinnamon. Top with the raisins, almonds and lemon zest. Starting from the 14-inch side, roll as for a jelly roll and cut equally into twelve rolls. Arrange the rolls cut side up in a greased 9-inch pie plate or baking pan. Let rise for 2 hours or until doubled in bulk. Preheat the oven to 350 degrees. Brush the rolls with the remaining 2 tablespoons butter and bake for 20 to 30 minutes or until light brown. Cool for 10 minutes and brush with a mixture of the confectioners' sugar and lemon juice.

sticky buns
$1/2$ cup packed brown sugar
$1/2$ cup (1 stick) butter
1 cup pecans, chopped

orange rolls
$1/2$ cup (1 stick) butter, softened
$1/2$ cup granulated sugar
2 tablespoons grated orange zest
    (2 large oranges)
$3/4$ cup confectioners' sugar
$1/4$ cup orange juice

To prepare the sticky buns, follow the directions for the cinnamon rolls, omitting the raisins and lemon zest and substituting toasted pecans for the toasted almonds. Mix the brown sugar, butter and 1 cup pecans in a bowl and spread over the bottom of a 9-inch pie plate or baking pan. Top with the rolls cut side up and let rise for 2 hours or until doubled in bulk. Bake for 20 to 30 minutes or until light brown. Let cool for 5 minutes and invert onto a plate.

To prepare the orange rolls, divide the basic dough into 2 equal portions. Roll each portion into a 9×13-inch rectangle, $1/4$ inch thick. Spread with a mixture of the butter, granulated sugar and orange zest. Starting from the 13-inch side, roll as for a jelly roll and cut into $3/4$-inch rolls. Arrange the rolls in greased muffin cups. Let rise for 2 hours or until doubled in bulk. Preheat the oven to 400 degrees and bake for 8 minutes or until light brown; do not overbake. Brush the warm rolls with a mixture of the confectioners' sugar and orange juice.

cook's note ■ For Basic or Savory Dinner Rolls, roll the dough on a lightly floured surface and cut into rounds using a biscuit cutter. Arrange the rounds on a buttered baking sheet or in a pie plate. Brush the rounds with melted butter or a mixture of melted butter and pressed garlic and let rise until doubled in bulk. Bake at 375 degrees for 10 to 15 minutes or until light brown. Serve warm.

Photograph for this recipe on page 36.

cowboy bread

[serves 12]

This flat bread, also known as pan de campo, dates back to trail-driving days and was traditionally made in a cast-iron Dutch oven over a mesquite fire.

8 cups unbleached all-purpose flour	4 teaspoons sugar
2 tablespoons plus 2 teaspoons	$1^1/_2$ cups corn oil
baking powder	3 cups milk
4 teaspoons salt	

Preheat the oven to 400 degrees. Mix the flour, baking powder, salt and sugar in a large bowl. Add the corn oil and stir until blended. Add the milk 1 cup at a time, mixing well after each addition; the dough will be slightly sticky.

Knead the dough on a lightly floured surface until easily handled. Divide the dough into 4 equal portions and shape each portion into a ball. Roll each ball $1/_2$ inch thick on a lightly floured surface using a rolling pin. Arrange the rounds on an ungreased baking sheet and bake for 20 to 25 minutes or until golden brown.

lemon basil bread

[serves 6 to 8]

The herbed butter with a hint of garlic gives this bread a fresh and unusual flavor.

1 baguette	1 tablespoon lemon pepper
$1/_2$ cup (1 stick) butter, melted	1 tablespoon lemon juice
$1/_4$ cup basil, chopped	2 garlic cloves, chopped or pressed
1 tablespoon parsley, chopped	

Preheat the oven to 350 degrees. Slice the baguette into 1-inch-thick slices, cutting to but not through the bottom. Arrange the baguette on a sheet of foil large enough to enclose.

Combine the butter, basil, parsley, lemon pepper, lemon juice and garlic in a bowl and mix well. Brush the butter mixture on the cut sides of each slice and over the top. Enclose the baguette with the foil and bake for 20 minutes or until heated through.

red booth garlic bread

[serves 6 to 8]

Yummy bread that takes you back to an old-fashioned steakhouse.

1 cup mayonnaise
3/4 cup (3 ounces) grated
    Parmesan cheese
6 garlic cloves, pressed
1 tablespoon cream
1/2 cup (2 ounces) shredded
    Cheddar cheese
1/4 teaspoon paprika
1 (16-ounce) loaf sourdough bread

Combine the mayonnaise, Parmesan cheese and garlic in a bowl and mix well. Combine the cream, Cheddar cheese and paprika in a saucepan and cook until the cheese melts, stirring constantly. Stir the Cheddar cheese mixture into the mayonnaise mixture. At this point the cheese mixture may be stored, covered, in the refrigerator until time of use.

Cut the bread loaf lengthwise into halves and arrange the halves cut side up on a baking sheet. Spread the cheese mixture evenly on the cut sides of the halves. Broil until brown and bubbly. Slice as desired.

cook's note ■ The topping can also be served as an appetizer. Spread on cocktail bread, top with cooked bay shrimp, and broil until bubbly.

There were five brothers in my husband's family who immigrated from Germany to the United States to build churches. They worked their way across Canada and the U.S., eventually arriving in California. One brother, my husband's great-grandfather, stopped building churches and got into the movie-making business as an actor in silent movies. The family has been in "The Biz" ever since.

Clockwise from left to right: Pear and Pomegranate Salad (page 67), Green Bean Salad (page 76), Orange Poppy Seed Salad (page 65)

salads & dressings

Indians and Yuccas Near Indian Hill
Millard Sheets, 1969

Horse Culture in California

When most people think of California, they envision beautiful beaches, palm trees, surfing, or the avenues of Hollywood teeming with celebrities on every street corner. The truth is, most of California remains rural, with sweeping spreads of farmland, orchards, and ranches gently laid between majestic mountain ranges, redwood forests, and blazing desert lands. And in the urban and rural areas alike, the horse remains an integral part of our community.

In the 1500s, with the Spaniards, came horses—and while Indians were not allowed to own them initially, they felt the connection between man and horse was "godlike" and named the horse God Dog or Big Dog. The entire makeup of the tribes took on greater significance when horses replaced the dog as the tribal pack animal; this expanded their existence from slow-moving villagers to nomadic wanderers and warriors. The Indians revered and mastered the horse, and we attribute the ancestry of almost all of the colored breeds to the Indian horse; the paint, palomino, appaloosa, and buckskin are those most familiar to us in modern times.

As our history evolved and raw land became farmland and ranches, the horse took on a greater working importance, not only in plowing out the fertile fields of our great growing valleys but also in the movement of livestock. The vaqueros and cowboys spent any idle time competing with one another in tasks related to their work duties. These expert horsemen honed cow punching, bulldogging, cutting, and reining to perfection and soon the rodeo evolved, becoming an event of great prestige and honor. Rodeos still draw huge crowds and pay out huge purses. The actual heyday of the cowboy was short lived, primarily spanning from the end of the Civil War to the completion of the railroad, but just as in a Hollywood movie, the legend lives big in our culture. We pay homage to the cowboy culture through music, film, festivals, and sporting events held throughout the state. Museums are filled with the lore of the Old West and every year our history and love of equestrian life is paraded down Colorado Boulevard in the world-famous Rose Parade®, where more than three hundred horses and riders participate annually in roping, riding, drill team, and acrobatic maneuvers to the delight of the crowd. Specialty horse shows and events dot the calendar in venues as far cast as the Cow Palace in San Francisco, to the Earl Warren Showgrounds in Santa Barbara, to the Los Angeles Equestrian Center near Griffith Park.

Horse racing in California was legalized in 1933, and since that time it has topped the field with fairground competition, harness racing, and full circuit thoroughbred racing, with some of the finest jockeys and trainers found in the United States. Where else but California, with its enviable climate, can you find a racetrack like Del Mar with views of the sparkling Pacific or Santa Anita, made famous by the legendary Seabiscuit, located at the foot of the sometimes snow-capped San Gabriel Mountains.

There is a thriving love for the horse in our culture that has carried through our history unabated. While open space is at a premium in our sprawling, modern, urban society, there is a desire to hold onto our past with the pull of a rein, and the click of our tongue. The horse has been our helper, our partner, and our history. It is by choice that we invite him to remain by our side in the future.

Food photography sponsored by Kandis and Jonathan Jaffrey
Mosaic photography sponsored by Cathy Woolway

lucky seven salad

Fruity and flavorful.

Prepare Creamy Dressing *for your favorite spinach salad one day in advance to allow the flavors to blend. Combine 1 cup vegetable oil, 5 tablespoons red wine vinegar, 1/4 cup sour cream or light sour cream, 2 tablespoons sugar, 1 1/2 teaspoons salt, 2 teaspoons parsley and 2 pressed garlic cloves in a jar with a tight-fitting lid and seal tightly. Shake to mix. Season to taste with pepper. Store, covered, in the refrigerator.*

balsamic dressing

1/2 cup grapeseed oil, walnut oil or vegetable oil
1/4 cup white wine vinegar
1/4 cup balsamic vinegar
1 teaspoon garlic powder
1/4 teaspoon freshly ground pepper
1/8 teaspoon sea salt

salad

1 head romaine, trimmed and torn into bite-size pieces
1 cup chopped apple
1/2 cup crumbled blue cheese
1/2 cup dried cranberries
1/2 cup chopped seeded peeled cucumber
1/2 cup pecans
1/2 cup thinly sliced red onion

To prepare the dressing, whisk the grapeseed oil, vinegars, garlic powder, pepper and salt in a bowl until combined.

To prepare the salad, toss the romaine, apple, cheese, cranberries, cucumber, pecans and onion in a bowl. Add the dressing and mix until coated.

cucumber grape salad

[serves 6 to 8]

Grapes add a refreshing change to this traditional tzatziki.

2 cups chopped seeded
    peeled cucumbers
1 1/2 teaspoons salt
1 cup plain yogurt
1 garlic clove, pressed
1 tablespoon finely chopped
    green onion

1 tablespoon fresh mint, chopped
1 tablespoon red wine vinegar
1 tablespoon olive oil
1 teaspoon chopped fresh dill weed,
    or 1/2 teaspoon dried dill weed
1 cup grapes, sliced

Toss the cucumbers and salt in a bowl. Chill, covered, for 1 hour. Drain the excess liquid from the cucumbers. Add the yogurt, garlic, green onion, mint, vinegar, olive oil and dill weed to the cucumbers and mix well. Chill, covered, for 1 hour. Stir in the grapes just before serving.

cook's note ▪ The flavor of this salad improves with age.

orange poppy seed salad

[serves 6]

The dressing turns a pale pink in the blender, making a lovely contrast to the green and orange of the salad.

poppy seed dressing
1/2 cup sugar
1 teaspoon salt
1 teaspoon dry mustard
1 cup vegetable oil
1/2 small red onion, finely chopped
1/2 cup cider vinegar
2 tablespoons poppy seeds

salad
1 or 2 heads romaine or butter
    lettuce, trimmed and torn into
    bite-size pieces
1 (11-ounce) can mandarin
    oranges, drained
1/2 cup chopped avocado
1/4 cup pine nuts, toasted
1/4 cup crumbled blue cheese

To prepare the dressing, process the sugar, salt, dry mustard, oil, onion and vinegar in a blender until combined. Pour the dressing into a jar with a tight-fitting lid and add the poppy seeds. Seal tightly and shake to mix.

To prepare the salad, gently toss the romaine, mandarin oranges, avocado, pine nuts and cheese in a salad bowl. Add the desired amount of dressing and mix until coated.

cook's note ▪ This recipe makes 1 pint of dressing, so there will be plenty left over for future salads. Store, covered, in the refrigerator.

Photograph for this recipe on page 61.

tricolor tomato salad

Fresh and good.

2 (6-ounce) jars marinated
    artichoke hearts
2 tablespoons balsamic vinegar
1 tablespoon Dijon mustard
1 teaspoon minced garlic
6 cups tricolor cherry tomatoes
1 fennel bulb, cut into
    paper-thin slices

1 cup pitted kalamata olives
1 large ball buffalo mozzarella,
    chopped
1 cup lightly packed fresh
    basil leaves
1/2 cup thinly sliced red onion
Freshly ground pepper to taste

Drain the artichokes, reserving 1/4 cup of the marinade. Whisk the reserved marinade, vinegar, Dijon mustard and garlic in a bowl until combined. Add the tomatoes, fennel, olives, cheese, basil, onion and pepper to the marinade mixture and toss gently to coat. Let stand for 2 to 3 hours before serving.

cook's note ■ If preparing this salad more than 4 hours in advance, do not add the basil until just before serving.

herb-marinated watermelon and feta cheese salad

Refreshingly different.

herb marinade
1/2 cup olive oil
1/4 cup white wine vinegar
2 tablespoons fresh basil, minced, or
    11/2 tablespoons dried basil
1 tablespoon fresh oregano, minced,
    or 2 teaspoons dried oregano
1 teaspoon coarse salt

1 dash of garlic powder
Freshly ground pepper to taste

salad
1/2 large seedless watermelon,
    chilled and cut into bite-size
    pieces
1 cup (or more) crumbled
    feta cheese

To prepare the marinade, whisk the olive oil, vinegar, basil, oregano, salt, garlic powder and pepper in a bowl until combined.

To prepare the salad, combine the watermelon and cheese in a salad bowl. Add the marinade and gently toss with a rubber spatula until coated. Let rest briefly and serve at room temperature or chill if desired.

cook's note ■ Substitute tomatoes, cucumbers, or any combination of summer vegetables for the watermelon.

pear and pomegranate salad

A wonderful salad that is equally beautiful served composed or tossed.

caramelized walnuts
2 tablespoons butter
1 tablespoon sugar
1/4 teaspoon salt
1 cup walnuts

pomegranate dressing
1/4 cup olive oil
3 tablespoons pure
    pomegranate juice
2 tablespoons walnut oil
2 tablespoons wine vinegar

1/2 teaspoon Dijon mustard
Salt and pepper to taste

salad
1 bunch baby spinach,
    stems removed
1 head butter lettuce, trimmed and
    torn into bite-size pieces
1 bunch watercress, stems removed
2 pears
1/2 cup crumbled feta cheese
1/2 cup pomegranate kernels

To prepare the walnuts, melt the butter in a small heavy saucepan. Add the sugar and salt and stir until blended. Stir in the walnuts. Cook over low heat until the sugar caramelizes, stirring occasionally. Spread the walnut mixture on a baking sheet lined with foil or pour into a small paper bag. Let stand until cool and break into pieces. Store in an airtight container for up to one week or freeze for up to one month.

To prepare the dressing, whisk the olive oil, juice, walnut oil, vinegar and Dijon mustard in a bowl until blended. Season with salt and pepper.

To prepare the salad, toss the spinach, lettuce and watercress in a bowl. Reserve 2 tablespoons of the dressing. Pour the remaining dressing over the spinach mixture and toss to coat. Divide the spinach mixture evenly among six plates. Cut the pears into halves and cut each half into six wedges. Arrange four pear wedges in a spoke pattern over each serving. Sprinkle evenly with the cheese, pomegranate kernels and 1/2 cup of the walnuts. Drizzle evenly with the reserved 2 tablespoons dressing. Or, serve as a tossed salad by combining the spinach, lettuce and watercress in a salad bowl. Top with the pear wedges, cheese, pomegranate kernels, 1/2 cup walnuts and dressing and toss gently to coat.

cook's note ■ If pomegranate seeds are not in season, substitute with 1/2 cup dried cranberries.

Photograph for this recipe on page 60.

armenian bulgur salad (eetch)

This is an easy, make-ahead salad that is great for vegetarians.

Serve Tabbouleh as a salad or as an appetizer with pita bread. Soak 1/2 cup bulgur in cold water for 10 minutes or until soft. Drain and press dry in cheesecloth or a tea towel. Mix the bulgur with 2 cups chopped seeded peeled tomatoes, 1 cup chopped fresh parsley, 1/2 cup chopped green onions, 1/2 cup minced fresh mint, 1/3 cup lemon juice, 1/2 teaspoon salt and 1/4 teaspoon pepper. Let stand for 30 minutes and stir in 1/3 cup extra-virgin olive oil.

2 large onions, finely chopped
1/2 cup olive oil
1 (16-ounce) can stewed tomatoes
1 (6-ounce) can tomato paste
1/2 cup water
Dash of paprika
Salt and pepper to taste
1/4 cup fresh lemon juice
2 cups fine bulgur
Chopped green onions for garnish

Sauté the onions in the olive oil in a large skillet until the onions begin to brown. Stir in the tomatoes, tomato paste, water, paprika, salt and pepper. Cook over low heat for 30 minutes, stirring occasionally. Stir in the lemon juice 3 to 5 minutes before the end of the cooking process.

Pour the tomato mixture over the bulgur in a large bowl and mix well; the bulgur will swell as it absorbs the liquid. Fluff with a fork and garnish with the green onions. Serve chilled or at room temperature.

cook's note ▨ Also serve as a filling for lettuce wraps, or in hollowed-out tomatoes or bell peppers.

tuscan bread salad

4 large tomatoes, cut into chunks
   (about 3 cups)
3 large garlic cloves, minced
2 tablespoons red wine vinegar
1/4 teaspoon salt
Freshly ground pepper to taste

1 (16-ounce) loaf country white bread
Olive oil to taste
Salt to taste
1/2 cup fresh basil, coarsely chopped
1/2 cup (2 ounces) freshly shaved
   Parmesan cheese

Preheat the oven to 300 degrees. Toss the tomatoes, garlic, vinegar, 1/4 teaspoon salt and pepper in a large bowl. Marinate for 30 minutes.

Tear the bread into bite-size pieces and arrange in a single layer on a baking sheet lined with foil. Drizzle the bread pieces with olive oil and season with salt to taste. Bake for 20 minutes or until golden brown, stirring occasionally. Add the toasted bread, basil and cheese to the tomato mixture and toss to mix. Serve immediately.

cook's note ■ Sourdough bread is not recommended for this recipe.

steak salad niçoise

Like a traditional niçoise salad from the south of France, but with steak instead of tuna.

niçoise dressing
1/2 cup olive oil
2 tablespoons red wine vinegar
2 tablespoons balsamic vinegar
1 teaspoon Dijon mustard
1 garlic clove, pressed
Dash of Worcestershire sauce
Pinch of sugar
Salt to taste (kosher preferred)
Pepper to taste

salad
2 red potatoes
Salt to taste
8 ounces fresh green beans, trimmed
3 large Roma tomatoes
1/2 small to medium red onion,
  thinly sliced
1/4 cup niçoise olives, sliced
1 1/2 pounds lean sirloin steak or
  tuna steak
Pepper to taste
Romaine

To prepare the dressing, whisk the olive oil, vinegars, Dijon mustard, garlic, Worcestershire sauce, sugar, salt and pepper in a large nonreactive bowl until blended. Taste and adjust the seasonings.

To prepare the salad, cook the potatoes in boiling salted water in a saucepan for 7 to 10 minutes or until tender; drain. Immediately plunge the potatoes into a bowl of ice water to stop the cooking process. Drain again and let stand until cool. Peel and slice the potatoes and stir the potatoes into the dressing.

Blanch the beans in boiling salted water in a saucepan for 3 minutes or just until tender and bright green; drain. Immediately plunge the beans into a bowl of ice water to stop the cooking process. Drain again and pat dry. Mix the beans with the potato mixture.

Peel, seed and cut the tomatoes into quarters. Add the tomatoes, onion and olives to the potato mixture and toss gently. The vegetables may be prepared in advance and marinated, covered, in the refrigerator. Bring to room temperature while the steak is being prepared.

Season the steak with salt and pepper. Broil, grill or pan-fry the steak over high heat until the outside is lightly seared and the interior is rare to medium. Cool to room temperature and cut into bite-size pieces. Add the steak to the potato mixture and gently mix. Serve over a bed of romaine.

cook's note ■ Add croutons or serve with garlic toast. Garnish with additional olives if desired.

flank steak salad

An easy weeknight dinner salad.

1 flank steak, cut into strips
Onion powder to taste
Salt and pepper to taste
1 tablespoon olive oil
1 tablespoon butter
2 teaspoons fresh oregano,
    coarsely chopped

1 or 2 garlic cloves, pressed
1/2 cup red wine vinegar
1 head firm lettuce such as romaine
    or iceberg, trimmed and torn
    into bite-size pieces
Feta cheese (optional)

Season the steak with onion powder, salt and pepper. Heat the olive oil in a large skillet over high heat. Pan-fry the steak in the hot oil until brown on all sides. Remove the steak to a plate using a slotted spoon, reserving the pan drippings. Reduce the heat to medium.

Heat the butter with the reserved pan drippings. Sauté the oregano and garlic in the butter mixture and stir in the vinegar. Add the lettuce and toss quickly to coat. Remove the lettuce mixture to a serving platter and top with the steak. Sprinkle with feta cheese and serve immediately.

chicken, apple and spinach salad

A delicious dinner salad that is not difficult to prepare.

wine vinaigrette
1/4 cup vegetable oil
3 tablespoons wine vinegar
1 teaspoon sugar
1/2 teaspoon prepared mustard
Salt and pepper to taste

salad
2 boneless skinless chicken breasts
Salt and pepper to taste

Plain bread crumbs for coating
1/4 cup vegetable oil
5 slices bacon, crisp-cooked and
    crumbled
1/3 cup sliced almonds, toasted
1 pound spinach, stems removed
1 avocado, chopped
1 apple, coarsely chopped
3 green onions, sliced

To prepare the vinaigrette, whisk the oil, vinegar, sugar, prepared mustard, salt and pepper in a bowl until blended.

To prepare the salad, season the chicken with salt and pepper and coat with bread crumbs. Sauté the chicken in the oil in a skillet for 20 minutes or until the juices run clear; drain. Cool slightly and chop into bite-size pieces.

Toss the chicken, bacon, almonds, spinach, avocado, apple and green onions in a salad bowl. Add the vinaigrette and mix until coated. Serve immediately.

cook's note ■ Leftover chicken works well in this recipe.

turkey waldorf salad

A great way to use those holiday leftovers.

Rose Bowl Game®
*The success of the
Tournament of Roses
Parade® led to the first
post-season football
match, which prompted
the construction
of Rose Bowl Stadium
in the Arroyo Seco.
In recent years, the
Rose Bowl Game® was
added to the Bowl
Championship Series,
and Pasadena has been
host to the national
championship game.
Rose Bowl Stadium is
used throughout the
year for a variety of
sports and concerts, and
on the third weekend
of each month it is the
location of the famous
Rose Bowl Swap Meet.*

cranberry relish
1 (12-ounce) package
    fresh cranberries
1 orange, sliced, seeded and
    cut into quarters
1 cup sugar
1 Granny Smith apple, cored

salad
2 cups chopped cooked turkey
    or chicken
1 cup sliced celery

2 large Granny Smith apples, peeled
    and chopped
1 orange, seeded and chopped
$1/2$ cup dried cranberries
$1/4$ cup sugar
1 tablespoon (or more) lemon juice
$1/2$ cup mayonnaise
1 tablespoon frozen orange
    juice concentrate
$3/4$ cup walnuts or pecans,
    coarsely chopped

To prepare the relish, combine the cranberries, orange and sugar in a food processor and pulse until coarsely chopped. Spoon the cranberry mixture into a bowl. Process the apple in the food processor until shredded and stir the apple into the cranberry mixture.

To prepare the salad, toss the turkey, celery, apples, orange, cranberries, sugar and lemon juice in a bowl until combined. Stir in $1/2$ cup of the relish, or the desired amount. Mix the mayonnaise and orange juice concentrate in a small bowl and stir into the turkey mixture. Sprinkle with the walnuts. Serve immediately or chill, covered, in the refrigerator until serving time.

cook's note ■ Prepare the Cranberry Relish even if there are no leftovers from your holiday meals. The relish is equally good with pork or chicken. For variety, add chopped fresh pears to the salad.

california MOSAIC

sweet mustard shrimp salad [serves 10 to 12]

Wonderful on a buffet.

1/2 cup Dijon mustard
1/2 cup cider vinegar
6 tablespoons sugar
1 to 2 tablespoons fresh lemon juice
1 teaspoon mustard seeds, toasted
2 teaspoons dry mustard
1/2 cup vegetable oil
2 tablespoons dried dill weed
2 tablespoons finely chopped red onion
1 teaspoon ground cinnamon
2 pounds medium shrimp
Salad greens

Combine the Dijon mustard, vinegar, sugar, lemon juice, mustard seeds and dry mustard in a bowl and mix well. Whisk in the oil until incorporated. Stir in the dill weed, onion and cinnamon. Chill, tightly covered, in the refrigerator. The marinade may be prepared up to one week in advance.

Steam, peel and devein the shrimp. Add the shrimp to the marinade and marinate in the refrigerator for 2 to 10 hours, stirring occasionally. Serve on a bed of salad greens.

cook's note ■ If time is of the essence, use pre-cooked frozen shrimp or purchase steamed, peeled, and deveined shrimp from the local seafood market or supermarket. As an appetizer, serve in a large glass bowl with cocktail picks.

West Indies Salad *is easy to prepare and quite impressive. Mix 1 pound drained and flaked crab meat, 1 finely chopped onion, 1/2 cup vegetable oil, 1/2 cup ice water and 6 tablespoons cider vinegar. Season to taste with salt and pepper. Marinate in the refrigerator before serving to enhance the flavor. Serve on a bed of lettuce with crostini or Triscuits.*

stuffed belgian endive salad

An elegant salad.

salad
3/4 cup crumbled blue cheese
3 ounces cream cheese, softened
3 tablespoons butter, softened
2 or 3 heads Belgian endive,
    separated into spears

dijon dressing and assembly
1/4 cup vegetable oil
2 tablespoons walnut oil
2 tablespoons white wine vinegar
1 small shallot, minced
1 teaspoon Dijon mustard
1 or 2 Granny Smith apples, sliced
1 cup Caramelized Walnuts (page 67)

To prepare the salad, blend the blue cheese, cream cheese and butter in a bowl. Thinly spread the cheese mixture on each spear and reshape the spears into endive heads. Chill, covered, in the refrigerator.

To prepare the dressing, combine the vegetable oil, walnut oil, vinegar, shallot and Dijon mustard in a jar with a tight-fitting lid and seal tightly. Shake to mix.

Drizzle 1 to 2 tablespoons of the dressing onto each of six chilled salad plates. Slice the chilled endive heads crosswise into rounds. Arrange the rounds and apple slices evenly on the prepared plates. Sprinkle with the walnuts and drizzle with the remaining dressing.

fresh lemon herb salad

A simple green salad that can be served with almost any entrée.

3 tablespoons olive oil
1 tablespoon lemon juice
1 tablespoon tarragon vinegar
2 heads butter lettuce, trimmed and
    torn into bite-size pieces

1 tablespoon chopped fresh chives
1 tablespoon chopped fresh
    dill weed
1 tablespoon chopped fresh tarragon
Salt and pepper to taste

Whisk the olive oil, lemon juice and vinegar in a small nonreactive bowl. Toss the lettuce, chives, dill weed and tarragon in a salad bowl. Add the olive oil mixture to the lettuce mixture just before serving and toss until coated. Season with salt and pepper.

fab spinach salad

"Deviled eggs on spinach." A beautiful presentation of sunny yellow dressing on bright green spinach. Easily doubled for a large crowd.

1 cup mayonnaise
2 tablespoons sugar
2 tablespoons tarragon vinegar or
    wine vinegar
2 tablespoons prepared
    yellow mustard
2 tablespoons prepared horseradish
10 ounces fresh spinach leaves,
    stems removed

^{1}/4 cup grated hard-cooked egg
^{1}/4 cup (1 ounce) shredded mild
    Cheddar cheese (optional)
4 slices bacon, crisp-cooked and
    crumbled (optional)
2 tablespoons chopped shallots

Mix the mayonnaise, sugar, vinegar, prepared mustard and prepared horseradish in a bowl. Toss the spinach, egg, cheese, bacon and shallots in a salad bowl. Add the desired amount of the mayonnaise mixture and toss until coated.

garbanzo chopped salad

Chopped salad is a staple at California restaurants.

2 (15-ounce) cans garbanzo
    beans, drained, rinsed and
    coarsely chopped
4 tomatoes, peeled, seeded
    and chopped
8 ounces Genoa or hard
    salami, julienned
6 tablespoons finely chopped
    green onions

1 cup drained pimento-stuffed green
    olives, sliced
1 large garlic clove, pressed
1 teaspoon coarse salt
1 cup tarragon vinegar
1 cup olive oil
1 head iceberg lettuce, trimmed and
    finely chopped

Combine the beans, tomatoes, salami, green onions and olives in a bowl and mix well. Mix the garlic and salt in a small bowl until of a paste consistency. Add the vinegar and olive oil to the garlic mixture and stir until blended.

Pour the vinegar mixture over the bean mixture and mix until coated. Toss the lettuce with the bean mixture in a salad bowl until combined.

cook's note ■ Omit the lettuce and serve as a side bean salad.

green bean salad [serves 4 to 6]

The mountains and hills that surround the Los Angeles area provide many natural amphitheaters, and the most famous of them all is the Hollywood Bowl. Nestled in Griffith Park in the Santa Monica Mountains, the Hollywood Bowl was founded in 1922 and is the summer home of the Los Angeles Philharmonic. It also hosts a variety of other types of music as well. The Bowl is a popular entertainment destination for all ages. SummerSounds is a series of weekday concerts and fine arts programs for children. In the evening, picnicking under the stars at a concert can be an elaborate affair. Though summer is the busiest season, there are a few concerts scheduled for the winter months, and the extensive grounds are open year round to visitors. The Bowl has also been a widely used location in Hollywood productions, including movies, television, and cartoons.

1/2 cup olive oil
1/3 cup white wine vinegar
1 teaspoon dill weed
1/2 teaspoon pressed garlic
1/4 teaspoon sea salt
1/4 teaspoon pepper

11/2 pounds fresh green beans, trimmed and cut into 1-inch pieces
1 cup pecans, toasted and coarsely chopped
1 cup crumbled feta cheese
1/2 cup chopped red onion

Whisk the olive oil, vinegar, dill weed, garlic, salt and pepper in a bowl until combined. Blanch the beans in boiling water in a saucepan for 2 to 5 minutes or until tender-crisp; drain. Immediately plunge the beans into a bowl of ice water to stop the cooking process. Drain again and pat dry.

Arrange the beans in a shallow serving dish and sprinkle with the pecans, cheese and onion. Add the olive oil mixture just before serving and toss until coated.

Photograph for this recipe on page 61.

armenian white bean salad (plaki) [serves 8 to 10]

A refreshing bean side dish that is wonderful for an evening concert picnic.

1/3 cup olive oil
1 large onion, chopped
1/2 to 3/4 cup chopped carrots
6 garlic cloves, chopped or pressed
Ground cumin to taste
Salt and pepper to taste

2 (15-ounce) cans white beans, drained
1/2 cup tomato sauce
1/4 cup lemon juice
1/4 cup parsley, chopped

Heat the olive oil in a saucepan over medium heat and add the onion, carrots, garlic, cumin, salt and pepper. Cook for 10 to 15 minutes, stirring occasionally. Remove from the heat and stir in the beans, tomato sauce, lemon juice and parsley. Taste and adjust the seasonings. Chill, covered, in the refrigerator.

cook's note ■ **Plaki** is when the ingredients are cooked. **Piaz** is when they are not. Any size or variety of white beans will work in this recipe. Cannellini, Great Northern, or white navy beans are good examples.

warm german potato salad [serves 6]

This recipe was brought by my grandmother when she immigrated to the United States.

1 beef bouillon cube
1 cup warm water
1 1/2 pounds red potatoes,
   thinly sliced
Salt to taste
6 slices bacon, chopped
1/2 cup finely chopped red onion
1/3 cup white wine

1/4 cup white wine vinegar
1 egg yolk, lightly beaten
1 to 2 teaspoons sugar
1 teaspoon salt
1/2 teaspoon pepper
1/4 cup fresh dill weed, chopped
Pepper to taste

Dissolve the bouillon cube in the warm water. Boil the potatoes in salted water in a saucepan for 7 to 10 minutes or until tender. Drain and cover to keep warm. Sauté the bacon in a large skillet over medium heat until crisp. Remove the bacon to a paper towel to drain using a slotted spoon, reserving the bacon drippings.

Sauté the onion in the reserved bacon drippings for 2 to 4 minutes or until tender. Whisk in the wine, 1/3 cup of the bouillon, the vinegar, egg yolk, sugar, 1 teaspoon salt and 1/2 teaspoon pepper. Simmer until the mixture is reduced to 3/4 cup, stirring occasionally. Remove from the heat. Add the potatoes to the reduced mixture and toss to coat. Sprinkle with the bacon and dill weed and toss gently. Season with salt and pepper to taste and spoon into a serving bowl. Serve warm.

japanese miso salad dressing [makes 3/4 cup]

This is a versatile Asian dressing that can be used in a variety of ways.

1/4 cup warm water
1/4 cup light yellow miso paste
2 tablespoons mayonnaise

4 teaspoons honey
1 tablespoon sesame oil
Wasabi to taste

Whisk the warm water and miso paste in a bowl until blended. Add the mayonnaise, honey and sesame oil and whisk until combined. Stir in the desired amount of wasabi. Serve over a green salad, drizzle over sautéed mushrooms in lettuce cups or toss with soba noodles. Or, serve as a dipping sauce with pot stickers.

The unusual combination of ingredients makes Shallot and Mustard Dressing a great addition to any green salad, and it can also be used as a marinade for grilled meats, chicken, or vegetables. Mix 1 minced large shallot and 1 tablespoon Dijon mustard. Whisk in 2 tablespoons balsamic vinegar. Gradually add 1/2 cup olive oil, whisking constantly until the oil is incorporated. Chop 1 1/2 tablespoons fresh thyme and stir into the olive oil mixture. Season with salt and pepper. If the vinegar flavor is too strong, just add a little honey.

Clockwise from left to right: Crab Cioppino (page 97), Yucatan Chicken Lime Soup (page 87), Cuban Vegetable Chili (page 84)

chili, soups & stews

The Story of Santa Cruz in 4 Different Mosaics
Carole Choucair Oueijan, 2005

Sea Harbor Life and Fishing Industry

From the glistening foamy waves crashing to the shore, to the shimmering scales of the garibaldi, our state fish, swimming around the kelp beds offshore, our California waters teem with wildlife that share their home with industry, transportation, and recreational vessels in the fair Golden State.

While most of California's coast is famous for its surfing beaches and scenic lookouts, there is an amazing abundance of sea life just below the surface. The Pacific Ocean directly off our coast is part of the migratory passage of many types of whales, including the California gray whale. From February through August these gentle and mesmerizing creatures travel up and down the coast as they complete their rounds of mating, birthing, and weaning their young. On their northern migration in the spring, they are most easily seen staying close to shore to avoid their natural predators—killer whales and sharks. Baby whales and their maternal guardians are often seen in the sheltered coves of Ventura, Santa Barbara, and the Central coast, where the noise of waves crashing upon rocks and shore provides a natural sound barrier to their enemies. Three species of dolphin, as well as California sea lions, harbor seals, and northern elephant seals, can be viewed year round in our waters frolicking with surfers and delighting beachgoers with their acrobatic antics. Overhead, multitudes of sea birds reveal the bounty below as they dive and bob for the hapless fish swimming too close to the surface.

Our fishing industry ranks California among the top five states in seafood production. With nearly three hundred varieties of fish and shellfish native to our coastline, this industry alone provides thousands of jobs ranging from fishermen, both professional and recreational, to processors, to longshoremen, as well as allied fields such as boat building, gear suppliers, exporters, markets, and restaurateurs—all the way down to the consumer.

The jagged coastline of California provides a multitude of small bays, inlets, marinas, and harbors that provide safe haven for many recreational watercraft and sailboats. The fishing, cruise, and shipping industries have access in two natural harbor formations, one in San Francisco, the other in San Diego, and two smaller natural bays in Humboldt and Monterey. The port cities of Los Angeles and Long Beach, while fabricated by man, are two additional gateways to the world. Millions of shipping containers pass through the Port of Los Angeles each year, ranking it as the busiest container port in the United States. In a mosaic that only nature could create, the coastal waters of California not only add wealth but also provide beauty with its varied riches.

Food photography sponsored by Bonnie and John DeWitt
Mosaic photography sponsored by Brenda and Steve O'Neil

après ski chili

Warm your soul after a hard day on the slopes.

Arboretum

The Los Angeles County Arboretum and Botanic Garden in Arcadia serves as a reminder of the many periods in California's history. The Arboretum is a 127-acre botanical garden and historical site jointly operated by the Los Angeles Arboretum Foundation and the Los Angeles County Department of Parks and Recreation. Original adobe homes, replicas of the Native American wickiups and National and State Historical Landmarks, such as the Queen Anne Cottage, the Coach Barn, and the Santa Anita Railroad Depot, can be found on the property. During the summer months, The Arboretum hosts the California Philharmonic Concerts on the Green.

2 tablespoons olive oil
1 cup chopped onion
1 garlic clove, pressed
3 pounds lean ground beef or
    ground turkey
8 ounces pork sausage
1 to 2 teaspoons salt, or to taste
2 (15-ounce) cans stewed tomatoes
1 (6-ounce) can tomato paste
2 (15-ounce) cans kidney beans

3 tablespoons (or more) chili powder
3 tablespoons ground cumin
1 tablespoon dill weed
2 teaspoons oregano
2 teaspoons basil
1 to 2 tablespoons prepared yellow
    mustard, or to taste
1 tablespoon lemon juice
1/4 cup brandy

Heat the olive oil in a large Dutch oven and add the onion. Sauté until the onion is tender. Stir in the garlic and cook for 1 minute. Add the ground beef and sausage and cook until brown and crumbly, stirring frequently and sprinkling with the salt during the cooking process; drain. Stir in the tomatoes and tomato paste. Add the undrained beans, chili powder, cumin, dill weed, oregano, basil, prepared mustard and lemon juice and mix well.

Simmer for 2 to 3 hours to allow the flavors to blend, stirring occasionally. You may chill or freeze the chili at this point for future use. If frozen, thaw in the refrigerator. Reheat the chili and stir in the brandy about 15 minutes before serving. Ladle into chili bowls.

two-alarm tex-mex chili

[serves 8 to 10]

An award-winning spicy chili for meat-lovers.

1 pound pork sausage,
    casings removed
8 to 9 pounds lean chuck roast or
    stew meat, chopped into
    1/2-inch pieces
2 yellow onions, finely chopped
2 cups finely chopped tomatoes
12 ounces tomato purée
6 tablespoons chili powder
2 1/2 tablespoons ground cumin

1 tablespoon paprika
1 tablespoon salt
1 tablespoon finely ground
    black pepper
2 teaspoons cayenne pepper
2 teaspoons fines herbes
1 teaspoon onion powder
2 garlic cloves, pressed
1 (12-ounce) bottle Mexican beer

Cook the sausage in a Dutch oven over medium-high heat just until light brown and add the chuck roast. Watch the heat carefully, as too high a heat will cause the sausage to shrink, imparting a rubbery taste. Cook until the roast is light brown and add the onions. Cook until the onions are golden brown. Stir in the tomatoes, tomato purée, chili powder, cumin, paprika, salt, black pepper, cayenne pepper, fines herbes, onion powder and garlic. Mix in half the beer. Cook over low heat for 1 1/2 hours, stirring occasionally. Gently stir in the remaining beer and cook for 1 1/2 hours longer. Ladle into chili bowls and serve with tortilla chips.

corn and chicken chili

[serves 4 to 6]

An old family recipe that uses corn instead of beans to add texture.

1 tablespoon corn oil or vegetable oil
1 onion, chopped
2 garlic cloves, minced
2 teaspoons ground cumin
3 boneless skinless chicken breasts,
    chopped into bite-size pieces
1 (15-ounce) can white
    hominy, drained
1 (15-ounce) can yellow corn
1 (15-ounce) can yellow
    cream-style corn

1 (15-ounce) can diced tomatoes
1 (12-ounce) jar salsa verde
2 (4-ounce) cans diced green chiles
1 cup chicken stock
1 tablespoon dried oregano
1 tablespoon chili powder
Salt and pepper to taste
1 cup (4 ounces) shredded Monterey
    Jack cheese for garnish
2 tablespoons chopped cilantro
    for garnish

Heat the corn oil in a Dutch oven and stir in the onion, garlic and cumin. Cook until the onion is tender and stir in the chicken. Cook until the chicken is cooked through, stirring occasionally. Add the hominy, corn, tomatoes, salsa verde, green chiles, stock, oregano and chili powder and mix well.

Cover and bring to a boil. Reduce the heat to low and simmer, covered, for 30 minutes. Season with salt and pepper. Ladle into chili bowls and sprinkle with the cheese and cilantro. Add additional stock for a thinner consistency or less stock for a thicker consistency.

cuban vegetable chili [serves 8]

A meatless chili that is chock-full of flavor from the vegetables and fresh herbs.

1 eggplant, cut into 1/2-inch pieces
1 tablespoon salt
1/4 cup olive oil
2 yellow onions, chopped
2 zucchini, chopped
1 red bell pepper, chopped
1 yellow bell pepper, chopped
4 large garlic cloves, minced
     or pressed
1/4 cup olive oil
8 fresh ripe or canned
     plum tomatoes
1 cup vegetable or chicken broth
1/2 cup Italian parsley, chopped
1/2 cup fresh basil, julienned
3 tablespoons chili powder

11/2 tablespoons ground cumin
1 tablespoon oregano
1 teaspoon pepper
2 cups soaked dried black beans,
     cooked, or 2 (15-ounce) cans
     black beans
11/2 cups frozen corn
1/2 cup fresh dill weed, chopped, or
     1/4 cup dried dill weed
1/4 cup lemon juice
1/2 cup Italian parsley, chopped
Sour cream for garnish
Shredded Monterey Jack cheese
     for garnish
Chopped green onions for garnish
Sprigs of dill weed for garnish

Place the eggplant in a colander and sprinkle with the salt. Let drain for 1 hour to remove any excess moisture; pat dry. Heat 1/4 cup olive oil in a large Dutch oven and add the yellow onions, zucchini, bell peppers and garlic. Sauté for 10 minutes.

Heat 1/4 cup olive oil in a skillet and add the eggplant. Cook for 10 minutes or until tender, stirring frequently. Add the eggplant to the sautéed vegetable mixture using a slotted spoon. Stir in the tomatoes, broth, 1/2 cup parsley, the basil, chili powder, cumin, oregano and pepper.

Cook over low heat for 30 minutes, stirring occasionally. Stir in the beans, corn, chopped dill weed and lemon juice. Cook for 15 minutes longer and stir in 1/2 cup parsley. Ladle into chili bowls and garnish with sour cream, cheese, green onions and/or sprigs of dill weed.

Photograph for this recipe on page 79.

avocado gazpacho

[serves 8]

The surprise of pineapple adds a nice zing to this cold summer soup.

8 cups fresh pineapple chunks
    or juice
4 avocados, cut into chunks
2 teaspoons salt
1 teaspoon Tabasco sauce

1 tomato, chopped
1 red bell pepper, chopped
1 avocado, chopped
Sour cream for garnish
Chopped fresh cilantro for garnish

Process the pineapple and 4 avocados in batches in a blender until puréed. Pour into a sealed container and stir in the salt and Tabasco sauce. You may prepare in advance to this point and store, covered, in the refrigerator.

Just before serving gently stir in the tomato, bell pepper and 1 chopped avocado. Ladle into chilled soup bowls and garnish each serving with a dollop of sour cream and chopped cilantro.

cook's note ■ Add the bell pepper just before serving. The flavor becomes too dominant if it is allowed to sit overnight.

hungarian soup

[serves 6]

Perfect on a cold winter weekend.

6 slices bacon, chopped
1/2 cup chopped onion
11/2 pounds ground beef
1 (28-ounce) can diced tomatoes
2 potatoes, chopped
3 carrots, thickly sliced
1 cup sliced celery with leaves

2 cups water
1 (10-ounce) can consommé
1 cup half-and-half or cream
11/2 teaspoons salt
1/4 cup cornstarch
1/2 teaspoon pepper
Grated Parmesan cheese for garnish

Sauté the bacon in a large Dutch oven until partially cooked. Add the onion and cook until the onion is golden brown. Add the ground beef and cook over medium heat until the ground beef is brown and crumbly, stirring frequently; drain. Stir in the tomatoes, potatoes, carrots, celery, water, consommé, half-and-half and salt. Bring to a boil and reduce the heat to low.

Simmer, covered, for 45 minutes, stirring occasionally. Blend the cornstarch with enough cold water in a small bowl to form a smooth paste. Add the cornstarch mixture to the soup and mix well. Bring to a boil and stir in the pepper. Ladle into soup bowls and garnish with cheese. Serve with crackers and/or crusty bread.

italian wedding soup

A brothy meatball and pasta soup that is a hit with both children and adults.

meatballs
8 ounces extra-lean ground beef
1 egg, lightly beaten
2 tablespoons dried bread crumbs
1 tablespoon grated Parmesan cheese
1/2 teaspoon dried basil
1/2 teaspoon onion powder

soup
5 3/4 cups chicken broth
1 cup orzo
1/3 cup finely chopped carrots
2 cups spinach leaves, sliced

To prepare the meatballs, combine the ground beef, egg, bread crumbs, cheese, basil and onion powder in a bowl and mix well. Shape the ground beef mixture into 3/4-inch balls.

To prepare the soup, bring the broth to a boil in a large saucepan over high heat and add the meatballs, pasta and carrots. Reduce the heat to medium and cook for 5 minutes. Stir in the spinach and cook for 5 minutes longer or until the pasta is tender, stirring frequently to prevent sticking. Ladle into soup bowls and serve with grated Parmesan cheese.

kielbasa, potato and leek soup

For a hearty meal, serve this German soup with a green salad and crusty bread.

6 slices bacon, coarsely chopped
1 (1-pound) head green cabbage,
    trimmed and shredded
1 onion, chopped
4 ribs celery, chopped
6 leeks, chopped

8 cups chicken broth
2 pounds potatoes, chopped
1 pound kielbasa, sliced
Shredded Cheddar cheese
    for garnish
Chopped fresh dill weed for garnish

Cook 6 slices bacon in a Dutch oven until crisp. Remove the bacon to a plate using a slotted spoon, reserving the bacon drippings and bacon. Cook the cabbage, onion, celery and leeks in the reserved bacon drippings until the vegetables are tender, stirring frequently. Stir in the broth and potatoes. Bring to a boil and reduce the heat to low.

Simmer for 1 hour, stirring occasionally. Add the kielbasa and cook for 15 minutes longer or until the sausage is heated through. Ladle into soup bowls and garnish with the reserved bacon, cheese and dill weed.

cook's note ■ For a richer soup, stir in 2 cups cream after the kielbasa has cooked for 15 minutes. Do not allow the soup to boil once the cream has been added.

yucatan chicken lime soup (sopa de lima)

Beyond its medicinal value, this is a tasty soup.

chicken stock
Sprigs of parsley and thyme
1 bay leaf
1 chicken
1 onion, cut into quarters
1 tomato, cut into quarters
2 carrots, cut into large chunks
2 ribs celery, cut into large chunks
4 garlic cloves

soup
4 (6-inch) corn or flour tortillas,
    cut into matchstick strips

1 tablespoon olive oil
1 onion, thinly sliced
8 garlic cloves, thinly sliced
1 to 4 serrano or jalapeño chiles,
    seeded if desired and
    thinly sliced
1/2 cup (or more) fresh lime juice
1 large tomato, cut into
    1/2-inch pieces
Salt and pepper to taste
1/4 cup coarsely chopped
    fresh cilantro

To prepare the stock, enclose the parsley, thyme and bay leaf in cheesecloth. Combine the cheesecloth bag, chicken, onion, tomato, carrots, celery and garlic in a stockpot. Add enough water to cover by 2 inches or more. Bring to a boil and skim the foam that rises to the surface. Reduce the heat to low and simmer for 1 hour, skimming the foam and fat as needed. Remove the chicken to a bowl and cover with ice water to cool quickly, reserving the stock.

Shred the chicken, discarding the skin and bones. Reserve 2 cups of the chicken for the soup; freeze the remaining chicken for another recipe. Strain the reserved stock, discarding the solids. Reserve 5 cups of the stock for the soup and freeze any remaining stock in 1-cup portions for future use.

To prepare the soup, preheat the oven to 400 degrees. Arrange the tortilla strips in a single layer on a nonstick or foil-lined baking sheet. Bake for 4 minutes or until light brown. Remove to a plate to cool.

Heat the olive oil in a large stockpot or saucepan and add the onion, garlic and serrano chile. Cook over medium heat for 5 minutes or until light brown. Stir in the reserved 5 cups chicken stock, the reserved 2 cups chicken, the lime juice and tomato. Simmer for 3 minutes or until the chicken is heated through. Season with salt and pepper and add additional lime juice if desired; the soup should be highly seasoned. Stir in the cilantro and ladle into soup bowls. Sprinkle with the tortilla strips.

cook's note ■ You may substitute a precut fryer for the chicken, but less meat will be available. Or, substitute with 12 ounces chopped boneless skinless chicken breasts. Reprinted with permission from the **Los Angeles Times**.

Photograph for this recipe on page 79.

The cure for the common cold? This soup helps provide relief from runny nose, congested nasal passages, rheumy eyes, and raw throat. The chiles blast open your sinuses; how much depends on whether you have scraped the seed-bearing veins from the interior of the chiles. The lime juice loads you up with vitamin C. The garlic is said to have immune system–enhancing properties. The steaming broth soothes your throat. The chicken nourishes you, while the cilantro revives your taste buds. Good stock is the secret, and Yucatan Chicken Lime Soup is definitely worth the minimal extra effort. But if you are too sick, canned stock will suffice. Also, do not even consider using bottled lime juice for this soup; fresh lime juice makes all the difference in the taste.

champagne chicken noodle soup

[serves 4]

A delicious way to use extra bottles of Champagne.

If you are a fan of blue cheese, this Blue Cheese Soup is sure to become a favorite. Bring 50 ounces homemade or canned chicken or vegetable stock just to the boiling point and stir in 8 ounces crumbled blue cheese of choice. Cook until the cheese melts and stir in 1 1/2 cups heavy whipping cream, salt and pepper. Simmer just until heated through; do not boil. Ladle into soup bowls. Beef stock or fish stock is not recommended for this recipe.

2 tablespoons all-purpose flour
1/4 teaspoon salt
1/4 teaspoon pepper
2 1/2 pounds boneless skinless
   chicken breasts or chicken
   tenders, cut into bite-size pieces
1 1/2 teaspoons olive oil
3 cups Champagne
3 cups chicken broth
3 carrots, cut into 1/2-inch pieces

3 large ribs celery, cut into
   1-inch pieces
2 tablespoons fresh parsley,
   chopped
Grated zest of 1 orange
   (1 tablespoon)
1/2 teaspoon thyme
8 ounces wide egg noodles
Salt to taste

Mix the flour, 1/4 teaspoon salt and the pepper in a sealable plastic bag. Pat the chicken dry and add to the flour mixture. Seal tightly and toss to coat.

Heat the olive oil in a Dutch oven and add the chicken. Cook until brown on all sides, stirring frequently. Stir in the Champagne, broth, carrots, celery, parsley, orange zest and thyme. Bring to a boil over medium heat and reduce the heat.

Boil gently for 45 minutes, stirring occasionally. Cook the noodles using the package directions in boiling salted water in a saucepan just until al dente; drain. Divide the warm noodles evenly among four shallow soup bowls and ladle the soup over the noodles. Serve immediately.

tortilla soup

This traditional Mexican soup is thickened by tortillas that dissolve in the broth.

1/3 cup chopped onion
3 garlic cloves, chopped
3/4 teaspoon ground cumin
3/4 teaspoon dried oregano
1/4 teaspoon chili powder
1/4 teaspoon pepper
8 cups reduced-fat chicken broth
1 (14-ounce) can diced tomatoes
1 (4-ounce) can diced green chiles
10 (6-inch) corn tortillas
11/2 pounds boneless skinless
   chicken breasts, cut into
   1/2-inch pieces

2 tablespoons chopped
   fresh cilantro
Salt to taste
1 avocado, cut into small pieces
   for garnish
Shredded sharp Cheddar cheese
   for garnish
Homemade tortilla chips for garnish
Sour cream for garnish
Chopped cilantro for garnish

Heat the onion, garlic, cumin, oregano, chili powder and pepper in a 5- to 6-quart nonstick saucepan over medium heat for 1 minute or until fragrant. Stir in the broth, undrained tomatoes and green chiles. Cover and bring to a boil over high heat.

Stack the tortillas and cut into 1/8-inch strips. Add the tortilla strips to the boiling broth and reduce the heat. Simmer, covered, for 15 minutes, stirring occasionally.

Add the chicken to the soup mixture and return to a boil over high heat. Reduce the heat and simmer, covered, for 5 minutes or until the chicken is cooked through. Stir in 2 tablespoons cilantro and season with salt. Ladle into soup bowls and garnish each serving with avocado, cheese, tortilla chips, sour cream and cilantro.

turkey matzo ball soup

This family recipe comes from a deli that two Holocaust survivors opened in New York City after the war.

soup

1 parsnip

2 or 3 turkey wings, or
    1 turkey breast

2 chicken thighs

3 carrots, cut into 1/2-inch slices

2 ribs celery, cut into large chunks

1 large onion, cut into large chunks

1 large garlic clove, coarsely chopped

1/4 teaspoon paprika

Salt and pepper to taste

3 sprigs of dill weed

matzo balls and assembly

6 eggs

1 cup matzo meal

1 cup stock or broth (from the soup
    or canned)

1 teaspoon salt

1/2 teaspoon pepper

To prepare the soup, chop the parsnip into large chunks, reserving the tops. Combine the turkey and chicken with enough water to generously cover in a large stockpot or Dutch oven. Turn the heat to high and as the water comes to a boil add the parsnip, carrots, celery, onion, garlic, paprika, salt and pepper. Skim the foam and fat as they rise to the top. Reduce the heat to low and simmer for 1 hour. Stir in the reserved parsnip tops and dill weed and simmer for 30 minutes longer.

To prepare the matzo balls, whisk the eggs in a large bowl until blended. Stir in the matzo meal, 1/2 cup of the stock, the salt and pepper. Chill, covered, for 40 minutes. Add the remaining stock to the matzo mixture a few tablespoons at a time until of the desired consistency. Shape the matzo mixture into balls the size of large golf balls. Less moisture creates hard matzo balls and more moisture creates lighter fluffier matzo balls.

Remove all the solids from the soup, except the carrots. Chop the turkey and chicken, discarding the skin and bones. Return the turkey and chicken to the soup or reserve for a future recipe. Add the matzo balls and cook until the matzo balls rise to the top. Ladle into soup bowls.

cook's note ■ For a shortcut, substitute 2 large cans plus 1 cup chicken broth for the homemade soup. Cook the carrots and dill weed together until the carrots are tender and add to the canned broth along with the matzo balls. Cook until the matzo balls rise to the top.

turkey mole soup

Mole is a traditional Mexican concoction that some say originated with the Aztecs. It has many variations but is usually a combination of chiles, chocolate, and spices such as cinnamon.

1 tablespoon vegetable oil
2 onions, chopped
1 1/2 teaspoons dried oregano
1 1/2 teaspoons ground cumin
1 1/2 pounds lean ground turkey
1/4 cup chili powder
2 bay leaves
1 tablespoon baking cocoa
1 1/2 teaspoons salt
1/4 teaspoon ground cinnamon

1 (28-ounce) can whole tomatoes
3 cups beef stock or canned
   beef broth
1 (8-ounce) can tomato sauce
3 (15-ounce) cans small white beans,
   drained and rinsed
Chopped red onion for garnish
Chopped fresh cilantro for garnish
Plain low-fat yogurt or light
   sour cream for garnish

Heat the oil in a large Dutch oven or stockpot over medium heat. Sauté 2 chopped onions in the hot oil for 10 minutes or until light brown and tender. Add the oregano and cumin and cook for 1 minute, stirring constantly. Increase the heat to medium-high and add the ground turkey.

Cook until the ground turkey is brown and crumbly, stirring frequently. Stir in the chili powder, bay leaves, baking cocoa, salt and cinnamon. Add the undrained tomatoes and break into smaller pieces with the back of a spoon. Stir in the stock and tomato sauce and bring to a boil. Reduce the heat to low.

Simmer for 45 minutes, stirring occasionally. Add the beans and cook for 10 minutes longer to allow the flavors to blend. Discard the bay leaves. You may prepare to this point up to one day in advance and store, covered, in the refrigerator. Reheat over medium-low heat. Ladle into soup bowls and garnish with chopped red onion, cilantro and/or yogurt.

Huntington Gardens
& Museums
*The Huntington
Library, Botanical
Gardens and Art
Collections are located
on a sprawling 120
acres in San Marino.
Originally the home
of Henry E. and
Arabella Huntington,
the Huntington estate
is now open to the
public and researchers
alike. Notable works
found in the Huntington
Collection include
Gainsborough's The
Blue Boy and a
Gutenberg Bible, along
with letters from
Washington, Jefferson,
Franklin, and Lincoln.
The Botanical Gardens
are arranged by themes,
such as the Japanese
Garden, the Shakespeare
Garden, the Subtropical
and Jungle Garden, the
Desert Garden, and
the Camellia Collection.*

texas oyster chowder

My Texas grandmother shared this chowder recipe with me. It is a wonderful supper on a chilly winter night.

2 (8-ounce) cans oysters
1/4 cup (1/2 stick) butter
1 yellow onion, coarsely chopped
2 shallots, finely chopped
1/4 teaspoon Worcestershire sauce
4 dashes of Tabasco sauce
1/4 teaspoon habanero chile sauce
1/2 cup chardonnay
1 cup water
1/4 teaspoon dried thyme

1/4 teaspoon dried summer savory
Salt and freshly ground pepper
   to taste
2 Yukon gold potatoes, sliced and
   cut into quarters
1 cup milk
1 cup half-and-half
2 tablespoons chopped fresh parsley
Chopped fresh parsley for garnish

Drain the oysters, reserving the liquor. Melt the butter in a stockpot. Add the onion, shallots, Worcestershire sauce, Tabasco sauce and habanero chile sauce to the butter and cook over medium heat for 8 minutes, stirring frequently. Add the wine and cook for 4 minutes or until the mixture is slightly reduced. Stir in the reserved liquor, water, thyme, savory, salt and pepper and bring to a boil. Stir in the potatoes.

Cook for 15 minutes or until the potatoes are cooked through but firm. Using a potato masher lightly mash a few of the potatoes to thicken the soup, leaving the majority of the potatoes intact. Stir in the milk and bring to a boil.

Boil for 2 minutes. Mix in the half-and-half and cook just until heated through; do not boil. Stir in the oysters and 2 tablespoons parsley. Cook for 5 minutes or until heated through. Taste and season with salt and pepper. Ladle into shallow soup bowls and garnish with parsley. Serve with toasted baguette slices.

cream of artichoke soup

A delicate soup with a hint of lemon. Lovely as a first course.

1 (12-ounce) can artichoke hearts
1 (13-ounce) can chicken broth
1 tablespoon lemon juice
3/4 teaspoon salt

Dash of pepper
1 cup heavy cream
6 thin lemon slices for garnish

Drain and rinse the artichokes. Process the artichokes and broth in a blender until puréed. Pour the artichoke purée into a saucepan and stir in the lemon juice, salt and pepper.

Bring just to the boiling point and remove from the heat. Stir in the cream and reheat if needed; do not allow to boil. Ladle into soup bowls and garnish with the lemon slices.

carrot and ginger soup

A creamy soup without the cream.

1/4 cup (1/2 stick) butter
2 pounds carrots, sliced
2 onions, chopped
2 garlic cloves, pressed
6 cups chicken broth

1 tablespoon grated fresh ginger, or
    1 teaspoon ground ginger
1 teaspoon salt
Pepper to taste
Crème fraîche or sour cream
    for garnish

Melt the butter in a saucepan and stir in the carrots, onions and garlic. Cook, covered, for 20 minutes or until the vegetables are tender. Add the broth and simmer for 30 minutes. Stir in the ginger, salt and pepper. Taste and adjust the seasonings.

Process the soup in a blender or using an immersion blender until puréed. Simmer just until heated through. Ladle into soup bowls and garnish with crème fraîche.

mushroom soup

The three different mushrooms add complexity to this easily prepared soup.

2 tablespoons butter
1 cup white mushrooms, chopped
1 leek bulb, chopped
1 garlic clove, pressed or chopped
2 (14-ounce) cans chicken broth
$1/3$ cup white mushrooms, sliced

$1/3$ cup shiitake mushrooms
$1/3$ cup chopped or sliced
    portobello mushroom
2 tablespoons snipped chives
    for garnish

Melt the butter in a saucepan and stir in chopped white mushrooms, leek and garlic. Sauté until the mushrooms and leek are tender. Stir in the broth, sliced white mushrooms, shiitake mushrooms and portobello mushroom.

Cook for 5 minutes or until heated through, stirring occasionally. Ladle into soup bowls and garnish with the chives.

pumpkin carrot soup

The splash of sherry gives this autumn soup a warm, smoky flavor.

1 tablespoon olive oil
$3^{1}/2$ cups chopped peeled pumpkin
    (about $1^{1}/2$ pounds)
$1^{1}/3$ cups chopped carrots
    (about 2 medium carrots)
1 cup chopped onion
1 tablespoon curry powder
$1^{1}/2$ teaspoons ground cumin

$1/2$ teaspoon cayenne pepper
1 tablespoon all-purpose flour
2 (14-ounce) cans chicken broth
$1/2$ teaspoon salt, or to taste
Chopped fresh parsley for garnish
Sour cream for garnish
Sherry for garnish

Heat the olive oil in a Dutch oven over medium-high heat and add the pumpkin, carrots, onion, curry powder, cumin and cayenne pepper. Sauté for 5 minutes. Stir in the flour and cook for 1 minute, stirring constantly. Mix in the broth and salt and bring to a boil. Reduce the heat to low.

Simmer, covered, for 25 minutes or until the vegetables are tender, stirring occasionally. Process the soup in batches in a blender until puréed. Return the purée to the Dutch oven and reheat over medium heat. Ladle into soup bowls and garnish with parsley, sour cream and a splash of sherry.

cook's note ■ Can easily substitute one 15-ounce can pumpkin purée for the fresh pumpkin. Stir in with the broth and salt.

lentil vegetable soup

The fresh vegetables together with the lentils make this a healthy and delicious soup.

3 tomatoes
7 cups vegetable or chicken broth
1 cup green or brown lentils, rinsed
3 carrots, chopped
1 red bell pepper, chopped
4 ribs celery, chopped
1 bay leaf
3 tablespoons olive oil

1 large red onion, finely chopped
1 leek, finely chopped
2 garlic cloves, pressed
1 pound spinach, trimmed and sliced
   (about 4 cups)
Salt and pepper to taste
Red wine vinegar to taste
Grated Parmesan cheese for garnish

Peel, seed and chop the tomatoes over a bowl, reserving the juice. Combine the reserved tomato juice, broth, lentils, carrots, bell pepper, celery and bay leaf in a stockpot and bring to a boil; skim the foam. Reduce the heat to a slow boil and cook until the lentils are tender, stirring occasionally.

Heat the olive oil in a skillet over medium-high heat and add the onion. Sauté for 3 minutes. Reduce the heat to medium and add the leek and garlic. Continue cooking until the onion is tender. Stir in the tomatoes and cook for 5 minutes longer. Add the tomato mixture to the lentil mixture and mix well.

Add the spinach in batches to the lentil mixture when the lentils are tender. Cook until the spinach wilts. Thin the soup with water if necessary. Discard the bay leaf and season with salt, pepper and vinegar. Ladle into soup bowls and garnish with Parmesan cheese.

cabbage patch stew

This hearty soup can be ready in a jiffy.

1 pound ground beef
2 onions, thinly sliced
1/2 small head cabbage,
   finely chopped
1/2 cup chopped celery
2 cups water (optional)
1 (15-ounce) can ranch-style beans
1 (15-ounce) can corn

1 (15-ounce) can diced tomatoes
1 garlic clove, pressed
1 teaspoon chili powder
1 teaspoon paprika
1 teaspoon salt
1 teaspoon pepper
1 teaspoon garlic salt

Brown the ground beef with the onions, cabbage and celery in a stockpot, stirring until the ground beef is crumbly; drain. Stir in the water and simmer for 15 minutes. Add the beans, corn, tomatoes, garlic, chili powder, paprika, salt, pepper and garlic salt and mix well. Simmer, covered, for 30 minutes, stirring occasionally. Ladle into soup bowls.

argentine beef stew in a pumpkin shell

Pumpkins are not just for Halloween. Everyone will love the show-stopping presentation of this delicious stew.

3 tablespoons olive oil
2 pounds beef stew meat, cut into
    1/2-inch pieces
2 cups chopped onions
11/2 cups chopped leeks
2 garlic cloves, pressed or minced
2 (10-ounce) cans beef consommé
2 large tomatoes, chopped
1 cup chopped green bell pepper
1/2 cup chopped celery
1/2 cup celery leaves, chopped
3 potatoes, peeled and chopped

3 yams, peeled and chopped
1 tablespoon salt
1 teaspoon sugar
1/2 teaspoon pepper
1 (15-ounce) can whole kernel corn
1 cup dried apricots
1/4 to 1/2 cup sherry
1 (10-pound) pumpkin
1/4 to 1/2 cup (1/2 to 1 stick)
    butter, melted
Salt and pepper to taste

Heat the olive oil in a Dutch oven over medium-high heat and add the beef, onions, leeks and garlic. Sauté until the beef is brown and stir in the consommé, tomatoes, bell pepper, celery, celery leaves, potatoes, yams, 1 tablespoon salt, the sugar and 1/2 teaspoon pepper. Simmer, covered, for 11/2 hours, stirring occasionally. Add the corn, apricots and sherry and mix well. Preheat the oven to 325 degrees. Cut the top from the pumpkin and discard. Scoop out the seeds and membranes. Brush the inside of the pumpkin with the butter and sprinkle with salt and pepper to taste. Arrange the pumpkin in a shallow baking pan. Ladle the beef mixture into the pumpkin and bake for 11/2 to 2 hours or until the pumpkin is tender. Place the pumpkin on a serving platter and ladle the stew into individual bowls, scraping some of the cooked pumpkin with each serving.

cook's note ■ The pumpkin may be omitted if unavailable. Add the corn, apricots and sherry to the beef mixture and simmer, covered, for 30 minutes.

crab cioppino

A special occasion recipe, when you want to take the time to make something delicious and hence make your guests feel special. Well worth the effort.

1/4 cup olive oil
4 onions, finely chopped
1 cup chopped celery
1 green bell pepper, chopped
1/2 cup parsley, chopped
5 green onions, chopped
8 garlic cloves, chopped or pressed
1 tablespoon red chili pepper flakes
1 tablespoon rosemary
1 tablespoon oregano
1 tablespoon Italian seasoning
1 tablespoon sage
1 tablespoon thyme
1 teaspoon basil
2 chicken bouillon cubes
2 beef bouillon cubes
1/2 teaspoon paprika
1/4 teaspoon poultry seasoning

1/4 teaspoon ground nutmeg
1/4 teaspoon ground allspice
Pinch of ground cinnamon
1 (28-ounce) can diced tomatoes
3 (8-ounce) cans tomato sauce
3 cups water
1 cup white wine
1 cup red wine
2 bay leaves
Meat of 3 Dungeness crabs
3 pounds clams, cleaned (optional)
3 pounds large prawns, peeled
   and deveined
8 ounces fresh white fish such as
   sea bass, rock cod or halibut,
   cut into chunks (optional)
1 lemon, sliced
Salt and pepper to taste

Crab Cioppino was my grandmother's version of the traditional Italian fish stew that she made when I was growing up in San Francisco. It was our traditional Christmas Eve dinner, and the smell of this dish cooking still transports me back to my childhood. I can still picture her in the kitchen.

Heat the olive oil in a large stockpot and add the onions, celery, bell pepper, parsley, green onions, garlic, red pepper flakes, rosemary, oregano, Italian seasoning, sage, thyme and basil. Sauté until the vegetables are wilted and brown. Stir in the bouillon cubes, paprika, poultry seasoning, nutmeg, allspice and cinnamon. Add the tomatoes, tomato sauce, water, wine and bay leaves and mix well.

Bring to a boil and reduce the heat. Simmer for 2 1/2 to 3 hours or until thickened, stirring occasionally. Stir in the crab meat, clams and prawns and cook for 1 to 1 1/2 hours, adding the fish and lemon slices during the last 30 minutes of the cooking process. Discard the bay leaves. Taste and season with salt and pepper and ladle into soup bowls. You may substitute deveined, peeled and steamed shrimp for the prawns. Add the shrimp a few minutes before the end of the cooking process and cook just until heated through.

Photograph for this recipe on page 78.

Clockwise from left to right: Caribbean Balsamic-Glazed Veal Chops (page 109), Grilled Brazilian Beer Chicken (page 120), Citrus-Roasted Salmon (page 130)

main dishes

The Will To Progress
El Deseo de Progresar
Ricardo Mendoza, 2004

Hispanic Influence in Our Culture

In 1769, Father Junipero Serra, a Franciscan missionary, founded the first of the California missions in San Diego. In the short span of years from 1769 to 1798, he was the person primarily responsible for founding the additional sixteen missions located along what is now known as the El Camino Real or California Mission Trail. These missions, not surprisingly, were situated on prime agricultural land, and as the Spanish quested for religious, civil, and military superiority over the Indians, the missions became the center of life for the regions they represented. From the very southern tip of California to the northernmost tip, the blueprint for future cities had been laid, and these prosperous communities swelled with wealth and converts to Christianity. The downfall of Spain's, and subsequently Mexico's, hold on the missions is ancient history now, but the lingering influence on our modern existence serves to enhance the patina of California culture and season our everyday lives.

The very name California is taken from a popular Spanish novel from 1510 called *Las Sergas de Esplandian* (The Exploits of Esplandian) by Garcia Ordonez de Montalvo. It describes a beautiful, mythical land whose name is an appropriate moniker for our state. Our street names, our foods, our freeways, our mountain ranges, everywhere we look we see the indelible mark of our Hispanic past surrounding us. Certainly, there are remnants of pueblos, ranchos, and historic settings in almost every county of the state, but Los Angeles boasts its very own traditional Mexican marketplace, Olvera Street.

Olvera Street was originally a small lane called Wine Street, but over time the street was extended and the name changed. There are several historic buildings along the lovely tree-lined street including the Avila Adobe, built around 1818 by former mayor Francisco Avila; the Pelanconi House, built in 1855 and the oldest brick house in the city; and the Sepulveda House, built in 1887 in the Eastlake Victorian style. Sadly, Olvera Street and its surrounding area fell into disrepair in the early twentieth century. But in 1926, a group of influential citizens led by socialite Christine Sterling, with publicity from the *Los Angeles Times*, started a campaign to revitalize the oldest part of Los Angeles. A corporation was established with the mission of establishing a colorful, vibrant Mexican marketplace and cultural center—a place where vendors could have the opportunity to sell traditional wares and present the customs and trades of early California. In 1930, Olvera Street reopened with LA's very first authentic Mexican restaurant, La Golondrina Café, located in the Pelanconi House, anchoring the many shops and booths that now bustle with tourists. Today, Olvera Street is the epicenter for the many festivals celebrating our Hispanic heritage, including Cinco de Mayo, Blessing of the Animals, Mexican Independence Day, Dia de Los Muertos, La Vergen de Guadelupe, and the beautiful Las Posadas. Our many Hispanic citizens continue the long-standing tradition of adding color and beauty to our community.

Food photography sponsored by Jennifer and Sam Cargill
Mosaic photography sponsored by Mara Lague

texas brisket with beer

Delicious with More Than Mashed Potatoes on page 155.

1 (5-pound) brisket, trimmed	1/4 cup chili powder
Salt and pepper to taste	2 tablespoons brown sugar
1 yellow onion, sliced	1 garlic clove, minced or pressed
1 (12-ounce) bottle beer	2 tablespoons all-purpose flour

Preheat the oven to 350 degrees. Season the brisket with salt and pepper and arrange fat side up in a large baking pan. Cover with the onion slices. Mix the beer, chili powder, brown sugar and garlic in a bowl and pour over the brisket. Bake, covered with foil, for 3 hours. Discard the foil and bake for 30 minutes longer.

Remove the brisket to a serving platter and place the onion slices in a food processor, reserving the pan drippings. Pulse until the onion is ground. Skim the excess fat from the reserved pan drippings. Combine the reserved pan drippings with enough water to measure 1 cup. Return the pan drippings mixture to the baking pan and blend in the flour and ground onion. Cook over medium heat to the desired consistency, stirring frequently. Slice the brisket and serve with the gravy.

cook's note ▦ Marinate the brisket for up to 24 hours to enhance the flavor. For a beautiful presentation, garnish the serving platter with kale and cherry tomatoes.

bavarian beef

1 (2 1/2- to 3-pound) boneless beef pot roast, trimmed	1/2 cup dry red wine or beef broth
1 tablespoon vegetable oil	1/2 cup German-style mustard
3 carrots, sliced	1/2 teaspoon coarsely ground pepper
2 parsnips, sliced	1/4 teaspoon ground cloves
2 leeks, chopped	2 bay leaves
1/2 onion, chopped	2 tablespoons all-purpose flour
2 large kosher dill pickles, chopped (3/4 cup)	2 tablespoons dry red wine or beef broth
3 ribs celery, sliced (1 cup)	Hot cooked spaetzle or noodles
	Chopped dill pickles for garnish

Brown the roast on all sides in the hot oil in a Dutch oven. Remove the roast to a platter, reserving the pan drippings. Mix the carrots, parsnips, leeks, onion, 2 dill pickles and celery with the reserved pan drippings and top with the roast.

Mix 1/2 cup wine, the mustard, pepper, cloves and bay leaves in a bowl and pour over the roast. Cook, covered, over low heat for 3 to 4 hours. Remove the roast to a platter. Skim the fat from the pan juices and discard the bay leaves. Stir in the flour and 2 tablespoons wine. Cook over medium heat until thickened, stirring frequently. Slice the roast and serve over spaetzle on a serving platter. Top with the cooked vegetables and thickened pan juices. Garnish with chopped dill pickles.

caribbean pot roast with sweet potatoes

[serves 6]

1 (3- to 5-pound) beef pot roast	1/2 bay leaf, crushed
2 tablespoons vegetable oil or bacon drippings	1 (8-ounce) can sliced water chestnuts (optional)
1/2 cup packed brown sugar	4 ribs celery, cut into 4-inch pieces
1/2 cup cider vinegar	4 sweet potatoes, peeled and sliced lengthwise into eighths
1/4 cup soy sauce	All-purpose flour (optional)
1/4 teaspoon salt	
1/8 teaspoon pepper	

Brown the roast on all sides in the hot oil in a Dutch oven. Mix the brown sugar, vinegar, soy sauce, salt, pepper and bay leaf in a bowl and pour over the top. Simmer, tightly covered, for 1 1/2 hours. Add the water chestnuts and celery.

Simmer, covered, for 30 minutes. Add the sweet potatoes and simmer, covered, for 1 hour longer or until the roast and vegetables are tender. Remove the roast and vegetables to a heated serving platter, reserving the pan drippings. If desired, thicken the reserved pan drippings by adding 1 1/2 tablespoons flour per cup of pan drippings and cooking to the desired consistency. Serve the gravy with the roast.

spicy lemon tri-tip

[serves 6]

Tri-tip is a California cut of beef that may require special ordering from the butcher in other parts of the United States. It is the triangular-shaped tip or butt of the bottom of the sirloin and is known for being a leaner cut of beef.

3 tablespoons grated lemon zest	1 tablespoon chili powder
3 tablespoons brown sugar	2 tablespoons salt
1 tablespoon garlic powder	2 tablespoons black pepper
1 tablespoon onion powder	1 1/2 teaspoons white pepper
1 tablespoon paprika	1 (3-pound) tri-tip

Mix the lemon zest, brown sugar, garlic powder, onion powder, paprika, chili powder, salt, black pepper and white pepper in a bowl. Rub the lemon zest mixture over the surface of the tri-tip. Chill, covered, for 3 to 4 hours or longer.

Arrange charcoal on one side of the grill and preheat. Arrange the tri-tip directly over the hot coals and sear on all sides for 1 minute. Move the tri-tip to the opposite side of the grill and grill over indirect heat for 30 to 45 minutes or to the desired degree of doneness. Slice across the grain to serve. Broil if desired.

cook's note ■ If using a gas grill, light only one side of the grill to sear the roast and then move to the other side to grill.

Yams versus sweet potatoes. True yams, sometimes called tropical yams, are very large tubers that are a staple in Africa and Southeast Asia, and are very rarely seen in America. Most have very tough skins and can be stored for long periods of time. Some have natural toxins that must be leeched from the meat through a very labor-intensive process. In America, root vegetables that are marketed as yams in some parts of the country, including California, are actually orange-fleshed sweet potatoes. They are indigenous to the Caribbean and tropical America, and are most frequently served in the United States during Thanksgiving. However, this delicious vegetable deserves more year-round attention not only because of its flavor, but also because it is full of vitamins and minerals. Be sure to try its whiter-fleshed cousins as well.

spicy cilantro flank steak

flank steak

$^2/_3$ cup soy sauce

$^1/_4$ cup medium-dry sherry

3 tablespoons sugar

1 tablespoon minced garlic

1 tablespoon Asian sesame oil

$^1/_2$ teaspoon dried hot red
   pepper flakes

1 (1$^1/_2$- to 2-pound) flank steak

Sprigs of cilantro for garnish

cilantro sauce

1$^1/_2$ cups cilantro, chopped

4$^1/_2$ tablespoons soy sauce

3 tablespoons vegetable oil

2 to 3 tablespoons lime juice

$^3/_4$ teaspoon minced garlic

$^3/_4$ teaspoon sesame oil

Dash of red pepper flakes (optional)

To prepare the steak, mix the soy sauce, sherry, sugar, garlic, sesame oil and red pepper flakes in a shallow dish until the sugar dissolves. Add the steak to the soy sauce mixture and turn to coat. Marinate, covered, in the refrigerator for 1 hour, turning occasionally.

Lightly coat the grill rack with oil and preheat the grill. Let the steak stand in the marinade at room temperature for 20 minutes. Grill to the desired degree of doneness. Slice as desired and arrange on a platter. Garnish with sprigs of cilantro.

To prepare the sauce, combine the cilantro, soy sauce, oil, lime juice, garlic, sesame oil and red pepper flakes in a bowl and mix well. Serve with the steak.

cook's note ■ You may use individual steaks.

flank steak spirals

Unique presentation that is dinner party-friendly.

2 flank steaks (about 3 pounds)
1/2 cup vegetable oil
1/2 cup soy sauce
2 tablespoons honey
2 tablespoons vinegar

1 green onion, finely chopped
1 1/2 teaspoons ginger
1 teaspoon garlic powder
1 teaspoon salt

Cut the steaks crosswise into 1/2- to 3/4-inch strips. Roll and secure with wooden picks. Arrange the rolls in a shallow dish.

Combine the oil, soy sauce, honey, vinegar, green onion, ginger, garlic powder and salt in a blender and process until blended. Pour the soy sauce mixture over the rolls and turn to coat. Marinate, covered, in the refrigerator for 8 hours or longer, turning occasionally.

Preheat the grill to medium. Arrange the rolls on the grill rack and grill for 8 minutes on each side or to the desired degree of doneness. Serve warm or at room temperature.

cook's note ■ Delicious served with either Grilled Pineapple Salsa on page 32, Tropical Salsa on page 113, or any other fruity salsa. For extra flavor with a little more mess, coat the steak strips with the marinade before rolling. Return the spirals to the marinade. This dish travels well and is a great addition to any picnic.

chinese stir-fried beef

1 tablespoon chili powder
2 teaspoons sugar
1 teaspoon garlic salt
1/2 teaspoon five-spice powder
3 tablespoons chunky peanut butter
3 tablespoons sherry
2 tablespoons soy sauce

1 tablespoon chopped fresh ginger
1 tablespoon sesame oil
Salt and pepper to taste
1 pound beef round steak,
    thinly sliced
1 tablespoon vegetable oil

Combine the chili powder, sugar, garlic salt, five-spice powder, peanut butter, sherry, soy sauce, ginger, sesame oil, salt and pepper in a large bowl or sealable plastic bag. Add the steak and toss to coat. Marinate, covered, in the refrigerator for 8 to 10 hours, stirring occasionally.

Heat the vegetable oil in a wok over medium heat. Add the undrained steak to the hot oil and stir-fry for 5 minutes or until the steak is brown. Serve with hot cooked rice.

south african beef casserole (bobotie)

Bobotie, pronounced Bo-Bwoatie, is a staple in South African homes.

1 slice white bread
1 cup milk
1 onion, finely chopped
1 tablespoon butter
1 tablespoon fines herbes
1 tablespoon curry powder
2 teaspoons salt

1 teaspoon turmeric
2 pounds ground beef
1/2 cup almonds, chopped
2 tablespoons apricot jam
2 tablespoons chutney
2 tablespoons lemon juice
3 eggs, lightly beaten

Soak the bread in 1/2 cup of the milk in a bowl until totally saturated. Press the excess milk from the bread into the remaining 1/2 cup milk, reserving the bread. Sauté the onion in the butter in a skillet until tender. Stir in the fines herbes, curry powder, salt and turmeric. Add the reserved bread, ground beef, almonds, jam, chutney and lemon juice and mix well. Cook until the ground beef is brown and crumbly, stirring frequently.

Preheat the oven to 350 degrees. Spoon the ground beef mixture into a baking dish. Whisk the eggs and remaining milk in a bowl until blended and pour the egg mixture over the prepared layer. Bake for 30 minutes or until set. Serve with hot cooked rice.

cook's note ■ Other ground meats may be substituted for the ground beef.

french-canadian tourtière

Tourtière is a French-Canadian meat pie that is usually served during the holidays. Serve as an entrée or as an appetizer.

1 pound lean ground beef
8 ounces ground pork
4 ounces ground veal
1 cup chopped onion
1 bay leaf
1 teaspoon sage
1/8 to 1/4 teaspoon ground cloves,
    or to taste

1 teaspoon poultry seasoning
Salt and pepper to taste
3 potatoes, peeled, cooked and
    mashed
2 unbaked (9-inch) pie shells
Sweet pickle relish for garnish
Ketchup for garnish

Brown the ground beef, ground pork and ground veal with the onion and bay leaf in a Dutch oven, stirring until the ground meats are crumbly; drain. Stir in the sage, cloves, poultry seasoning, salt and pepper. Mix in the mashed potatoes and let stand until cool. Taste and add additional spices if needed. Chill, covered, for 8 to 10 hours. Discard the bay leaf. Preheat the oven to 300 to 325 degrees. Spoon the ground beef mixture evenly into one of the pie shells and top with the remaining pie shell, sealing the edge and cutting vents with a knife. Bake for 45 to 60 minutes or until brown. Garnish with pickle relish and ketchup.

cook's note ■ Any combination of ground meats may be used in this recipe.

killer steak marinade

[makes 1 cup]

The onions take this to the next level.

3 red onions, sliced
1/2 cup soy sauce
1/4 cup olive oil
1/4 cup sherry

3 garlic cloves, minced
1 tablespoon flat-leaf parsley
1 tablespoon oregano

Combine the onions, soy sauce, olive oil, sherry, garlic, parsley and oregano in a bowl and mix well. Pour the onion mixture over the desired cut of beef and marinate, covered, in the refrigerator for 8 to 10 hours. Drain, reserving the onions. Grill the beef and the onions over hot coals to the desired degree of doneness.

cook's note ▦ Use with any cut of beef, or with lamb, pork, or chicken.

stroganoff sauce

[serves 4 to 6]

1/4 cup (1/2 stick) butter
2 cups thinly sliced onions
8 ounces mushrooms, thinly sliced
1 cup sour cream

2 tablespoons all-purpose flour
2 teaspoons paprika
1 teaspoon salt

Melt the butter in a large skillet and stir in the onions and mushrooms. Cook over low heat for 15 minutes or until tender and slightly crisp. Mix the sour cream, flour, paprika and salt in a bowl and add to the mushroom mixture. Cook over low heat until heated through, stirring frequently. Serve with grilled steak.

cook's note ▦ For Creamy Onion Sauce, increase the amount of onions to 4 cups and omit the mushrooms.

Descanso Gardens
The Descanso Gardens are located on 160 acres in La Canada and feature a bird sanctuary, lakes, streams, and thousands of flowers. The Gardens were originally the home of E. Manchester Boddy, the publisher of the Los Angeles Daily News. Boddy bought the property in 1937 and built a stately twenty-two-room mansion that now serves as a museum. Known for its fantastic display of camellias, daffodils, azaleas, roses, and toyon berries, the Descanso Gardens are open to the public daily and are a popular location for local weddings.

osso buco

A traditional recipe from the Italian countryside.

veal

6 veal shanks, 2 inches thick
Salt and pepper to taste
1/2 cup all-purpose flour
3 tablespoons olive oil
1/2 cup (1 stick) butter
1 cup finely chopped onion
3/4 cup finely chopped carrots
3/4 cup finely chopped celery
2 garlic cloves, minced
1 cup chicken broth

2 cups dry white wine
1 cup finely chopped fresh tomato
1 tablespoon parsley
1/2 teaspoon minced thyme
3 bay leaves

gremolata

1 tablespoon flat-leaf parsley
1 grated teaspoon lemon zest
1/4 teaspoon minced garlic

To prepare the veal, preheat the oven to 350 degrees. Season the shanks with salt and pepper and coat with the flour. Heat 2 tablespoons of the olive oil and 1/4 cup of the butter in a large skillet until the butter melts. Add the shanks and cook until brown on all sides. Remove the shanks to a Dutch oven or covered baking pan using a slotted spoon, reserving the pan drippings.

Heat the remaining 1 tablespoon olive oil and remaining 1/4 cup butter with the reserved pan drippings and add the onion, carrots, celery and garlic. Cook for 6 to 8 minutes or until the vegetables are tender. Spoon the onion mixture over the shanks.

Deglaze the skillet with the broth and pour the broth mixture over the shanks. Pour the wine over the shanks, adding additional wine or broth if the shanks are not covered by three-quarters. Add the tomato, parsley, thyme and bay leaves to the shank mixture. Bake, covered, for 2 hours. Discard the bay leaves.

To prepare the gremolata, mix the parsley, lemon zest and garlic in a small bowl. Sprinkle over the Osso Buco before serving.

caribbean balsamic-glazed veal chops

[serves 4]

Simple but elegant. This recipe is from a restaurant on the Caribbean island of Anguilla.

2/3 cup balsamic vinegar
1/2 cup olive oil
4 veal chops or pork chops

Salt and freshly ground pepper
   to taste
Sprigs of thyme for garnish

Preheat the grill. Mix the vinegar and olive oil in a small bowl and pour half the vinegar mixture into a shallow dish. Arrange the veal chops in the vinegar mixture and turn to coat. Marinate at room temperature for 30 minutes.

Grill the veal chops for 3 minutes per side for medium or to the desired degree of doneness, basting occasionally with the remaining vinegar mixture. Sprinkle with salt and pepper and garnish with sprigs of thyme. Serve immediately. The veal chops may be broiled.

Photograph for this recipe on page 98.

Serve Roasted Red Pepper and Raisin Sauce with veal or pork. Mix 6 coarsely chopped roasted large red bell peppers, 1/2 cup golden raisins, 1/4 cup olive oil, 3 tablespoons balsamic vinegar and 2 minced large garlic cloves. Serve with Caribbean Balsamic-Glazed Veal Chops, chicken or pork.

tamari lamb

[serves 8]

1 (4- to 6-pound) boneless
   leg of lamb
Tamari
Orange juice

3 large garlic cloves, sliced
Chopped fresh rosemary
Dijon mustard

Place the lamb in a double layer of two large sealable plastic bags. Mix equal portions of tamari and orange juice in a bowl and pour over the lamb. Seal tightly and turn to coat. Marinate in the refrigerator for 12 to 24 hours, turning once or twice.

Preheat the oven to 350 degrees. Remove the lamb to a roasting pan just large enough to hold, reserving the marinade. Make small slits in the surface of the lamb and insert the garlic and rosemary into the slits. Tie the lamb with kitchen twine. Spread Dijon mustard over the surface of the lamb and then pour the reserved marinade over the top.

Roast for 1 1/2 to 2 hours or until a meat thermometer inserted into the thickest portion of the lamb registers 145 degrees for medium-rare, basting with the pan drippings several times. Remove the lamb from the oven and tent with foil. Let stand for 15 minutes before slicing. Serve with the pan drippings.

cook's note ▦ Tamari is a stronger soy sauce.

armenian layered lamb and cabbage casserole

This is traditional dolmas unwrapped in a casserole.

This recipe was created because the cook became tired of watching her children immediately unwrap all the dolmas she had labored over for so long and then dumping the contents onto their plates.

1 1/4 pounds ground turkey
1 (8-ounce) can tomato paste
1 cup short grain rice
1 tomato, chopped
1/2 bell pepper, chopped
1 teaspoon salt
1/2 teaspoon black pepper
1/2 teaspoon Aleppo/Syrian hot pepper or cayenne pepper
1 to 2 cups chicken broth

1 to 2 pounds lamb (smaller bone-in cuts preferred such as shoulder chops/neck/riblets)
Salt and pepper to taste
Olive oil or vegetable oil
1 large head cabbage, chopped into bite-size pieces
Plain yogurt for garnish
Dried mint for garnish

Combine the ground turkey, 1/2 of the tomato paste, the rice, tomato, bell pepper, salt, black pepper and hot pepper in a bowl and mix well. Mix the remaining tomato paste with the broth in a bowl.

Season the lamb with salt and pepper and cut into smaller pieces if necessary. Braise the lamb in a small amount of olive oil in a large Dutch oven. Top the lamb with half the cabbage. Cover the cabbage evenly and completely with the turkey mixture. Pierce holes in the turkey mixture so the broth mixture can seep through more easily. Layer with the remaining cabbage and pour the broth mixture over the top. The liquid should not cover the top cabbage layer but should be seen if the Dutch oven is tilted.

Simmer, covered, for 45 to 60 minutes. Let stand for 10 minutes before serving. Spoon onto serving plates with lips. Garnish each serving with yogurt and mint or serve on the side. Serve with toasted pita chips or garlic toast.

lamb curry

curry

1/2 cup (1 stick) butter
1 Granny Smith apple, chopped
1 large onion, chopped
4 ribs celery, chopped
2 pounds cooked lamb, chicken,
    beef or shrimp, chopped into
    bite-size pieces
1 cup evaporated milk
1 tablespoon Kitchen Bouquet
1 cup raisins

1 teaspoon (heaping) curry powder
1 teaspoon (heaping)
    all-purpose flour

condiments

Toasted coconut
Crushed peanuts
Chopped crisp-cooked bacon
Chutney
Chopped green onions
Chopped hard-cooked eggs

To prepare the curry, melt the butter in a large skillet and add the apple, onion and celery. Sauté until tender and stir in the lamb, evaporated milk, Kitchen Bouquet, raisins, curry powder and flour. Cook until the lamb is heated through, stirring occasionally. Serve with hot cooked rice and one or more of the condiments.

cook's note ▓ To roast a boneless leg of lamb, sprinkle with salt and pepper and roast at 350 degrees for 30 minutes per pound. Cut into chunks. If making multiple batches of the Lamb Curry, make each batch separately. To serve 24, multiply by 8 and use 2 bunches of celery, two 15-ounce packages of raisins, and five 12-ounce cans of evaporated milk plus enough water to equal 8 cups. At this point, the curry may be frozen; defrost in the refrigerator before heating. Combine all the batches in a roasting pan and heat at 350 degrees for 25 to 30 minutes.

Hearst Castle

Built on forty thousand acres by newspaper mogul William Randolph Hearst, Hearst Castle is located in San Simeon, California. During the heyday of Hearst Castle in the 1920s, popular movie stars and politicians were frequent visitors to the palatial estate, including Charlie Chaplin, Cary Grant, Winston Churchill, and the Marx Brothers. Hearst had the buildings designed in styles of famous European structures, including a Spanish cathedral and a Roman temple. In all, Hearst Castle has fifty-six bedrooms, sixty-one bathrooms, nineteen sitting rooms, 127 acres of gardens, indoor and outdoor swimming pools, tennis courts, a movie theater, an airfield, and the world's largest private zoo. In 1957 the Hearst family donated the estate to the state, and it is open for public tours.

roasted pork with
caramelized apples

Fills your home with an amazing spicy aroma.

spice rub

2 tablespoons brown sugar
2 teaspoons ground cumin
1 teaspoon ground cinnamon
1 teaspoon garlic powder
3/4 teaspoon salt
1/2 teaspoon black pepper
1/4 teaspoon ground ginger
1/4 teaspoon cayenne pepper
1/4 teaspoon ground cloves

pork

1 (31/2-pound) boneless pork loin
    roast, trimmed

Vegetable oil
1/2 cup chopped onion
1 (14-ounce) can chicken broth
1/2 cup chopped dried apricots
1/2 cup thawed frozen orange
    juice concentrate
1/3 cup golden raisins
2 tablespoons butter
4 Granny Smith apples, each cut
    into 8 wedges
2 tablespoons brown sugar
1 teaspoon ground cinnamon
1 tablespoon balsamic vinegar

To prepare the spice rub, mix the brown sugar, cumin, cinnamon, garlic powder, salt, black pepper, ginger, cayenne pepper and cloves in a bowl.

To prepare the pork, rub the surface of the pork with the spice rub. Chill, covered, for 2 hours or longer. Preheat the oven to 425 degrees.

Heat a small amount of oil in a large Dutch oven over medium-high heat and add the pork. Sear for 4 minutes or until brown on all sides. Add the onion and cook for 1 to 2 minutes or until the onion is softened, stirring constantly. Stir in the broth, apricots, orange juice concentrate and raisins and bring to a boil.

Bake, covered, for 30 minutes. Reduce the oven temperature to 325 degrees and bake for 20 minutes longer or until a meat thermometer inserted into the thickest portion of the pork registers 160 degrees (slightly pink). Remove the pork to a platter and tent with foil, reserving the cooking liquid. Remove the apricots and raisins from the cooking liquid to a bowl using a slotted spoon. Bring the reserved cooking liquid to a boil over high heat and boil until reduced by one-half. Remove from the heat.

Melt the butter in a heavy skillet over medium heat. Add the apples, brown sugar and cinnamon and stir until coated. Cook for 20 minutes or until the apples are tender. Add the vinegar and toss to coat. Stir in the reserved apricot mixture and reduced cooking liquid. To serve, spoon the apple mixture around the pork on the platter.

apricot-glazed pork loin with tropical salsa

Super easy and delicious.

pork

3/4 cup soy sauce
1/4 cup honey
5 garlic cloves, chopped or pressed
1 tablespoon (rounded) apricot
    preserves
2 pounds pork roast, tenderloin or
    thick chops

tropical salsa

1 large Granny Smith apple,
    finely chopped
1/2 orange, seeded and chopped
1/2 cup chopped pineapple
1 cucumber, peeled, seeded
    and chopped
1 red bell pepper, seeded
    and chopped
1 jalapeño chile, seeded and
    chopped (optional)
1/4 cup fresh lime juice
1/4 cup pineapple juice
1/4 cup orange juice
2 tablespoons fresh cilantro,
    finely chopped
1 teaspoon salt

To prepare the pork, mix the soy sauce, honey, garlic and preserves in a bowl. Pour over the pork in a shallow dish, turning to coat. Marinate, covered, in the refrigerator for 3 hours or longer, turning occasionally. Drain, reserving the marinade.

Preheat the oven to 375 degrees. Heat a cast-iron skillet or heavy ovenproof skillet over high heat. Sear the pork in the hot skillet for 5 minutes or until brown on all sides, turning frequently. Remove from the heat and pour the reserved marinade over the pork. Bake for 25 minutes or to the desired degree of doneness. Slice as desired.

To prepare the salsa, combine the apple, orange, pineapple, cucumber, bell pepper and jalapeño chile in a bowl. Stir in the lime juice, pineapple juice, orange juice, cilantro and salt. Chill, covered, until serving time. Serve with the pork.

cook's note ▥ Can easily be grilled. Boar fillets or any other meat can be substituted for the pork. Toss leftovers with a little barbecue sauce for sandwiches.

kentucky bourbon
pork tenderloin

Bourbon can only apply to whiskey made in Kentucky because of the higher lime content of the water in that state. The lime is also what makes the grass "blue."

My father and his family moved to California from Texas in the late 1940s. They moved out here mainly due to the job opportunities that were available at the time. Almost any job that you wanted could be found here in California. My father said that the great year-round weather and natural beauty was another factor in moving out west. He would refer to California as "The Land of Milk and Honey," and it truly was.

1/3 cup bourbon
3 tablespoons brown sugar
3 tablespoons soy sauce
1 small garlic clove, pressed
1 1/2 teaspoons salt (optional)
1/4 teaspoon curry powder
1/4 teaspoon ginger
2 pounds pork tenderloin

Combine the bourbon, brown sugar, soy sauce, garlic, salt, curry powder and ginger in a bowl and mix well. Pour the bourbon mixture over the pork in a shallow dish, turning to coat.

Marinate, covered, in the refrigerator for 2 to 12 hours, turning occasionally. Preheat the grill. Grill the pork over hot coals until a meat thermometer inserted in the center registers 155 degrees.

cook's note ▪ Whiskey, rum, or sherry may be substituted for the bourbon.

cheesy pork chops

An all-in-one meal.

cheese sauce

2 tablespoons butter

2 tablespoons all-purpose flour

2 cups milk

2 cups (8 ounces) shredded sharp
   Cheddar cheese

1/4 cup white wine

1/2 teaspoon salt

1/2 teaspoon white pepper

1/2 teaspoon garlic powder

pork chops

2 large or 4 small potatoes, peeled
   and thinly sliced

1 large onion, thinly sliced

Salt and pepper to taste

4 to 6 pork chops

To prepare the sauce, melt the butter in a saucepan and stir in the flour until blended. Cook for 2 to 3 minutes or until bubbly and smooth, stirring constantly. Remove from the heat and gradually mix in 1 cup of the milk, 1 cup of the cheese and the wine. Return the saucepan to medium-low heat and stir in the remaining 1 cup milk, remaining 1 cup cheese, the salt, white pepper and garlic powder. Cook until blended and thickened, stirring frequently.

To prepare the pork chops, preheat the oven to 350 degrees. Layer the potatoes and onion in an 8×10-inch or a 9×13-inch baking dish. Season with salt and pepper. Spread the prepared layers with the cheese sauce and top with the pork chops.

Bake, covered, for 1 hour or until the potatoes are tender and the chops are cooked through. Remove the cover 15 minutes before the end of the baking process to allow the pork chops to brown.

cook's note ▦ For a weeknight shortcut for the cheese sauce, substitute one 10-ounce can Cheddar cheese soup.

a californian's memphis barbecue

The secret to Memphis barbecue is slow cooking over low heat, allowing the smoke to flavor the meat. It is a process that cannot be rushed, and a little practice is needed to develop the technique. But do not worry; even your practice batches are sure to please.

I met my husband when he flew to Memphis to go on a blind date with me. While his father was in Memphis working on a project, my future father-in-law was invited to a party where he met a family friend. This family friend kept telling me her new beau had a son I just had to meet, and she eventually arranged for him to come to Memphis for the weekend. Thus began a two-year cross-country courtship, eventual marriage, and two children, and the rest, as they say, is history. During this whole process, my husband has been "bubbafied" by my family. He has also fallen in love with Memphis barbecue, and we must have it at least once a trip on our visits to Memphis. The next two pages contain his version.

dry rub
1/4 cup paprika
1 tablespoon salt
1 tablespoon onion powder
1 tablespoon garlic powder
1 tablespoon white pepper
1/2 teaspoon cayenne pepper
1/2 teaspoon ground cinnamon

basting sauce (aka the mop)
1/2 cup (1 stick) butter
1/2 cup cider vinegar
6 garlic cloves, pressed
2 tablespoons Worcestershire sauce

awesome barbecue sauce
1/2 onion
3 large garlic cloves
1/4 cup (1/2 stick) butter
11/2 cups ketchup
3/4 cup cider vinegar
1/4 cup Worcestershire sauce
2 tablespoons brown sugar
1 teaspoon black pepper

1/2 teaspoon salt
1/8 teaspoon cayenne pepper
Dash of ground cinnamon

baby back ribs
Hickory chips
2 to 4 pounds baby back pork ribs

pulled pork sandwiches
5 to 10 pounds pork shoulder butt,
    bone in
Sandwich buns

simple slaw
1 head cabbage, trimmed
    and shredded
11/2 carrots, grated
1 cup mayonnaise
3 tablespoons cider vinegar
2 teaspoons prepared
    yellow mustard
2 teaspoons sugar
1 teaspoon salt
1/2 teaspoon pepper

To prepare the rub, mix the paprika, salt, onion powder, garlic powder, white pepper, cayenne pepper and cinnamon in a bowl. Makes 1/2 cup.

To prepare the basting sauce, melt the butter in a small saucepan. Stir in the vinegar, garlic and Worcestershire sauce. Makes 1 cup.

To prepare the barbecue sauce, process the onion and garlic in a food processor until ground. Melt the butter in a saucepan and stir in the onion mixture. Sauté until the mixture is translucent. Stir in the ketchup, vinegar, Worcestershire sauce, brown sugar, black pepper, salt, cayenne pepper and cinnamon and bring to a boil. Reduce the heat to low and simmer for 15 minutes or longer. Store in the refrigerator until serving time. Best if served warm but can be served chilled or at room temperature. Makes 3 cups.

To prepare the ribs, soak hickory chips in water for 8 to 10 hours; drain. Prepare the ribs by removing all membranes. Using a sharp knife, loosen one edge of the membrane, grasp with a paper towel and pull to remove. Coat the ribs with the dry rub. Let stand at room temperature for 30 minutes or chill for 8 to 10 hours.

A smoker works best for this process, but if one is not available, build a fire on one side of a charcoal grill. If using a gas grill, light only one side of the grill. When the coals are covered in ash, add a handful of hickory chips to the hot coals and arrange the ribs on the grill rack away from the coals. Cover and open the smoker vents so that the smoke is pulled across the ribs.

Turn the ribs every 30 minutes, switching the position for even cooking and basting with the basting sauce. Add more hickory chips each time the ribs are turned and ten to twelve briquettes as needed. Smoke the ribs for 3 to 5 hours or until the rib meat begins to pull from the bones. Brush the ribs with the barbecue sauce during the last 30 minutes of smoking. Remove the ribs from the grill and let rest for 30 minutes before serving. Reheat the remaining barbecue sauce and serve with the ribs.

To prepare the sandwiches, follow the procedure above for smoking, omitting the spice rub. Smoke the shoulder for 6 to 10 hours over low heat or until the pork easily pulls from the bones. Remove the pork from the grill and let rest for 45 minutes. Shred the pork. Serve on buns topped with the barbecue sauce and Simple Slaw. The smoked pork will be pink, but is thoroughly cooked through.

To prepare the slaw, toss the cabbage and carrots in a bowl. Mix the mayonnaise, vinegar, prepared mustard, sugar, salt and pepper in a bowl. Add the mayonnaise mixture to the cabbage mixture and mix well. Taste and adjust the seasonings.

cook's note ▦ The Dry Rub and Awesome Barbecue Sauce can also be used on chicken. For a delicious appetizer, dust summer sausage with the rub and grill until heated through. Serve the sausage on a platter with cubed Cheddar cheese and jalapeño chiles lightly dusted with additional rub.

zucchini stuffed with italian sausage

A great way to use up the extra-large zucchini from your summer garden.

salsa de pomodoro

2 cups Italian plum tomatoes
  or whole tomatoes,
  coarsely chopped
1/2 cup chopped onion
2 tablespoons olive oil
1 tablespoon fresh basil, or
  1 teaspoon dried basil
1/2 teaspoon salt

zucchini

2 medium or 2 large zucchini
1/4 cup olive oil

8 ounces hot or mild Italian
  sausage or turkey sausage,
  casings removed
1/2 cup chopped onion
1/2 teaspoon chopped garlic
1/2 cup bread crumbs
1 egg, lightly beaten
1 tablespoon grated
  Parmesan cheese
1 teaspoon salt
1/2 teaspoon dried oregano
1/4 teaspoon pepper
Olive oil for drizzling

To prepare the salsa, mix the tomatoes, onion, olive oil, basil and salt in a bowl.

To prepare the zucchini, preheat the oven to 350 degrees, Cut the zucchini horizontally into halves. Scoop out the pulp carefully, leaving the shells intact. Chop the pulp.

Heat 1/4 cup olive oil in a skillet and add the zucchini pulp, sausage, onion and garlic. Cook until the sausage is brown and crumbly and the onion is tender, stirring frequently; drain. Stir in the bread crumbs, egg, cheese, salt, oregano and pepper. Spoon the sausage mixture evenly into the zucchini shells. You may prepare to this point and freeze for future use.

Cover the bottom of a shallow baking dish with the salsa and arrange the stuffed shells over the salsa. Drizzle with olive oil and bake, covered with foil, for about 1 hour.

cook's note ■ For a shortcut for the salsa, combine one 16-ounce can Italian-style diced tomatoes with a little olive oil, basil, chopped onion, salt and/or oregano.

chicken breasts in sherry with baked butter rice

[serves 8]

baked butter rice

1/4 cup (1/2 stick) butter
3 cups long grain rice, rinsed
  and drained
1 small onion, finely chopped
2 tablespoons butter
6 cups chicken broth (made from
  chicken bouillon cubes)
Salt and pepper to taste

chicken

1/2 cup (1 stick) butter
8 chicken breasts
1 large onion, thinly sliced
1 cup tomato juice
1 cup water
3/4 cup sherry
Salt and pepper to taste

To prepare the rice, preheat the oven to 375 degrees. Melt 1/4 cup butter in a heavy skillet and add the rice. Braise until the butter begins to bubble and the rice begins to brown. Sauté the onion in 2 tablespoons butter in a skillet until golden brown. Stir the onion, broth, salt and pepper into the rice. Spoon the rice mixture into a buttered baking dish and bake for 30 to 45 minutes. Remove from the oven, stir and bake for 10 minutes longer or until the rice is tender. Cover to keep warm. Maintain the oven temperature.

To prepare the chicken, melt the butter in a large skillet and add the chicken. Cook over low heat for 20 minutes or until brown on both sides. Remove the chicken to a 9×11-inch baking dish using a slotted spoon, reserving the pan drippings. Brown the onion in the reserved pan drippings and stir in the tomato juice, water, sherry, salt and pepper. Pour the onion mixture over the chicken and bake for 30 minutes. Turn the chicken and bake for 30 minutes. Turn again and bake for 15 minutes longer.

Arrange 1 chicken breast on each of eight serving plates. Spoon equal portions of the rice onto each plate and drizzle with the sherry sauce. Serve immediately.

cook's note ■ The secret to the rice is to braise it long enough.

Pasadena Historical Museum

In 1924 the Pasadena Historical Museum was founded to preserve the unique and colorful history of Pasadena. Located on the Fenyes Estate situated on what was once known as "Millionaire's Row," the museum is home to a number of California impressionist paintings and lavish antique furnishings. The Fenyes Estate also served as the first Finnish Consulate located in the West before it became the Historical Museum. A Finnish Folk arts museum can be found today on the grounds as a reminder of the property's rich history.

french chicken with cream and port

[serves 2]

2 chicken breasts, or half a chicken
Salt and pepper to taste
4 ounces mushrooms, sliced
1/4 cup (1/2 stick) butter

1/2 cup brandy
1/2 cup heavy cream
3 tablespoons port
Chopped fresh parsley for garnish

Preheat the oven to 350 degrees. Season the chicken with salt and pepper. Sauté the mushrooms in 2 tablespoons of the butter in a Dutch oven or covered ovenproof baking dish until tender. Remove the mushrooms to a bowl using a slotted spoon, reserving the pan drippings. Heat the remaining 2 tablespoons butter with the reserved pan drippings and add the chicken.

Sauté until golden brown. Remove from the heat. Pour the brandy over the chicken and ignite. Allow the flames to subside. Bake, covered, for 30 to 40 minutes or until the chicken is cooked through. Remove the chicken to a plate and stir the cream and wine into the pan drippings.

Cook over low heat until thickened and of a sauce consistency, stirring frequently. Return the chicken and mushrooms to the Dutch oven. You may prepare in advance to this point and store in the refrigerator. Bake, covered, for 15 minutes longer. Remove the chicken to a serving platter and drizzle with the sauce. Garnish with parsley.

cook's note ■ This recipe can easily be doubled.

grilled brazilian beer chicken

[serves 4 to 6]

2 cups Brazilian beer
1/2 cup vegetable oil
1/2 cup Dijon mustard
1 tablespoon sweet paprika
1 teaspoon ground pepper

1 onion, thinly sliced
10 garlic cloves, thinly sliced
2 bay leaves
2 pounds chicken breasts, bone in
Sprigs of rosemary for garnish

Combine the beer, oil, Dijon mustard, paprika and pepper in a bowl and mix well. Stir in the onion, garlic and bay leaves. Pour the beer mixture over the chicken in a shallow dish, turning to coat. Marinate, covered, in the refrigerator for 6 hours or for up to 2 days, turning occasionally.

Preheat the grill. Drain the chicken, reserving the marinade. Grill the chicken over hot coals until cooked through, turning occasionally and basting with the reserved marinade several times. Remove the chicken to a serving platter and garnish with sprigs of rosemary. Serve immediately.

cook's note ■ A Brazilian beer is best but can be difficult to find, so Mexican beer may be substituted. Dark meat chicken pieces also work well with the marinade.

Photograph for this recipe on page 99.

moroccan chicken with olives and potatoes

An unusual combination and quite delicious.

2 chicken breasts	$1/4$ teaspoon pepper
2 chicken thighs	$4^3/4$ cups water
1 large onion, chopped	1 (14-ounce) jar pimento-stuffed
$1/3$ cup olive oil	Spanish olives, drained
4 teaspoons ground ginger	4 potatoes, peeled and cut into
2 teaspoons salt	4 to 6 chunks
$1/4$ teaspoon turmeric	$1^1/2$ cups water

Combine the chicken, onion, olive oil, ginger, salt, turmeric and pepper in a large saucepan. Add $3/4$ cup of the water and cook over high heat for 5 minutes, stirring constantly. Cook, covered, for 5 minutes and stir in the remaining 4 cups water. Reduce the heat to medium and cook, covered, for 45 minutes. Soak the olives in warm water in a bowl while the chicken cooks. Drain the olives and add the olives, potatoes and $1^1/2$ cups water to the chicken mixture. Cook for 30 minutes longer. Serve in bowls with crusty bread.

cook's note ■ You may substitute 4 chicken breasts or 1 whole chicken for 2 chicken breasts and 2 chicken thighs.

chicken adobo

A delicious classic Philippine dish.

$1/2$ cup cider vinegar	1 teaspoon coarsely cracked
$1/4$ cup soy sauce	black pepper
1 tablespoon minced garlic	1 bay leaf, or 2 Turkish bay leaves
1 head of garlic, separated into	4 whole chicken legs, cut into legs
cloves and peeled	and thighs (about $2^1/2$ pounds)
1 tablespoon black peppercorns	

Mix the vinegar, soy sauce, minced garlic, garlic cloves, peppercorns, cracked pepper and bay leaf in a bowl. Pour the vinegar mixture over the chicken in a sealable plastic bag. Seal tightly, pressing out the air, and turn to coat. Marinate in the refrigerator for 2 to 10 hours, turning occasionally. Preheat the oven to 425 degrees. Arrange the chicken in a single layer in a 9×13-inch baking pan and pour the marinade over the chicken. Bake on the middle oven rack for 30 to 35 minutes or until the chicken is cooked through. Skim the fat from the pan juices and discard the bay leaf. Serve the chicken with the pan juices and hot cooked rice.

For crispier chicken, broil the baked chicken 4 inches from the heat source for 2 to 3 minutes or to the desired crispness. For thicker pan juices, pour the juices into a small saucepan and discard the bay leaf. Bring to a boil and boil until reduced and thickened.

cook's note ■ This recipe can easily be doubled.

mexicali chicken

These crunchy tortilla-crusted chicken breasts will delight friends and family.

3/4 cup (3 ounces) shredded
 Cheddar and Monterey
 Jack cheese
1 (4-ounce) can diced green chiles
1 (2-ounce) can sliced olives

3 tablespoons finely chopped onion
4 boneless skinless chicken breasts,
 pounded or butterflied
1/3 cup butter or margarine, melted
1 cup tortilla chips, crushed

Preheat the oven to 375 degrees. Mix the cheese, green chiles, olives and onion in a bowl. Sprinkle the green chile mixture on the chicken breasts and roll or fold to enclose the filling. Dip in the butter and coat with the chips.

Arrange the chicken rolls in a single layer in a shallow baking dish. Bake for 30 to 40 minutes or until cooked through. Serve with sour cream and salsa.

cook's note ■ You may prepare in advance and store, covered, in the refrigerator. Bake just before serving.

gilroy garlic chicken

Gilroy, California, is the home of the world-famous Garlic Festival.

8 garlic cloves, finely chopped
3 tablespoons lime juice
2 tablespoons Dijon mustard
2 tablespoons honey

Salt and freshly ground pepper
 to taste
4 boneless skinless chicken breasts
2 tablespoons olive oil

Mix the garlic, lime juice, Dijon mustard, honey, salt and pepper in a shallow dish. Add the chicken and toss to coat. Marinate for 10 minutes, turning occasionally. Drain the chicken, reserving the marinade.

Heat the olive oil in a large sauté pan and add the chicken. Cook until brown on both sides, turning occasionally. Add the reserved marinade to the sauté pan and reduce the heat. Cook for 7 minutes longer or until the chicken is cooked through. Serve with hot cooked rice or pasta.

cook's note ■ The sauce can be thinned with white wine. Prepare in advance and store, covered, in the refrigerator. Reheat just before serving.

pistachio-crusted chicken

The pistachios add a nutty crunch to this easy chicken recipe.

4 boneless skinless chicken breasts
1/2 teaspoon salt
1/2 teaspoon black pepper
1/4 teaspoon cayenne pepper

1 egg
1 cup pistachios, coarsely ground
1 tablespoon vegetable oil

Pound the chicken 1/2 inch thick between sheets of foil or waxed paper using a meat mallet. Mix the salt, black pepper and cayenne pepper in a small bowl. Whisk the egg in a shallow dish until blended.

Sprinkle the chicken with the salt mixture. Dip in the egg and coat with the pistachios. You may prepare in advance to this point and store, covered, in the refrigerator until just before cooking.

Heat the oil in a large skillet over medium to medium-high heat. Add the chicken to the hot oil and cook for 4 minutes or until brown on both sides, turning once. Cook, covered, for 2 minutes longer or until the juices run clear.

hawaiian chicken kabobs

A flavorful island combination.

8 boneless skinless
   chicken breasts, cubed
1 pineapple, cut into chunks
4 red bell peppers, cut into chunks
4 onions, cut into chunks
1 cup pineapple juice
1 cup coconut milk
2 tablespoons soy sauce

1 teaspoon ginger powder or
   slivered fresh ginger
1 garlic clove, minced
Hot cooked rice
Chopped macadamia nuts
   for garnish
Toasted coconut for garnish

Thread the chicken, pineapple, bell peppers and onions alternately on skewers and arrange in a single layer in a shallow dish. Mix the pineapple juice, coconut milk, soy sauce, ginger and garlic in a bowl and pour over the kabobs, turning to coat. Marinate, covered, in the refrigerator for 2 to 12 hours, turning occasionally.

Preheat the grill. Grill the kabobs over hot coals until the chicken is cooked through, turning occasionally. Arrange the kabobs over rice on a serving platter. Garnish with macadamia nuts and coconut.

cook's note ▪ Serve with Grilled Pineapple Salsa on page 32. You may bake at 350 degrees for 20 minutes or until the chicken is cooked through if desired.

chicken tikka masala

[serves 6]

California
Fusion Cuisine

In the mid-1980s several California chefs began preparing dishes that mixed seemingly opposite styles of cooking, such as French and Japanese, and fusion cuisine was born. This new cooking style quickly gained in popularity, especially with the help of celebrity clientele who began frequenting these establishments. Fusion cuisine is the ultimate example of California's amazing agricultural availability and diverse cultural heritage combining to create our own unique style of cooking.

curry marinade

1/2 cup plain yogurt
1/4 cup lemon juice
1 (2-inch) piece fresh ginger, minced
2 garlic cloves, pressed
1 to 2 teaspoons curry powder
1 teaspoon chili powder
1 teaspoon ground cumin

chicken

4 boneless skinless chicken breasts,
    cut into bite-size pieces

2 tablespoons vegetable oil
1 onion, finely chopped
1 (1-inch) piece fresh ginger, minced
1 garlic clove, pressed
2 tomatoes, chopped
1/2 teaspoon ground cumin
1/2 teaspoon ground coriander
Salt to taste
1/4 cup sour cream
Hot cooked couscous or rice

To prepare the marinade, combine the yogurt, lemon juice, ginger, garlic, curry powder, chili powder and cumin in a bowl.

To prepare the chicken, toss the chicken with the marinade in a shallow dish and marinate for 20 minutes. Heat the oil in a large skillet and add the onion, ginger and garlic.

Sauté until the onion is golden brown. Stir in the undrained chicken and simmer for 8 to 10 minutes or until the chicken is cooked through, stirring occasionally. Add the tomatoes, cumin, coriander and salt and cook for 5 minutes or until the tomatoes are tender. Add the sour cream gradually, stirring constantly. Cook just until heated through. Serve over couscous or rice.

cook's note ■ Delicious with Couscous with Herbs and Lemon on page 161.

chicken maque choux with corn bread topping

Maque choux is a Cajun term meaning corn that has been fried and then simmered.

chicken

1 pound boneless skinless
    chicken breasts,
    coarsely chopped
Creole seasoning to taste
1 1/2 tablespoons vegetable oil
1/2 cup chopped red bell pepper
1 cup chopped yellow onion
2 garlic cloves, minced or pressed
2 teaspoons ground cumin
1 teaspoon salt
1 bay leaf
1/2 teaspoon Creole seasoning
1 cup fresh, canned or frozen
    corn kernels

2 cups chopped tomatoes with juice
1 cup chicken broth
1/4 cup fresh parsley, chopped

corn bread topping

3/4 cup cornmeal
1/4 cup all-purpose flour
1 1/2 teaspoons baking powder
1/2 teaspoon salt
1/2 cup milk
1 egg, lightly beaten
2 tablespoons vegetable oil
1 cup (4 ounces) shredded Cheddar
    cheese (optional)
Sour cream for garnish

To prepare the chicken, season the chicken with Creole seasoning to taste. Heat 1 tablespoon of the oil in a cast-iron skillet or ovenproof skillet over medium-high heat. Add the chicken to the hot oil and cook for 5 minutes or until brown. Remove the chicken to a platter, reserving the pan drippings.

Heat the reserved pan drippings with the remaining 1/2 tablespoon oil and add the bell pepper and onion. Sauté for 3 minutes and stir in the garlic, cumin, salt, bay leaf and 1/2 teaspoon Creole seasoning. Cook for 30 seconds, stirring constantly. Stir in the corn and cook for 3 minutes or until the corn begins to color. Add the tomatoes and broth and mix well.

Bring to a boil and cook for 10 minutes or until thickened, stirring occasionally. Return the chicken to the skillet and cook for 3 to 5 minutes longer. Remove from the heat and discard the bay leaf. Stir in the parsley. Taste and adjust the seasonings.

To prepare the topping, preheat the oven to 400 degrees. Combine the cornmeal, flour, baking powder and salt in a bowl and mix well. Add the milk, egg and oil and stir just until moistened. Spread the topping over the chicken mixture to within 1/2 inch of the edge of the skillet. Bake for 15 minutes or until the topping is golden brown. Remove from the oven and immediately sprinkle with the cheese. Serve hot garnished with sour cream.

cook's note ▪ Save time by substituting precooked chicken for the chicken breasts, increasing 1/2 teaspoon Creole seasoning to 2 teaspoons.

verde chicken enchiladas [serves 6]

California Missions

The California Missions were built by the Spanish Catholic church in the eighteenth century and served as outposts in the New World. The distance between each mission was a day's journey. They were used to introduce European crops and livestock to California. Catholic monks, led by Father Junipero Serra, taught the locals new methods of farming along with Christian doctrine. When the Mexican Congress voted to secularize the missions in 1833, the church abandoned the missions, and the Native Americans were forced to leave the properties. Today the twenty-one missions located along El Camino Real have been repaired or reconstructed and are open to the public.

1 3/4 cups sour cream
4 ounces cream cheese, softened
1 (7-ounce) can diced green chiles
1/2 cup fresh cilantro, chopped
4 green onions, chopped
1 1/2 teaspoons ground cumin
3 boneless skinless chicken breasts, cooked and shredded
1 cup (4 ounces) shredded Monterey Jack cheese

Salt and pepper to taste
2 (16-ounce) jars verde salsa
12 corn tortillas
1/4 cup sour cream
1 cup (4 ounces) shredded Monterey Jack cheese
Sour cream for garnish
Chopped fresh cilantro for garnish

Preheat the oven to 350 degrees. Combine 1 3/4 cups sour cream, the cream cheese, green chiles, 1/2 cup cilantro, the green onions and cumin in a bowl and mix well. Stir in the chicken and 1 cup Monterey Jack cheese. Season with salt and pepper.

Heat 1/2 cup of the salsa in a small skillet. Heat the tortillas one at a time in the warm salsa for 30 seconds to soften, turning once. Spoon 1/2 cup of the chicken filling down the center of each tortilla and roll to enclose the filling. Arrange the enchiladas seam side down in a buttered 9×13-inch baking dish. You may prepare in advance to this point and chill, covered, in the refrigerator for up to 3 hours.

Mix the remaining salsa and 1/4 cup sour cream in a bowl and spoon over the top of the enchiladas. Bake, covered, for 45 minutes or until the enchiladas are heated through and the sauce is bubbly. Remove the cover and sprinkle with 1 cup Monterey Jack cheese. Bake for 5 minutes longer or until the cheese melts. Garnish with sour cream and cilantro.

cook's note ▦ For a shortcut, purchase roasted chicken from your favorite market. Kick up the spice by substituting minced jalapeño chiles for the green chiles.

Photograph for this recipe on page 204.

turkey burgers
with caramelized onions

The sweetness of the caramelized onions contrasts beautifully with the savory burgers.

caramelized onions

1 tablespoon unsalted butter
1 tablespoon olive oil
2 large onions, cut into
   1/4-inch slices
1 teaspoon sugar
1/2 teaspoon salt
1/4 teaspoon ground pepper
2 teaspoons dried thyme

turkey burgers

2 pounds ground turkey
2 green onion bulbs, minced
1 shallot, minced
2 teaspoons Worcestershire sauce
1 1/2 teaspoons salt
1 teaspoon Tabasco sauce
1/2 teaspoon lemon pepper
4 hamburger buns

To prepare the onions, heat the butter and olive oil in a skillet until the butter melts and add the onions. Cook, covered, for 10 minutes or until the onions are tender, stirring occasionally. Stir in the sugar, salt and pepper and increase the heat. Cook for 25 to 30 minutes or until the onions are golden brown, stirring occasionally. Stir in the thyme.

To prepare the burgers, preheat the grill. Combine the turkey, green onions, shallot, Worcestershire sauce, salt, Tabasco sauce and lemon pepper in a bowl and mix well. Shape the ground turkey mixture into four patties. Grill the patties for 7 minutes on each side or until cooked through. Serve on the buns topped with the caramelized onions and dressed as desired.

cook's note ■ If you prefer, the turkey burgers may be cooked in a skillet.

turkey cottage pie

A great way to use Thanksgiving leftovers.

5 sprigs of parsley	1 cup turkey gravy
1/2 teaspoon dried thyme	1 cup chicken stock or canned
1 bay leaf	chicken broth
3 tablespoons butter	2 1/2 cups chopped cooked turkey
1 cup (1/2-inch) slices celery	1 cup stuffing
1 cup (1/2-inch) slices carrots	1 cup cooked peas
1 cup coarsely chopped onion	Salt and pepper to taste
2 teaspoons minced garlic	2 cups mashed potatoes
3 tablespoons all-purpose flour	Melted butter to taste

Place the parsley, thyme and bay leaf in a cheesecloth bag for bouquet garni. Melt 3 tablespoons butter in a saucepan over medium heat. Add the celery, carrots, onion and garlic to the butter and cover the pan. Sweat the vegetables and garlic for 5 minutes and stir in the flour. Cook for 3 minutes, stirring constantly. Add the bouquet garni, gravy and stock. Cook for 20 minutes, stirring occasionally. Preheat the oven to 350 degrees. Discard the bouquet garni and stir the turkey, stuffing, peas, salt and pepper into the vegetable mixture. Bring to a simmer and spoon the turkey mixture into a 1 1/2-quart baking dish. Spread the mashed potatoes over the prepared layer and drizzle with melted butter. Bake for 30 minutes or until bubbly. Broil just until brown and serve immediately. Do not use any leftover stuffing that contains shellfish in this recipe.

wild duck poppers

Contrary to popular belief, there is a thriving hunting culture in California that has easy access to an incredible amount of wilderness and all kinds of game.

2 cups apple cider vinegar	1 pound sliced hickory-smoked bacon
1 cup Worcestershire sauce	10 wild duck breasts
3/4 cup honey	20 pickled jalapeño chile slices
7 tablespoons Tabasco sauce or	16 ounces cream cheese, cubed
Louisiana hot sauce	and softened
2 tablespoons granulated garlic	Dry Rub on page 116, or Creole
2 tablespoons granulated onion	seasoning to taste

Combine the vinegar, Worcestershire sauce, honey, Tabasco sauce, granulated garlic and granulated onion in a bowl and mix well. Pour the vinegar mixture over the bacon and duck in a shallow dish, turning to coat. Marinate, covered, in the refrigerator for 2 to 10 hours, turning occasionally.

Preheat the grill to medium; use hickory wood. Make a pocket in each duck breast using a sharp knife. Mix the jalapeño chiles and cream cheese in a bowl until combined. Stuff each pocket evenly with the cream cheese mixture. Wrap the duck breasts with the sliced bacon and secure with wooden picks. Generously sprinkle with Dry Rub. Grill the stuffed duck breasts for 2 minutes per side; do not overcook. Medium-rare is the best way to eat wild game.

cook's note ■ Chicken or turkey may be substituted for the duck.

venezuelan white, red and green fish

An attractive presentation and a tasty combination of flavors.

2 large yellow onions, thinly sliced
Olive oil
1 tablespoon sugar
1 pound potatoes, sliced
2 pounds white fish such as halibut,
    cod, ono or sea bass

Salt and pepper to taste
1 pound (or more) tomatoes, sliced
1 (14-ounce) jar pimento-stuffed
    green olives
Fresh lime juice

Preheat the oven to 450 degrees. Cover the bottom of a greased 9×13-inch baking dish with the onions and drizzle with olive oil. Sprinkle with the sugar. Layer with the potatoes and fish and sprinkle with salt and pepper.

Top the prepared layers with the tomatoes and olives and drizzle with olive oil and lime juice. Bake for 30 minutes or until the potatoes are tender and the fish flakes easily when tested with a fork.

halibut with shiitake mushrooms

3 tablespoons soy sauce
2 tablespoons peanut oil
1 teaspoon sesame oil
1 pound fresh green beans, trimmed
8 ounces shiitake or oyster
    mushrooms, stems removed

2 (8-ounce) halibut fillets,
    1 inch thick
Salt and pepper to taste
Orange Miso Sauce (page 30)

Preheat the oven to 450 degrees. Mix the soy sauce, peanut oil and sesame oil in a shallow dish. Add the green beans and mushrooms and toss to coat. Remove the bean mixture to a rimmed baking sheet using a slotted spoon and spread in a single layer, reserving the soy sauce mixture. Add the fillets to the reserved soy sauce mixture and toss gently to coat.

Arrange the fillets over the green bean mixture and drizzle with the remaining soy sauce mixture. Sprinkle with salt and pepper. Roast until the fillets are opaque in the middle and the beans are tender-crisp. Divide the fillets and vegetables evenly between two serving plates. Serve with Orange Miso Sauce.

cook's note ▤ For variety, substitute Chinese long beans (dow gok) or haricots verts for the fresh green beans.

easy elegant salmon

This delightful salmon makes its own sauce as it bakes.

2 pounds salmon, shark, tuna,
    halibut or sea bass fillets
1/2 cup (2 ounces) grated
    Parmesan cheese

1/2 cup mayonnaise
1/2 cup lemon juice
1/4 cup capers

Preheat the oven to 400 degrees. Line a large shallow baking dish with foil and arrange the fillets skin side down in the prepared baking dish. Mix the cheese, mayonnaise, lemon juice and capers in a bowl.

Spoon the mayonnaise mixture over the fillets. Bake for 25 to 30 minutes or until the fillets flake easily when tested with a fork. Serve immediately.

citrus-roasted salmon

The citrus zest gives the salmon a wonderful flavor and is well worth the effort. Use a microplane to speed up the zesting process.

1 orange
1 lemon
Grated zest of 1 lime
1 teaspoon coarse salt

1 teaspoon coriander seeds, crushed
1/2 teaspoon pepper
1 (11/2-pound) salmon fillet with skin
1 tablespoon olive oil

Zest the orange and lemon. Cut the orange and lemon into 1/4-inch slices. Mix the orange zest, lemon zest, lime zest, salt, coriander and pepper in a bowl.

Arrange the fillet skin side down in a large glass or ceramic baking dish. Rub the fillet with the zest mixture. Chill, covered with plastic wrap, for 1 to 2 hours. Let stand at room temperature for 20 minutes.

Preheat the oven to 400 degrees. Remove the fillet to a platter. Reserve several of the orange slices and several of the lemon slices. Arrange the remaining orange slices and remaining lemon slices in a single layer in the baking dish. Layer with the fillet skin side down. Place the reserved orange slices and reserved lemon slices on top of the fillet and drizzle with the olive oil. Roast for 17 to 25 minutes or until the fillet flakes easily. Cut crosswise into four equal portions and serve immediately.

Photograph for this recipe on page 98.

salmon with mango and avocado relish

This colorful dish is sure to please.

salmon
1/2 cup grapefruit juice
1/4 cup lemon juice
1/4 cup olive oil
1 teaspoon ground cumin
2 (8-ounce) salmon fillets

mango and avocado relish
2 mangoes, chopped
1 large avocado, chopped

2 tomatoes, seeded and chopped
1/2 cup chopped yellow bell pepper
1/4 cup chopped red onion
1/4 cup chopped cilantro
1/4 teaspoon ground cumin
1/4 teaspoon cayenne pepper,
  or to taste
Salt and black pepper to taste

To prepare the salmon, mix the grapefruit juice, lemon juice, olive oil and cumin in a bowl. Pour the grapefruit juice mixture over the salmon in a shallow dish, turning to coat. Marinate, covered, in the refrigerator for 2 to 4 hours, turning occasionally.

Preheat the grill. Grill for 5 minutes or until the salmon flakes easily. Cut into strips to serve.

To prepare the relish, gently toss the mangoes, avocado, tomatoes, bell pepper, onion, cilantro, cumin and cayenne pepper in a bowl. Season with salt and black pepper. Serve with the salmon.

cook's note ▧ Substitute other varieties of fish, chicken, or beef for the salmon. If using beef, increase the cumin to 1 tablespoon, add 1/2 teaspoon pressed garlic, and salt and pepper to taste to the marinade. Serve the leftover Mango and Avocado Relish with a variety of dishes, including beef, pork, quesadillas, and tacos. Also can be served on a bed of lettuce as a salad or with rice pilaf as a main entrée.

shanghai swordfish

2 pounds swordfish, salmon, halibut,
    tuna or sea bass steaks
3 tablespoons soy sauce
3 tablespoons fresh lemon juice
3 tablespoons cooking sherry
1 1/2 tablespoons wasabi

1 tablespoon vegetable oil
2 teaspoons sugar
1 teaspoon finely chopped
    fresh ginger
3 green onions with tops, chopped

Make three or four shallow slashes in each side of each steak. Arrange the steaks in a single layer in a nonreactive dish. Mix the soy sauce, lemon juice, sherry, wasabi, oil, sugar, ginger and green onions in a bowl and pour over the steaks. Marinate, covered, in the refrigerator for 1 hour, turning several times.

Preheat the broiler. Drain the steaks, reserving the marinade. Arrange the steaks on a greased broiler rack in a broiler pan. Broil 4 inches from the heat source for 8 to 10 minutes per side or until the steaks flake easily when tested with a fork, brushing with the reserved marinade several times. Serve with steamed white rice and vegetables. Bring the remaining marinade to a boil in a saucepan and boil for 2 minutes. Use to flavor rice and/or vegetables if desired.

lemon dill trout in foil

This recipe is great for camp-outs.

3 or 4 lemons, sliced
1 bunch dill weed, trimmed
    and chopped
8 teaspoons butter, cut into
    1-teaspoon portions

2 whole trout, sea bass, halibut, tuna
    or salmon, dressed
Kosher salt to taste
Lemon pepper to taste
2 tablespoons white wine

Preheat the grill. Cut two sheets of heavy-duty foil twice as long as the whole trout. Line each piece of foil with lemon slices, some of the dill weed and 2 teaspoons of the butter. Season the trout with salt and lemon pepper and arrange 1 trout on each prepared sheet of foil.

Top each trout with 2 teaspoons of the remaining butter, the remaining dill weed and the remaining lemon slices. Drizzle 1 tablespoon of the wine over each trout. Fold the foil over to cover and crimp the edges to seal. Grill for 15 to 20 minutes or until the trout flakes easily. To serve, remove the trout from the packets carefully and arrange on serving plates. Spoon the juices from the packets over the trout.

dungeness crab thermidor

[serves 6]

A Pacific Northwest twist on an old favorite.

3 tablespoons butter
1/4 cup all-purpose flour
1 teaspoon salt
1/8 teaspoon ground nutmeg
Dash of paprika
2 cups whipping cream
1/4 cup sherry
2 pounds Dungeness crab meat, drained and flaked
3/4 cup (3 ounces) shredded mild Cheddar cheese

Melt the butter in a medium saucepan and stir in the flour. Cook until the mixture is light brown, stirring constantly. Add the salt, nutmeg and paprika and mix well. Gradually add the cream and sherry, stirring constantly. Cook over medium heat until smooth and thickened and of a sauce consistency, stirring constantly.

Preheat the oven to 350 degrees. Add the crab meat to the sauce about 10 minutes before serving and simmer over medium heat until heated through, stirring constantly. Spoon the crab meat mixture into a buttered baking dish and sprinkle with the cheese. Bake for 4 minutes or until the cheese melts. Serve with hot cooked rice or noodles.

Soft-shell crabs are young crabs that are caught just after shedding their hard outer shell. Blue crabs are the most common variety of soft-shell crabs available in the United States. They are seasonal and can be found fresh from May through August and frozen in the off-season. If buying fresh, be sure to have the fishmonger clean them before purchasing. The entire crab is eaten, legs and all.

To prepare Maryland Soft-Shell Crabs, *melt butter in a skillet over medium heat until hot and season to taste with garlic powder. Sauté 2 blue crabs per guest for 5 minutes on one side and 4 minutes on the remaining side. Drain on paper towels. Thinly slice the crabs and serve on buns dressed with lettuce, tomato and mayonnaise, or serve over garlic mashed potatoes as an entrée.*

lobster quesadillas with brie

Quesadillas go uptown.

2 lobster tails, grilled or broiled
8 flour tortillas
8 ounces Brie cheese, sliced
8 ounces Pepper Jack
   cheese, shredded
1 small onion, chopped

1 red bell pepper, chopped
1 small serrano chile, minced
1 tomato, chopped
Butter
Pineapple Mango Salsa (page 141)
1 avocado, mashed

Remove the lobster meat from the tails and coarsely chop. Arrange 4 of the tortillas on a hard work surface. Layer the tortillas evenly with the cheese, onion, bell pepper, serrano chile, tomato and lobster meat. Top with the remaining tortillas.

Sauté the quesadillas in butter in a skillet until golden brown on both sides, turning once. Cut each quesadilla into quarters and serve with the salsa and mashed avocado. Any fruit salsa will work well with this recipe.

bangkok mussels with red curry sauce

The sweet and spicy sauce flavors the rice of this wonderful Thai dish.

1 (14-ounce) can coconut milk
$1/2$ cup sugar
$1/2$ cup finely chopped lemon grass
$1/4$ cup finely chopped green onions
$1/4$ cup fresh basil, finely chopped
2 tablespoons finely chopped
   fresh ginger

1 tablespoon minced or
   pressed garlic
2 tablespoons Thai red curry paste
3 pounds mussels
$1/2$ cup sake or white wine
Hot cooked rice

Combine the coconut milk, sugar, lemon grass, green onions, basil, ginger and garlic in a heavy saucepan and bring to a boil. Reduce the heat to low and simmer until the sauce is reduced by half, stirring frequently. Whisk in the curry paste and simmer for 5 minutes longer, stirring occasionally. Remove from the heat and cover to keep warm.

Rinse the mussels with cold water. Discard any with broken shells or any that remain open when tapped. Remove any beards. Combine the mussels and wine in a large saucepan. Steam, tightly covered, over high heat for 5 minutes or just until the mussels begin to open. Remove from the heat and discard any unopened mussels. Stir in the sauce and serve immediately over hot cooked rice with crusty bread on the side.

stir-fry sesame asparagus and scallops

1/4 cup peanut oil
1 1/2 pounds fresh asparagus or
    green beans, trimmed and
    cut into 2-inch pieces
1 1/2 pounds scallops or shrimp
1 onion, sliced
1/4 cup cashews, chopped

1 (8-ounce) can water chestnuts,
    drained and sliced
4 teaspoons soy sauce
1 tablespoon sesame seeds, toasted
2 teaspoons Asian garlic chili sauce
1 teaspoon salt (optional)

Heat the peanut oil in a wok or large skillet over high heat. Add the asparagus, scallops and onion to the hot oil. Stir-fry for 3 to 5 minutes or until the scallops are opaque and the vegetables are tender-crisp. Stir in the cashews, water chestnuts, soy sauce, sesame seeds, chili sauce and salt and stir-fry just until heated through. Serve with hot cooked rice.

scallops and wild mushrooms en croûte

2 tablespoons butter
1 tablespoon peanut oil
1 pound assorted wild mushrooms
    such as chanterelle or shiitake,
    cut into 1-inch pieces
1 red onion, coarsely chopped
2 garlic cloves, minced or pressed
3 tablespoons all-purpose flour
2 teaspoons fresh thyme, chopped

2 teaspoons parsley, chopped
1/2 cup sherry
3 cups chicken broth
1 cup heavy cream
Kosher salt and freshly ground
    pepper to taste
12 scallops
1 sheet puff pastry
1 egg, lightly beaten

Preheat the oven to 400 degrees. Heat the butter and peanut oil in a skillet until the butter begins to brown. Stir in the mushrooms. Cook until the mushrooms begin to caramelize, stirring frequently. Add the onion and garlic and cook until the onion is tender. Stir in the flour, thyme and parsley and cook until the flour is absorbed. Mix in the sherry and cook for 1 minute. Add the broth and cream and bring to a boil.

Reduce the heat to medium-low and cook for 12 minutes or until the mixture begins to thicken, stirring frequently. Season with salt and pepper and remove from the heat. Spoon the mushroom mixture evenly into four 2-cup ramekins. Arrange 3 scallops over the top of each. Cut the puff pastry into 4 equal portions and fit each ramekin with 1 portion of the puff pastry. Cut vents and brush with the egg. Bake for 15 minutes or until the pastry is golden brown.

cook's note ■ Can be served without the puff pastry in a scallop shell as coquilles St. Jacques, adding the scallops with the cream and broth.

killer shrimp

This is my mother's original Killer Shrimp recipe. It is very good and easy to prepare. The sauce has a sweetness that complements the shrimp. Any hard liquor works, but it is Black Label Scotch at my house.

1 tablespoon sugar
2 tablespoons soy sauce
1 tablespoon hard liquor or
 sherry
1/4 cup vegetable oil

1 pound unpeeled medium shrimp
2 tablespoons minced green onions
1 tablespoon julienned fresh ginger
8 small bok choy leaves,
 cut into halves

Mix the sugar, soy sauce and liquor in a bowl. Heat a large wok or skillet over medium heat until hot and add the oil. Heat until the oil begins to smoke and add the shrimp.

Cook until the shrimp turn pink and start to curl. Stir in the soy sauce mixture, green onions, ginger and bok choy. Stir-fry for 2 to 3 minutes. Serve with hot cooked rice and steamed or garlic stir-fried vegetables.

cook's note ■ Substitute onion powder and ginger powder for the green onions and ginger if fresh is not available; just use half the amount.

shrimp and artichoke fettuccine
[serves 8 to 10]

A rich and creamy casserole that is fit for company.

16 ounces spinach fettuccine
1/2 cup (2 ounces) shredded
    Parmesan cheese
1/2 cup sour cream
1/4 cup mayonnaise
1/2 teaspoon salt
2 pounds shrimp, cooked, peeled
    and deveined

2 (8- or 9-ounce) jars artichoke pesto
1 (6-ounce) jar marinated artichokes,
    drained and chopped
2 cups (8 ounces) shredded Italian
    5-cheese blend
Juice of 1 lemon

Preheat the oven to 350 degrees. Cook the pasta using the package directions and drain. Mix the Parmesan cheese, sour cream, mayonnaise and salt in a bowl and stir in the pasta. Combine the shrimp, pesto, artichokes, 5-cheese blend and lemon juice in a bowl and mix well.

Spoon the pasta mixture into a 9×13-inch baking dish and spread with the shrimp mixture. Bake for 1 hour. Serve with Fresh Lemon Herb Salad on page 74.

shrimp fried rice
[serves 4]

Fried rice is a "leftover" dish in Chinese households using extra cooked rice. My grandmother used to make this for me when I was a child.

1/2 cup vegetable oil
2 eggs, beaten
1/2 cup mushrooms, chopped
1/2 cup fresh or thawed frozen
    green peas
1/2 cup snow peas, chopped
1/2 cup chopped carrots
1/4 cup minced green onions

12 fresh or thawed frozen shrimp,
    peeled and deveined
2 1/2 cups cooked rice (preferably
    sticky short grain rice)
1 tablespoon soy sauce
1 teaspoon sea salt
1 teaspoon pepper

Heat the oil in a large skillet over medium-high heat and add the eggs. Fry until they begin to solidify. Stir in the mushrooms, green peas, snow peas, carrots and green onions. Lightly stir-fry the vegetables and add the shrimp.

Stir-fry until the shrimp turn pink and curl. Stir in the rice, soy sauce, salt and pepper. Stir-fry until the rice is fried and slightly hardened.

cook's note ▦ Substitute chopped cooked chicken for the shrimp if desired.

quick and easy paella

Paella is a traditional Spanish one-pan dish with myriad variations. It gets its name from the pan it is usually cooked in, which is called a paellera.

1 (8-ounce) package Spanish-style
  yellow rice with saffron
3 ounces spicy link sausage such as
  linguiça or Louisiana hot
  links, chopped
1 large boneless skinless chicken
  breast, chopped
1 tablespoon olive oil
1 cup chopped onion
1 cup chopped red bell pepper

2 large garlic cloves, minced
1 1/2 pounds medium shrimp, peeled
  and deveined
1 cup cherry tomato halves
1/2 cup dry white wine
Salt and pepper to taste
1/2 cup peas
3 tablespoons chopped cilantro
  leaves for garnish

Cook the rice using the package directions in a medium saucepan. Brown the sausage and chicken in a large nonstick skillet over medium-high heat. Remove the sausage mixture to a platter using a slotted spoon, reserving the pan drippings. Heat the olive oil with the reserved pan drippings over medium heat and stir in the onion, bell pepper and garlic.

Cook for 2 minutes or until the vegetables are tender. Add the shrimp, tomatoes and wine and cook until the shrimp turn bright pink and are just cooked through. Season with salt and pepper. Stir in the sausage mixture and peas. Fluff the rice with a fork. Add the shrimp mixture to the rice and toss to combine. Garnish with the cilantro.

cook's note ▓ Serve with garlic bread and a simple salad for a complete meal. You can add any meat or seafood such as clams, mussels, scallops, and/or fish. Chorizo works beautifully, but there are two types. If using solid link, brown with the chicken. If using ground chorizo, remove from the casings and cook in a separate pan before adding to the shrimp mixture.

rotelle with seafood and capers

16 ounces rotelle
1/2 cup (1 stick) butter
1/4 cup olive oil
1 pound large shrimp, peeled and deveined
8 ounces scallops
8 ounces fresh crab meat, drained and flaked
1/4 cup minced garlic
1 teaspoon salt
Freshly ground black pepper to taste
1 cup fresh lemon juice
3/4 cup parsley, chopped
Grated zest of 1 lemon
1/2 lemon, thinly sliced
1 tablespoon capers
1/2 teaspoon hot red pepper flakes

Cook the pasta using the package directions and drain. Heat the butter and olive oil in a heavy saucepan over medium-low heat until the butter melts and stir in the shrimp, scallops, crab meat, garlic, salt and black pepper.

Sauté for 5 minutes or until the shrimp turn pink and the scallops turn white. Remove from the heat. Add the lemon juice, parsley, lemon zest, lemon slices, capers and red pepper flakes and mix well. Toss the shrimp mixture with the pasta in a large bowl. You may substitute any variety of pasta for the rotelle.

In 1971, we came to the United States from South Korea for a better future for our family. We moved to Ohio to be near my father's relatives. My mother sponsored my grandparents to come, but they moved to Los Angeles because of the larger Korean community. (Today, Southern California has the largest Korean/ Korean-American population outside of South Korea.) My immediate family moved to California to be near my relatives after my father passed away in 1984. Both my parents and grandparents passed their U.S. citizenship exams. My generation and those following are very blessed to have parents who thought of our future for a better life in the States.

baja tequila taco bar

Entertain your friends with a taco bar. Offer a variety of fish, shrimp, and/or chicken with a selection of salsas to satisfy every taste. Have lots of cold Mexican beer and margaritas on hand.

baja tequila marinade
1/4 cup fresh lime juice
    (about 2 limes)
1/4 cup tequila
2 tablespoons lemon juice
2 tablespoons olive oil
1/4 cup chopped fresh cilantro
1 teaspoon salt
2 garlic cloves, minced
1/2 teaspoon crushed dried
    red chiles

pico de gallo
5 tomatoes, coarsely chopped
1 small red onion, chopped
1/4 cup chopped cilantro
1/4 cup fresh lime juice
3 jalapeño chiles, finely chopped
1 serrano chile, finely chopped
2 garlic cloves, minced

spicy tomato salsa
mayonnaise
1/2 cup mayonnaise

tomatillo salsa verde
1 pound fresh tomatillos, husked
    and quartered
1 cup cilantro leaves (1 bunch)
2 garlic cloves
1 teaspoon salt
1/2 cup chopped white onion
1/4 cup lime juice (1 lime)
2 jalapeño chiles, seeded
    and chopped
1 serrano chile, seeded
    and chopped

To prepare the marinade, mix the lime juice, tequila, lemon juice, olive oil, cilantro, salt, garlic and red chiles in a bowl and mix well. Marinate chicken for 30 minutes, shrimp for 30 minutes and fish for 10 minutes. Be careful not to allow the fish to marinate longer than 10 minutes.

To prepare the pico de gallo, mix the tomatoes, onion, cilantro, lime juice, jalapeño chiles, serrano chile and garlic in a bowl. Store, covered, in the refrigerator until serving time. To lower the level of spiciness, reduce the number or size of the chiles.

To prepare the mayonnaise, mix 2 cups of the Pico de Gallo with the mayonnaise in a bowl. Store, covered, in the refrigerator until serving time.

To prepare the salsa verde, combine the tomatillos, cilantro, garlic, salt, onion, lime juice, jalapeño chiles and serrano chile, in a food processor. Process to the desired consistency. Store, covered, in the refrigerator until serving time.

pineapple mango salsa

2 cups chopped fresh pineapple
1 cup chopped fresh mango
1 red bell pepper, chopped
1/2 chopped red onion
1/2 cup fresh cilantro, chopped
1 jalapeño chile, chopped
1 tablespoon garlic chile sauce

baja fish tacos

1 pound fresh fish fillets, cut into
      1×2-inch strips
12 miniature corn tortilla shells

baja shrimp tacos

1 pound shrimp, peeled
      and deveined
12 miniature corn tortilla shells

To prepare the pineapple mango salsa, combine the pineapple, mango, bell pepper, onion, cilantro, jalapeño chile and garlic chile sauce in a bowl and mix well. Store, covered, in the refrigerator until serving time.

To prepare the fish tacos, preheat the grill. Marinate the fish in the Baja Tequila Marinade in a shallow dish for 10 minutes, turning once or twice; drain. Grill the fish until cooked through. Spoon the fish evenly into the shells and serve with Pico de Gallo, Pineapple Mango Salsa, Cabbage and Jicama Slaw (cook's note), shredded jicama and/or sliced avocado.

To prepare the shrimp tacos, preheat the grill. Marinate the shrimp in the Baja Tequila Marinade in a shallow dish for 30 minutes, turning occasionally; drain. Thread wooden skewers with approximately 6 shrimp each. Grill the skewers until the shrimp turn pink. Arrange the shrimp in the tortilla shells. Serve with Cabbage and Jicama Slaw (cook's note), Pico de Gallo, Spicy Tomato Salsa Mayonnaise and/or Pineapple Mango Salsa. Soak wooden skewers in water in a bowl for 30 minutes before use.

cook's note ■ Cabbage and Jicama Slaw is a combination of coarsely shredded red and green cabbage with shredded jicama. Toss with red wine vinegar, vegetable oil, and sugar to taste.

Photograph for this recipe on page 205.

Clockwise from left to right: Carrots and Parsnips Marrakesh (page 151), Orzo with Prosciutto and Asparagus (page 163),
Swiss Chard with Orange Gremolata (page 151)

vegetables & side dishes

Untitled
Millard Sheets, 1977
(Scenes from the rural lifestyle of an earlier era)

Farms, Farmers, and Farmers' Markets

Setting California's table is as easy as putting a mosaic piece into place. From our northern regions, through our central valleys, all the way to our southernmost counties, agriculture is our leading industry and an integral part of our life; there is very little that cannot be brought to market from the farms and ranches that adorn our state.

California leads the nation in the production of fruits and vegetables, and almost every part of the state has large regions dedicated to the agricultural industry. The great Central Valley extends almost four hundred miles down the middle of the state and is commonly called America's Breadbasket. Almost every type of nontropical fruit, vegetable, and nut is grown in this region. The northern and central counties are famous for producing some of the country's finest wines. Our coastal farms provide tender field lettuce, cabbage, carrots, celery, garlic, and strawberries and perfume the air with miles of fragrant and colorful flowers. Our southern farms provide squash, broccoli, dates, hothouse flowers, peppers, and tomatoes. While our economy depends on the export of wine, grapes, cotton, oranges, and flowers, our highest-income crop has little to do with seeds and blossoms. It is our dairy cow and the milk it gives that brings the largest share of farm income and leads the nation in milk production. California has more than two thousand dairy farms with 1.7 million dairy cows, which supply milk to 139 in-state dairy plants that produce fluid milk, cheese, ice cream, butter, and other dairy products.

While dairy cows dominate our livestock industry, domestic cattle have been present in the New World for five hundred years and have been an important component of California's economic and social fabric since the establishment of the first Spanish mission in San Diego in the early 1700s. Today, California's ranching enterprises are as diverse as any in the world. Ranchers own or manage roughly thirty-eight million acres of either privately or publicly owned rangeland. Most California ranches are family-owned and operated, and many have been in the same family for generations.

Throughout the state, local farmers' markets, some temporary and some permanent, allow regional farmers to sell their wares and, depending on where you live, afford you a plate of the freshest ingredients available—some even let you have the pleasure of going into the field to pick your own produce. There are more than 360 certified farmers' markets in California, many of them filled with produce from farms that are certified organic, and the number continues to grow each year. Of these, $250 million in sales was recorded, and this does not account for the number of regional farmers' markets that spring up from town to town during the growing seasons. One of the most famous markets in Los Angeles is Farmers' Market at 3rd and Fairfax. Established in 1934, it has become a worldwide tourist experience that includes more than one hundred vendors selling groceries, farm fresh produce, homemade confections, and delicious international foods. There are also clothing shops, key makers, a bank, and yes, even a lottery booth where the next California millionaire can purchase the winning ticket.

Just after dawn, as the sun stretches its warm nurturing rays across the perfectly furrowed fields and orchards, a cow lows, a rooster crows, and the shick-shick of the irrigators breaks the valley's silence. A California farmer begins his day, like every other, by putting into action the tools that help feed and nourish a very hungry nation.

Food photography sponsored by Susan McDonnell
Mosaic photography sponsored by Amy and David Lamb

fire-roasted artichokes

A versatile recipe.

Juice of 2 lemons	1 tablespoon fresh cilantro, chopped
Salt to taste	1 tablespoon paprika
4 artichokes	1 teaspoon salt
1/2 stick (1/4 cup) butter, melted	1 teaspoon garlic powder

Fill a large saucepan halfway with water and add the lemon juice and salt to taste. Cut the stems from the artichokes to form a flat base. Cut 1/3 off the top of each artichoke and scrape the fuzzy chokes from the centers. Place the artichokes in the lemon water and bring to a boil. Cook for 20 to 25 minutes; drain.

Preheat the grill. Mix the butter, cilantro, paprika, 1 teaspoon salt and the garlic powder in a bowl. Carefully remove the artichokes from the lemon water using a slotted spoon and arrange each artichoke on a piece of foil large enough to completely enclose. Drizzle with the butter mixture and seal.

Grill or bake in a 500-degree oven for 8 minutes, turning occasionally. To serve, fill the artichoke cavities with melted butter, mayonnaise or any other dipping sauce. Serve warm or chilled.

cook's note ▦ Great for picnics and buffets. Easily prepared in advance. The butter spice mixture is delicious on any grilled vegetable such as corn, asparagus, or potato wedges. Place the vegetables in foil packets and grill or bake to the desired degree of crispness.

Broccoli Cauliflower Salad is quick and easy to prepare and makes a great side dish for most any entrée. Chop 1 head of cauliflower and 1 bunch of broccoli into bite-size pieces and combine with 1/2 chopped red onion. Add a mixture of 1 cup mayonnaise, 1/4 cup cider vinegar and 2 tablespoons or less sugar. Store, covered, in the refrigerator until serving time.

asparagus chinoise

A sophisticated stir-fry.

36 fresh asparagus spears	3 tablespoons soy sauce
1/4 cup (1/2 stick) butter	1/8 teaspoon salt

Snap off the woody ends of the asparagus spears and discard. Cut the remaining spears diagonally into 1/4-inch slices. Melt the butter in a large skillet and add the asparagus.

Sauté for 6 minutes or until tender. Stir in the soy sauce and salt about 2 minutes before the end of the sautéing process.

french beans with shallots

Haricots verts are longer and more delicate than regular green beans.

1 pound French string beans or
    haricots verts
Kosher salt to taste
2 tablespoons butter

1 tablespoon olive oil
3 large shallots, chopped
1/2 teaspoon pepper

Blanch the beans in boiling salted water in a saucepan for 1 1/2 minutes. Drain and immediately plunge the beans into a bowl of ice water to stop the cooking process; drain again.

Heat the butter and olive oil in a sauté pan over medium heat until the butter melts and add the shallots. Sauté for 5 to 10 minutes or until light brown, stirring occasionally. Add the beans to the shallot mixture and sauté just until heated through. Season with the pepper and serve immediately. If substituting with green beans, blanch for 3 minutes.

green beans in prosciutto

Beautiful and delectable bundles.

2 pounds green beans
1 pound mozzarella cheese,
    thinly sliced
8 ounces prosciutto, thinly sliced
3/4 cup olive oil
1/3 cup red wine vinegar

2 tablespoons chopped fresh
    dill weed
2 tablespoons chopped fresh basil
1/2 teaspoon salt
1/4 teaspoon cracked pepper

Trim the beans and cut about the same size. Cook the beans in boiling water in a saucepan for 5 to 6 minutes or until tender-crisp. Drain and immediately plunge the beans into a bowl of ice water to stop the cooking process. Drain again and pat dry.

Arrange the beans in bundles of 6 or 7 beans and wrap each bundle with a slice of cheese and a slice of prosciutto. Place the wrapped bundles on a platter. Whisk the olive oil, vinegar, dill weed, basil, salt and pepper in a bowl until thickened. Pour the olive oil mixture over the bean bundles. Chill, covered, until serving time.

cook's note ▥ Prepare the night before and serve at room temperature. Wonderful on a picnic.

herbed green beans

To dress up this simple recipe, use haricots verts.

1 pound fresh green beans,
    wax beans, purple beans or
    haricots verts, trimmed
1/2 cup (1 stick) butter
1 small onion, chopped
1 teaspoon garlic salt

1 teaspoon fresh basil, or
    1/2 teaspoon dried basil
1 teaspoon fresh oregano, or
    1/4 teaspoon dried oregano
1/4 teaspoon marjoram

Blanch the beans in boiling water in a saucepan for 2 to 5 minutes or until tender-crisp. Drain and immediately plunge the beans into a bowl of ice water to stop the cooking process; drain again.

Melt the butter in a skillet and add the onion. Sauté until the onion begins to soften and stir in the beans. Turn off the heat and sprinkle the bean mixture with the garlic salt, basil, oregano and marjoram. Turn the heat on low just before serving and cook just until the beans are heated through. Substitute summer savory for the oregano if desired.

texas spicy beans

These beans have a real kick.

2 (16-ounce) cans pork and beans
1 (16-ounce) can kidney beans
1 (15-ounce) can chili beans
1 onion, chopped
1 green bell pepper, chopped
3 tablespoons ketchup
3 tablespoons molasses

1 tablespoon cider vinegar
1 teaspoon chili powder
1 teaspoon salt
1 teaspoon black pepper
1 teaspoon Tabasco sauce
1 teaspoon Worcestershire sauce
1/2 teaspoon crushed red pepper

Preheat the oven to 350 degrees. Combine the beans, onion and bell pepper in a bowl and mix well. Stir in the ketchup, molasses, vinegar, chili powder, salt, black pepper, Tabasco sauce, Worcestershire sauce and red pepper. Spoon the bean mixture into a shallow baking dish and bake for 30 to 45 minutes or until bubbly.

baked heirloom beets with balsamic vinegar

Heirloom beets come in a variety of colors, so mix and match for a colorful presentation.

1 pound (golf ball-size) beets of
    various colors, leaves and
    stems trimmed
10 garlic cloves, pressed

$1/4$ cup fresh marjoram or oregano
Salt and pepper to taste
$3/4$ cup balsamic vinegar
$1/3$ cup olive oil

Preheat the oven to 400 degrees. Arrange the beets, garlic and marjoram on a sheet of foil large enough to enclose. Season generously with salt and pepper and bring the sides of the foil up. Pour a mixture of the vinegar and olive oil over the beet mixture and seal the foil.

Bake for 1 hour or until the beets are tender. Let stand until cool enough to handle. Peel and slice or chop the beets, reserving the juices. Serve the beets with the reserved juices over watercress or mixed salad greens or as a side to grilled meats. Serve at room temperature if desired.

brussels sprouts with bacon

This Bavarian-style recipe will tempt even the most finicky eater.

2 pounds fresh brussels sprouts
3 slices bacon or pancetta, cut into
    thin strips
1/2 cup red wine vinegar

Salt to taste
1 to 2 tablespoons red wine vinegar
    (optional)
1/4 cup pine nuts, toasted

Trim the brussels sprouts, removing any outer leaves that are too dark or damaged. Trim the base and make an "X" 1/4 to 1/2 inch deep in each base. Steam over boiling water for 5 to 7 minutes or just until tender-crisp. Let stand until cool and cut lengthwise into quarters.

Cook the bacon in a skillet over medium-low heat until brown and crisp. Increase the heat to high and stir in 1/2 cup vinegar. Cook for 3 minutes or until the strong smell disappears. Reduce the heat and stir in the brussels sprouts.

Cook just until heated through and season with salt and 1 to 2 tablespoons vinegar. Stir in the pine nuts and serve immediately. You may substitute any green vegetable for the brussels sprouts.

red cabbage with apples

Tangy and delicious. Serve with beef roast or pork chops.

1 small head red cabbage, trimmed
    (about 2 pounds)
2 tablespoons vegetable oil or butter
3 tablespoons finely chopped onion
1 large green apple, peeled and
    cut into matchsticks or grated

3 tablespoons red wine vinegar
2 1/2 tablespoons honey
1 teaspoon salt
1/8 teaspoon caraway seeds

Cut the cabbage into quarters and thinly slice each quarter crosswise. Immerse the cabbage in a bowl of cold water for 5 minutes; drain. Heat the oil in a skillet over medium heat and add the onion. Cook until golden brown, stirring frequently.

Mix the cabbage with the onion. Stir in the apple, vinegar, honey, salt and caraway seeds. Cook, covered, over low heat for 1 to 1 1/2 hours or until the cabbage is very tender, adding boiling water if needed for additional moisture and stirring occasionally.

carrots and parsnips marrakesh [serves 4 to 6]

The much over-looked parsnip shares center stage in this wonderful dish.

1 pound carrots, sliced
8 ounces parsnips, sliced
Salt to taste
2 tablespoons butter
1/4 cup slivered almonds

1 tablespoon sugar
1/2 teaspoon ground cumin
1/4 teaspoon coriander
1/4 teaspoon ground cinnamon
1/8 teaspoon ground nutmeg

Combine the carrots, parsnips and salt with enough water to cover in a saucepan. Bring to a boil and boil for 15 to 20 minutes or until tender. Drain and remove the carrot mixture to a bowl. Melt the butter in the saucepan and add the almonds. Cook over medium-low heat for 3 minutes or until the almonds are light brown, stirring constantly. Stir in the carrots, parsnips, sugar, cumin, coriander, cinnamon and nutmeg. Cook over low heat for 5 to 10 minutes or until most of the liquid is absorbed and the carrots and parsnips are glazed.

Photograph for this recipe on page 142.

swiss chard with orange gremolata [serves 4]

Gremolata is a colorful Italian garnish that adds flavor to many dishes. It is primarily composed of orange and/or lemon zest, garlic, and parsley.

orange gremolata
3 large garlic cloves, minced
    or pressed
2 tablespoons Italian parsley, minced
2 tablespoons julienned orange zest
1 teaspoon julienned lemon zest

swiss chard
2 tablespoons butter
1 tablespoon olive oil

1/4 cup chicken broth
2 tablespoons frozen orange
    juice concentrate
1 tablespoon lemon juice
1 pound Swiss chard, trimmed and
    cut into bite-size pieces
Salt and pepper to taste

To prepare the gremolata, mix the garlic, parsley, orange zest and lemon zest in a bowl.

To prepare the Swiss chard, heat the butter and olive oil in a large skillet over medium-high heat. Reserve 1 tablespoon of the gremolata and stir the remaining gremolata into the butter mixture. Cook for 30 seconds, stirring constantly. Add the broth, orange juice concentrate and lemon juice and mix well. Bring to a simmer and stir in the Swiss chard. Cook, covered, for 5 to 10 minutes or until tender, stirring occasionally. Toss the Swiss chard mixture and spoon into a serving bowl. Season with salt and pepper and sprinkle with the reserved 1 tablespoon gremolata.

cook's note ▦ For variety, substitute green beans, brussels sprouts, broccoli, or your favorite vegetable for the Swiss chard.

Photograph for this recipe on page 142.

southern greens

On New Year's Day, Southerners always eat greens to bring money, and black-eyed peas to bring luck, during the coming year.

1 pound greens (mustard, turnip, collard or spinach)	2 precooked spicy sausage links such as Louisiana Hot Links, cut into $1/4$-inch slices
1 tablespoon olive oil	1 (15-ounce) can chicken broth
1 onion, chopped	Salt and pepper to taste
2 garlic cloves, minced	Red wine vinegar (optional)

Trim the tough ends from the greens and discard. Cut the greens into bite-size pieces. Heat the olive oil in a Dutch oven over medium heat and add the onion and garlic. Cook until the onion is tender and stir in the greens, sausage and broth. Simmer over low heat for 35 to 40 minutes or until the greens are tender. Season with salt and pepper and a splash of vinegar.

cook's note ▥ For more Traditional Slow-Cooked Greens, combine 1 ham hock with 1 to 2 cups water in a Dutch oven. Bring to a boil and add the trimmed greens along with a dash of red pepper flakes, a pinch of salt, and a pinch of sugar. Reduce the heat to low and simmer for $3^1/2$ hours. Add additional water as needed.

corn and onion pudding

2 tablespoons all-purpose flour	2 cups chopped sweet onions
$1^1/2$ cups milk	1 tablespoon chopped garlic
1 cup (4 ounces) shredded sharp Cheddar cheese	$1/2$ teaspoon salt
$1/2$ teaspoon each salt, black pepper and dried thyme	$1/2$ teaspoon black pepper
$1/8$ teaspoon cayenne pepper	$1/8$ teaspoon cayenne pepper
1 tablespoon vegetable oil	2 eggs, lightly beaten
	$2^1/2$ cups fresh corn kernels (cobs scraped with back of knife)

Pour the flour into a medium heavy saucepan and whisk in about $1/4$ cup of the milk. Stir until a paste forms. Mix in the remaining milk and cook over medium heat for 5 minutes or until thickened, stirring constantly. Continue cooking, adding the cheese $1/3$ cup at a time and whisking constantly until blended. Remove from the heat and stir in $1/2$ teaspoon salt, $1/2$ teaspoon black pepper, the thyme and $1/8$ teaspoon cayenne pepper. Let stand until cool. Preheat the oven to 375 degrees. Heat the oil in a large skillet and stir in the onions. Cook for 5 minutes or until tender. Stir in the garlic and cook for 5 minutes longer. Mix in $1/2$ teaspoon salt, $1/2$ teaspoon black pepper and $1/8$ teaspoon cayenne pepper and remove from the heat. Whisk the eggs into the cooled cheese sauce until combined and stir in the onion mixture and corn. Spoon the corn mixture into an 8×8-inch baking dish. You may chill, covered, at this point for up to 24 hours. Bake on the middle oven rack for 35 to 40 minutes or until set. Cool for 5 to 10 minutes before serving.

cook's note ▥ Frozen or canned corn may be substituted for the fresh corn, but purée a small portion before adding.

brie and onion pie

The hot jalapeño jelly adds a beautiful glaze and a sweet, spicy finish.

1/4 cup (1/2 stick) butter
1 cup crushed Carr's whole wheat
   crackers, gingersnaps or
   butter crackers
2 to 3 cups thinly sliced sweet or
   yellow onions
2 tablespoons butter

3/4 cup milk
2 eggs
1 teaspoon salt
1/4 teaspoon white pepper
8 ounces Brie cheese
1/4 cup hot jalapeño jelly

Preheat the oven to 350 degrees. Melt 1/4 cup butter in a 9-inch pie plate and stir in the cracker crumbs. Pat the crumb mixture evenly over the bottom and side of the pie plate.

Sauté the onions in 2 tablespoons butter in a skillet until tender and brown. Spoon into the prepared pie plate. Whisk the milk, eggs, salt and white pepper in a bowl until blended and pour over the onions.

Remove the rind from the Brie and discard. Cut the Brie into 1/2-inch wedges. Arrange the wedges in a spoke fashion over the top of the prepared layers. Flatten the remaining Brie wedges with your fingers and fill in the gaps until the surface is almost covered. Bake for 30 minutes or until the cheese melts and begins to brown. Heat the jelly in a saucepan until melted and drizzle over the top of the pie.

cook's note ▥ A milder pepper jelly will work, but the hot jelly adds more contrast to this rich pie. Delicious as a brunch entrée or as a side to grilled meats and chicken.

braised italian cipollini onions

These caramelized Italian onions have a sweet orange glaze.

3 pounds small fresh cipollini onions
   or pearl onions
1/4 cup extra-virgin olive oil

1 cup orange juice
1 cup balsamic vinegar

Trim and peel the onions, leaving the cores intact. Heat the olive oil in a large nonstick skillet over high heat and add the onions. Sauté for 9 minutes or until golden brown. Add the orange juice and vinegar and bring to a boil, scraping the bottom of the skillet to release any browned bits.

Reduce the heat to medium-low. Simmer, covered, for 8 minutes or just until the onions are tender and the liquid is reduced, stirring occasionally.

cook's note ▥ Serve as an accompaniment to roasted meats, on a buffet, or with cocktails.

green peas and cauliflower [serves 6 to 8]

Surprisingly delicious.

Cuban Celery and
Pea Salad *is a simple
and refreshing salad.
Chop 1 bunch of celery
(about 3 to 4 cups)
and soak in a bowl of
ice water. Cook one
10-ounce package
frozen green peas for
3 minutes and allow to
cool in the cooking
liquid. Drain the celery
and peas and toss in a
salad bowl. Mix in
8 ounces cubed cream
cheese. Add a mixture
of 1/2 cup vegetable
oil, 1/3 cup (or more)
red wine vinegar, salt
and coarsely ground
pepper and toss until
coated. Chill until
serving time.*

3 cups sliced cauliflower
2 tablespoons butter
1/4 cup chopped onion
2 tablespoons all-purpose flour
1 teaspoon salt
1/4 to 1/2 teaspoon ground nutmeg

1 cup milk
1/2 cup half-and-half
1 (10-ounce) package frozen peas,
    partially thawed and separated
1/3 cup grated Parmesan cheese

Preheat the oven to 350 degrees. Cook the cauliflower in a small amount of boiling water in a saucepan until tender-crisp; drain. Melt the butter in a skillet and add the onion. Sauté until the onion is tender. Stir in the flour, salt and nutmeg and cook until bubbly. Add the milk and half-and-half and mix well.

Cook until thickened, stirring constantly. Stir in the cauliflower, peas and half the cheese. Spoon the cauliflower mixture into a baking dish and sprinkle with the remaining cheese. Bake for 20 to 25 minutes or until brown and bubbly.

asian snow peas [serves 6]

11/2 pounds snow peas, trimmed
3 tablespoons soy sauce
1 tablespoon toasted sesame oil
1 tablespoon oyster sauce

1 teaspoon sugar
6 garlic cloves, pressed or minced
2 tablespoons sesame seeds, toasted
    for garnish

Cook the snow peas in boiling water in a saucepan for 3 to 4 minutes or until tender-crisp; drain. Mix the soy sauce, sesame oil, oyster sauce and sugar in a small bowl.

Spray a wok or 10-inch skillet with nonstick cooking spray and heat over medium-high heat. Add the garlic to the hot wok and stir-fry for 20 to 30 seconds or until softened. Stir in the snow peas and stir-fry for 2 minutes. Add the soy sauce mixture and stir-fry for 1 to 2 minutes or until most of the liquid is absorbed. Spoon the snow peas into a serving bowl and garnish with the sesame seeds.

cook's note ▦ Asparagus, green beans, and/or broccoli may be substituted for the snow peas.

more than mashed potatoes

[serves 8 to 10]

Good on a buffet. Prepare one day in advance and reheat just before serving.

8 to 10 russet potatoes, peeled
and quartered
Salt to taste
8 ounces cream cheese, softened
1 cup sour cream
1/2 cup minced green onions
and tops
1/2 cup minced celery
1/4 cup minced green bell pepper

1/4 cup (1/2 stick) butter or
margarine, melted
1 tablespoon minced fresh parsley
1 teaspoon salt
1/2 teaspoon garlic powder
Freshly ground pepper to taste
1/2 teaspoon paprika
2 tablespoons butter or margarine

Cook the potatoes in boiling salted water in a saucepan until tender. Drain and return the potatoes to the saucepan. Cook over low heat until all the moisture has evaporated, shaking the saucepan constantly. Remove from the heat and cover to keep warm.

Preheat the oven to 375 degrees. Combine the cream cheese and sour cream in a mixing bowl and beat until blended. Add the hot potatoes one at a time, beating constantly at high speed until light and fluffy. Reduce the speed to low and add the green onions, celery, bell pepper, 1/4 cup butter, the parsley, 1 teaspoon salt, the garlic powder and pepper. Beat until combined.

Spoon the potato mixture into a 2 1/2- to 3-quart baking dish. Sprinkle with the paprika and dot with 2 tablespoons butter. Bake for 25 minutes or until heated through and the top is golden brown.

swiss potatoes au gratin

[serves 8]

One of the ultimate comfort foods.

3 pounds russet potatoes, peeled
and cut into 1/8-inch slices
Salt and pepper to taste
1 1/2 cups sour cream or
crème fraîche

1 1/2 cups (6 ounces) shredded
Gruyère cheese, Jarlsberg
cheese or any Swiss cheese
2 tablespoons parsley, chopped
for garnish

Preheat the oven to 400 degrees. Arrange half the potatoes slightly overlapping in a generously buttered 9×13-inch baking dish. Sprinkle generously with salt and pepper. Spread with half the sour cream and sprinkle with half the cheese. Repeat the layers with the remaining potatoes, salt and pepper, remaining sour cream and remaining cheese.

Bake for 30 minutes. Reduce the oven temperature to 350 degrees and bake for 45 minutes longer or until the potatoes are tender and the top is golden brown. Cover with foil if needed to prevent overbrowning. Let stand for 10 minutes and garnish with the parsley.

butternut squash and mashed potatoes

Bring this to your next holiday gathering and really WOW the crowd.

3 pounds butternut squash
1 teaspoon garlic powder
Olive oil
2 pounds potatoes, peeled
   and quartered
Salt to taste
1/4 cup (1/2 stick) butter
1/2 cup heavy cream

1 teaspoon salt
1/4 teaspoon ground nutmeg
Freshly ground pepper to taste
1/2 cup (2 ounces) grated
   Parmesan cheese
3/4 cup (or more) crushed
   gingersnaps or amaretti
2 tablespoons butter

Preheat the oven to 350 degrees. Cut the squash lengthwise into halves and remove the seeds. Sprinkle the cut sides with the garlic powder. Arrange the squash cut side down on a baking sheet coated with olive oil. Bake for 45 minutes or until the squash is tender. Let stand until cool enough to handle and scoop the pulp into a large bowl; mash lightly. Maintain the oven temperature.

Boil the potatoes in boiling salted water in a saucepan for 25 to 30 minutes or until tender; drain. Cool until easily handled and push the potatoes through a ricer. Add the potatoes to the squash and mash until combined.

Bring 1/4 cup butter and the cream to a simmer in a saucepan. Stir in 1 teaspoon salt, the nutmeg and pepper. Add the cream mixture and cheese to the squash mixture and mix well. Spoon the squash mixture into a baking dish and top with the cookie crumbs. Dot with 2 tablespoons butter and bake for 20 to 30 minutes or until brown and bubbly.

Sugar-Browned Potatoes *will complement most any entrée. Boil 1 1/2 pounds small firm potatoes for 15 to 20 minutes or until tender. Drain and rinse with cold water to stop the cooking process. Peel the potatoes and cut into wedges. Heat 3 tablespoons sugar in a heavy skillet over medium heat until the sugar melts and turns light brown. Stir in 3 tablespoons butter and cook until the butter melts, stirring constantly. Add the potatoes and cook for 10 minutes or until the potatoes are evenly glazed and heated through, shaking the saucepan constantly. Substitute red potatoes, yams, or sweet potatoes for a different twist.*

creamed spinach

4 pounds fresh spinach leaves, or
   3 pounds frozen chopped spinach
1 1/2 tablespoons butter or olive oil
1 onion (12 ounces), finely chopped
3 tablespoons all-purpose flour
3/4 teaspoon dried thyme

1/4 teaspoon ground nutmeg
1 1/2 cups skimmed chicken broth
1 1/2 cups whipping cream
1 1/2 teaspoons salt
1 cup (4 ounces) shredded Gruyère
   cheese or Swiss cheese

Fill a 6- to 8-quart saucepan with some of the spinach and cook over high heat for 8 to 10 minutes or until the spinach wilts and shrinks, turning frequently with a wide spatula and adding the remaining spinach as the saucepan allows. Cook for 1 minute longer, stirring constantly. Remove the spinach to a colander to drain. Rinse the saucepan and pat dry. Preheat the oven to 375 degrees. Melt the butter in the same saucepan over medium-high heat and add the onion. Cook for 5 minutes or until tender. Stir in the flour, thyme and nutmeg and cook for 1 to 2 minutes or until the flour is golden brown, stirring constantly. Remove from the heat and whisk in the broth, cream and salt. Bring to a boil over high heat and reduce the heat to low. Simmer for 5 minutes to allow the flavors to blend. Coarsely chop the spinach and add to the cream sauce. Cook until bubbly and spoon the spinach mixture into a shallow 3-quart baking dish. Bake for 6 to 8 minutes or until bubbly. Sprinkle with the cheese and bake for 5 minutes or until the cheese melts.

cook's note ▥ This recipe may be prepared up to 1 day in advance. Store, covered, in the refrigerator after spooning the mixture into a baking dish. Remove the cover and bake in a preheated 375-degree oven for 25 minutes or until the center is hot and the edges are bubbly. Sprinkle with the cheese and bake for 5 minutes longer or until the cheese melts.

squash rice casserole

Vegetarian comfort food.

6 to 8 cups mashed drained cooked
   summer squash (yellow squash,
   zucchini or pattypan squash)
2 cups cooked brown rice
1 cup sour cream
1/2 cup (2 ounces) shredded
   Cheddar cheese
2 eggs, beaten

2 tablespoons grated
   Parmesan cheese
1/2 teaspoon salt
1 cup shredded cooked chicken
   breast (optional)
1/2 cup (2 ounces) shredded
   Cheddar cheese
2 tablespoons grated
   Parmesan cheese

Preheat the oven to 350 degrees. Combine the squash, rice, sour cream, 1/2 cup Cheddar cheese, the eggs, 2 tablespoons Parmesan cheese, the salt and chicken in a bowl and mix well. Spoon the squash mixture into a greased 9×13-inch baking dish and sprinkle with 1/2 cup Cheddar cheese and 2 tablespoons Parmesan cheese. Bake for 40 minutes. Broil for 5 minutes or until brown and bubbly.

cook's note ▥ For additional flavor, cook the squash and brown rice in vegetable or chicken broth. Vegetables such as broccoli, spinach, or Swiss chard may be substituted for the squash.

butternut squash soufflé

[serves 6 to 8]

A great alternative to sweet potatoes on the holiday table.

3 cups steamed chopped peeled
   butternut squash
3/4 cup sugar
1/2 cup milk
1/4 cup (1/2 stick) butter, melted

3 tablespoons all-purpose flour
2 egg yolks, beaten
1 teaspoon vanilla extract
Splash of Grand Marnier (optional)
2 egg whites

Preheat the oven to 350 degrees. Mash the squash in a bowl. Stir the sugar, milk, butter, flour, egg yolks, vanilla and liqueur into the squash. Beat the egg whites in a mixing bowl until stiff peaks form and fold into the squash mixture.

Spoon the squash mixture into a soufflé dish or large baking dish. Bake for 1 hour or until a wooden pick inserted in the center comes out clean.

panko-coated fried squash blossoms

[serves 6]

Panko, Japanese bread crumbs, is crispier than regular bread crumbs. Panko can be found in the Asian section of most supermarkets.

1 cup (or more) all-purpose flour
Italian seasoning to taste
Seasoned salt to taste
Pepper to taste
12 squash blossoms

1 egg, beaten
1 cup (or more) panko
Peanut oil for frying
Grated Parmesan cheese for garnish

Mix the flour, Italian seasoning, salt and pepper in a shallow dish. Coat the squash blossoms with the flour mixture. Dip in the egg and roll in the panko.

Add enough peanut oil to a skillet to measure 1/4 inch and heat over medium heat. Add the squash blossoms to the hot oil and fry until brown on all sides. Drain on paper towels and garnish with cheese. If using an electric skillet, set the temperature on 350 degrees.

cook's note ▥ Sliced green or firm red tomatoes may be substituted for the squash blossoms.

Although sweet enough to serve as a dessert, Baked Apricots is a wonderful hot fruit side dish for the holidays. To prepare, preheat the oven to 300 degrees. Layer two 28-ounce cans drained apricots, two 1-pound packages light brown sugar, one 16-ounce package crushed butter crackers and a generous dotting of butter in a greased 9×13-inch baking dish until all of the ingredients are used, ending with the butter. Bake for 1 hour or until brown and crusty on top. To speed the process, drain the apricots the night before and drizzle with lemon juice.

stuffed tomatoes

The delicate balance of tomato and thyme contrasts with the cheesy rice stuffing.

2 cups water
1 cup basmati rice
1 tablespoon salt
1 teaspoon butter
12 tomatoes

2 tablespoons fresh thyme
8 ounces asiago cheese or fontina
    cheese, grated
Salt and pepper to taste

Combine the water, rice, 1 tablespoon salt and the butter in a saucepan and bring to a boil. Reduce the heat to low and cook for 20 minutes or until the rice is tender. Let stand until cool.

Preheat the grill or oven to 350 degrees. Slice the top from the tomatoes and scoop out the pulp using a spoon or melon baller. Mix the rice, thyme, cheese and salt and pepper to taste in a bowl. Spoon the rice mixture into the tomato shells and wrap in foil. Grill or bake for 25 minutes.

zucchini pancakes

2 cups shredded zucchini or other
    summer squash
2 tablespoons chopped fresh
    Italian parsley
1 egg, lightly beaten
Salt and pepper to taste

1/4 cup all-purpose flour
1/2 teaspoon baking powder
1 tablespoon (or more) olive oil or
    vegetable oil
1/2 cup (2 ounces) shredded
    Parmesan cheese

Drain the zucchini on paper towels for 10 minutes. Combine the zucchini, parsley, egg, salt and pepper in a bowl and mix well. Stir in a mixture of the flour and baking powder. Let stand at room temperature for 30 minutes.

Heat the olive oil in a large skillet until hot. Drop the zucchini mixture by tablespoonfuls into the hot oil. Cook for 1 minute or until bubbles form on the surface of the pancakes, the edges are dry and the bottoms are golden brown. Turn and cook until brown on the remaining side. Repeat the process until all of the zucchini mixture is used, adding additional olive oil as needed. Serve the pancakes immediately or keep warm in a 200-degree oven. Sprinkle with the cheese just before serving.

cook's note ▓ Serve as an appetizer topped with crème fraîche or sour cream and caviar.

To prepare Curried Tomato Halves, *preheat the oven to 350 degrees. Slice 2 tomatoes crosswise into halves and arrange the halves cut side up in a buttered baking pan. Mix 1/2 cup sour cream, 1/2 cup mayonnaise and 1/2 teaspoon curry powder and spread the sour cream mixture evenly over the tops of the tomato halves. Bake for 20 to 30 minutes or until the tomatoes are tender and heated through. A new twist to an old favorite.*

baked barley with portobello mushrooms

This barley dish has the creamy texture of a risotto without the labor and makes a nice complement to grilled steak or grilled chicken. Makes a nice vegetarian entrée.

2 tablespoons butter	4 cups vegetable broth or water
3 onions, chopped	1 tablespoon soy sauce
8 ounces button mushrooms, sliced	1 tablespoon sherry
8 ounces portobello	1 teaspoon balsamic vinegar
mushrooms, sliced	1/2 teaspoon salt
1 1/2 cups pearl barley	1/4 teaspoon pepper

Preheat the oven to 350 degrees. Melt the butter in a Dutch oven over medium heat and add the onions. Cook, covered, over low heat until golden brown, stirring frequently. Stir in the mushrooms and cook until the mushrooms are brown. Add the barley and toss until coated.

Stir the broth, soy sauce, sherry, vinegar, salt and pepper into the barley mixture and bring to a boil. Bake, covered, for 1 hour or until the barley is tender. Let stand for 10 minutes before serving.

cheesy corn grits

Grits go uptown.

4 cups water	1/2 cup (2 ounces) shredded
1 teaspoon salt	Romano cheese or
1 cup quick-cooking grits	Parmesan cheese
1 cup fresh or frozen corn kernels	1/4 cup chopped green onions
(about 2 ears fresh corn)	1 tablespoon butter
3/4 cup milk	1/4 teaspoon Tabasco sauce
1/2 cup (2 ounces) shredded	1/4 teaspoon pepper
Cheddar cheese	

Bring the water and salt to a boil in a saucepan. Add the grits to the boiling water and stir until smooth. Reduce the heat to low and cook for 8 minutes, stirring occasionally. Stir in the corn and milk and cook for 2 minutes longer. Remove from the heat.

Add the cheese, green onions, butter, Tabasco sauce and pepper to the grits mixture and mix well. Serve immediately as a side dish for game birds, ham, pork chops or omelets.

wedding pilaf

Wedding Pilaf is a traditional Middle Eastern dish served on special occasions. Great with beef, chicken, or ham.

pilaf

1/2 cup (1 stick) butter or margarine
1/2 cup broken vermicelli or
   thin spaghetti
2 cups rice
2 tablespoons plus 2 teaspoons dried
   minced onion
3 1/2 to 4 tablespoons
   bouillon granules
4 cups hot water

1 teaspoon onion powder
1/4 teaspoon celery salt
Salt to taste

date and apricot topping

1/4 cup (1/2 stick) butter
   or margarine
1 cup almond slivers, blanched
3/4 cup pitted dates, chopped
3/4 cup dried apricots, chopped

To prepare the pilaf, melt the butter in a heavy saucepan or Dutch oven and stir in the pasta. Cook until golden brown, stirring constantly with a wooden spoon. Add the rice and dried minced onion and mix well. Cook for 2 to 3 minutes or until the rice is coated, stirring constantly.

Dissolve the bouillon in the hot water in a bowl and stir in the onion powder and celery salt. Stir the bouillon mixture into the rice mixture. Simmer, covered, for 20 to 25 minutes or until the liquid is absorbed, checking after 10 minutes. Stir the pilaf and let stand, covered, for 20 minutes before serving. Season with salt.

To prepare the topping, melt the butter in a saucepan and stir in the almonds, dates and apricots. Cook for 2 to 3 minutes or until heated through, stirring constantly. Sprinkle over the pilaf just before serving.

cook's note ▮ Onion soup mix may be substituted for the bouillon, dried minced onion, onion powder, and celery salt.

couscous with herbs and lemon

Couscous is ground semolina pasta that is popular in North African and Middle Eastern cuisine.

1 tablespoon extra-virgin olive oil
1 onion, finely chopped
1 garlic clove, minced
1 (10-ounce) can chicken broth
3/4 cup water
1 1/2 cups (10 ounces) couscous

1/2 cup finely chopped parsley
1/2 cup finely chopped basil
1/3 cup finely chopped mint
1 tablespoon extra-virgin olive oil
1 tablespoon lemon juice, or to taste
Salt and pepper to taste

Heat 1 tablespoon olive oil in a 2- or 3-quart heavy saucepan over medium heat. Add the onion and cook for 3 minutes or until golden brown, stirring occasionally. Add the garlic and cook for 30 seconds, stirring constantly. Stir in the broth and water and bring to a boil. Stir in the couscous and remove from the heat.

Let stand, covered, for 5 minutes. Fluff with a fork and stir in the parsley, basil, mint, 1 tablespoon olive oil, the lemon juice, salt and pepper.

lemon basil capellini

Light, fresh, quick, and delicious. Delightful as an entrée on a warm summer evening.

Julienned zest and juice of 1 lemon
1 1/2 tablespoons unsalted butter
1 1/2 tablespoons extra-virgin
    olive oil
8 fresh basil leaves, finely sliced
2 teaspoons finely chopped parsley

3 ounces capellini
Salt and freshly ground pepper
    to taste
Freshly grated Parmigiano-
    Reggiano cheese to taste

Combine the lemon zest, lemon juice, butter, olive oil, basil and parsley in a bowl large enough to hold the cooked pasta. Cook the pasta using the package directions until al dente and drain.

Immediately add the hot pasta to the lemon mixture and toss to coat. Divide the pasta mixture evenly between two bowls and season with salt and pepper. Sprinkle with Parmigiano-Reggiano cheese.

kugel with apricots and cranberries

A traditional Jewish dish that is a staple on the Seder table.

12 ounces egg noodles
2 tablespoons butter
1/2 cup chopped dried apricots
1/2 cup dried cranberries
3 eggs
2 cups sour cream

2 cups cottage cheese or
    ricotta cheese
3/4 cup sugar
1/2 teaspoon vanilla extract
Cinnamon and sugar to taste

Preheat the oven to 350 degrees. Cook the noodles using the package directions until al dente. Drain and place the noodles in a greased 9×13-inch baking pan. Immediately dot the hot noodles with the butter to allow the butter to melt. Gently stir in the apricots and cranberries.

Whisk the eggs in a bowl until blended and stir in the sour cream, cottage cheese, sugar and vanilla. Pour the egg mixture over the noodle mixture and sprinkle generously with cinnamon and sugar. Bake, covered with foil, for 35 minutes. Remove the foil and bake for 40 minutes longer or until firm in the center and puffed and light brown on the top. Serve hot or at room temperature. Add raisins, currants or any other variety of dried fruit as desired.

orzo with prosciutto and asparagus [serves 6]

Colorful and delicious as either a side dish or entrée.

1 pound asparagus
1/4 cup (1/2 stick) butter
2 ounces prosciutto, thinly sliced and
    cut into strips
1 1/4 cups orzo
2 cups chicken broth
1 cup white wine

1/4 cup (1 ounce) grated
    Parmigiano-Reggiano cheese or
    Parmesan cheese
Salt and pepper to taste
Shaved Parmigiano-Reggiano cheese
    or Parmesan cheese for garnish

Snap off the thick woody ends of the asparagus spears and discard. Cut the spears diagonally into 1/2-inch pieces. Melt 2 tablespoons of the butter in a large skillet over medium-high heat and add the prosciutto. Sauté until crisp. Remove the prosciutto to a platter using a slotted spoon, reserving the pan drippings.

Increase the heat to high and heat the remaining 2 tablespoons butter with the reserved pan drippings. Stir in the pasta and sauté for 1 to 2 minutes. Add the broth and wine and bring to a boil. Reduce the heat to medium-low.

Simmer, covered, for 8 minutes, stirring occasionally. Add the asparagus and simmer, covered, for 5 minutes or until the asparagus is tender. Remove the cover and simmer until the liquid is absorbed. Remove from the heat and stir in the prosciutto and 1/4 cup cheese. Season with salt and pepper and garnish with additional cheese.

Photograph for this recipe on page 143.

penne with sun-dried tomatoes, capers and olives [serves 4]

This recipe comes by way of the Caribbean island of Anguilla.

16 ounces penne
Salt to taste
3/4 cup chopped oil-pack
    sun-dried tomatoes
1/2 cup pitted kalamata olives,
    cut into halves

1/2 cup chopped fresh basil
1/3 cup grated Parmesan cheese
1/4 cup chopped fresh parsley
1/4 cup capers, drained and rinsed
1/4 cup olive oil
Pepper to taste

Cook the pasta in boiling salted water in a large saucepan over high heat until tender. Drain and return the pasta to the saucepan. Stir in the tomatoes, olives, basil, cheese, parsley, capers and olive oil. Taste and season with salt and pepper. Serve immediately with additional Parmesan cheese. Add minced garlic if desired.

Clockwise from left to right: Strawberry Rhubarb Mousse (page 175), Decadent Chocolate and Tangerine Mousse Cake (page 185), Basic Fruit Crisp (page 173), White Chocolate and Pistachio Cookies (page 200)

desserts

Watts Towers
Simon Rodia, 1921 to 1954

Watts Towers

When we think of the great Italian artists and their masterpieces, our minds burst with dramatic visions of Michelangelo's *David*, Leonardo da Vinci's *Mona Lisa*, Sandro Botticelli's *The Birth of Venus*, and of course, Simon Rodia's famous *Watts Towers* located in the south Los Angeles community of the same name.

Rodia, you ask? You may not know the name, but you may recognize his work. His unique and fascinating monument may not rank at the pinnacle of fine Italian art, and for the purposes of this book it may not necessarily be a mosaic by its truest definition, but it most certainly earns its place as a gargantuan testament to one man's vision of spirit, ingenuity, and determination, and his ability to bring together many parts to create a whole work of art.

Sabato "Simon" Rodia, an Italian immigrant born in Campania, Italy, in 1879, arrived in the United States at the age of twelve. By working age, he had taken odd jobs crisscrossing the country and landed finally in California. His work was varied during those years, undertaking jobs as a quarryman, logger, railroad hand, construction worker, and tile setter, which probably laid a good foundation for what was to become his signature accomplishment—Nuestro Pueblo, or "our town," as he called it.

Simon Rodia wanted to celebrate his new country. So in 1921, working alone with a vision in his head, utilizing no special equipment except for a window washer's belt and buckle and simple tile setter tools, he began construction on his dream—construction that would be completed more than thirty years later, in 1954. He began his project on a pie-shaped residential lot by forming three slender towers made up of steel rods and pipes, wrapped in wire mesh and then coated with mortar. The tallest tower stretches nearly 100 feet high and is considered the tallest column of unreinforced concrete in the world. When he was finished, he had completed seventeen separate sculptural forms including a patio, a gazebo, a multi-tiered circular bench, three bird baths, a thirty-eight-foot structure he called "The Ship of Marco Polo," and a wall surrounding it all. The entire structure is embedded with a mosaic of surplus pieces of tile from his jobs, rock, porcelain, seashells, hand drawings, and glass bottles he would get from the neighborhood children.

There is nothing quite as satisfying as seeing the human spirit alive and driven by its passion. The *Watts Towers* speak to those ambitious souls with a positive nod of motivation. For those less ambitious, they stand as a beacon of determination and dreams realized—that anything is possible if you simply want it bad enough and are willing to try. Simon Rodia is quoted as saying, "I had in my mind to do something big, and I did!" For dreamers everywhere, that is all that is necessary.

The *Watts Towers* are one of only nine works of art classified as "folk art" listed on the National Registry of Historic Places in the United States, and one of four National Historic Landmarks located in Los Angeles. Falling under the administration of the California State Parks Department, the *Watts Towers* are managed by the Los Angeles City Cultural Affairs Department through the Watts Towers Art Center. The public is welcome to tour and explore the vision of this amazing man and his tangible masterpiece on Fridays, Saturdays, and Sundays year-round.

Food photography sponsored by Ginny and Gene Noll
Mosaic photography sponsored by Avery Dennison

sherried macaroons

Try this Drinking
Dessert *the next time
you have company.
Soften 1/2 gallon
vanilla ice cream
and stir in 5 jiggers
crème de menthe
and 4 jiggers brandy.
Freeze until firm.
Soften slightly
before serving and
stir. Spoon into wine
glasses. Or try this
combination. Soften
1/2 gallon coffee
ice cream and stir
in 5 jiggers Kahlúa
and 4 jiggers
brandy. Proceed
as directed above.*

1 (8-ounce) can almond paste
1 cup sugar
2 egg whites
Sliced almonds
2/3 cup sherry or cream sherry

Preheat the oven to 300 degrees. Line a cookie sheet with baking parchment. Combine the almond paste, sugar and egg whites in a bowl and knead until blended. Drop the dough by spoonfuls onto the prepared cookie sheet and sprinkle with almonds.

Bake for 30 minutes. Cool on the cookie sheet for 2 minutes. Remove the baking parchment to a wire rack and let stand until the cookies are cool. Moisten the bottom side of the baking parchment to make removal of the macaroons easy.

Crumble the macaroons into a bowl and stir in the sherry. Soak for 5 minutes. Serve as a topping for ice cream or pound cake. Or, mix the macaroon mixture with 2 quarts softened vanilla ice cream and refreeze until firm. Spoon into dessert bowls or goblets.

chocolate peanut butter cheesecake

This cheesecake will satisfy any peanut butter cup craving.

chocolate wafer crust

1 cup chocolate wafer crumbs
1/4 cup packed brown sugar
5 tablespoons butter, melted

peanut butter filling

2 cups creamy peanut butter
2 cups sugar

16 ounces cream cheese, softened
2 tablespoons butter, melted
2 teaspoons vanilla extract
1 1/2 cups whipping cream
4 ounces semisweet
    chocolate, chopped
3 tablespoons plus 2 teaspoons
    hot coffee

To prepare the crust, preheat the oven to 350 degrees. Mix the wafer crumbs, brown sugar and butter in a bowl. Press the crumb mixture over the bottom and halfway up the side of a 9-inch springform pan. Bake for 8 to 10 minutes.

To prepare the filling, combine the peanut butter, sugar, cream cheese, butter and vanilla in a large mixing bowl and beat until smooth. Beat the whipping cream in a mixing bowl until soft peaks form. Fold the whipped cream into the peanut butter mixture and spoon into the crust. Chill, covered, for 6 hours or longer. Mix the chocolate and hot coffee in a heatproof bowl until blended. Spread the chocolate mixture over the top of the pie and chill until set.

cook's note ▪ Allow at least 7 hours chilling time.

Millard Sheets

Millard Sheets, one of the featured artists of California Mosaic, *was a leader in art and art education in Southern California and across the United States. Born, reared, and educated in Southern California, Sheets (1907–1989) studied at Chouinard Art Institute, Los Angeles, and was a member of the executive committee overseeing the first New Deal art projects. From the late 1930s until 1955, he headed the art departments at Scripps College and Claremont Graduate School, and in 1953 he became the director of Otis Art Institute, now Otis/ Parsons. During this period he was also Director of Fine Arts at the Los Angeles County Fair, and his legacy continues there today at the Millard Sheets Gallery.*

lemon swirled cheesecake [serves 12 to 16]

A vibrant lemon flavor infuses this creamy cheesecake.

Arroyo Seco

Pasadena is home to a massive gorge, 132 acres in all, called the Arroyo Seco that carves through the western border of the city. The Arroyo Seco was created by a stream system that flows from the San Gabriel Mountains. Today, two of Pasadena's most notable landmarks, the Colorado Street Bridge and the Rose Bowl, find their home in the Arroyo Seco, as well as Kidspace Children's Museum (a former Junior League of Pasadena project), the Aquatic Center, and Brookside golf course. It is a popular recreation area, with miles of hiking trails, an archery center, a casting pond, a playground, stables, and numerous soccer fields.

almond crust

5 ounces (1 1/2 cups) almonds, toasted and ground
1/2 cup panko (see page 158)
1/4 cup sugar
2 tablespoons all-purpose flour
1/4 teaspoon salt
3 tablespoons butter, melted

lemon filling

40 ounces Neufchâtel cheese
1 3/4 cups sugar
3 tablespoons all-purpose flour
2 1/2 teaspoons grated lemon zest
2 teaspoons vanilla extract
1/4 teaspoon salt
5 eggs
1 cup Lemon Curd (page 186)

To prepare the crust, preheat the oven to 375 degrees. Combine the almonds, panko, sugar, flour and salt in a bowl and mix well. Add the butter and stir until crumbly. Press the crumb mixture over the bottom of a 9-inch springform pan. Place the pan on the middle oven rack and bake for 10 minutes. Cool on a wire rack. Reduce the oven temperature to 325 degrees.

To prepare the filling, beat the cream cheese in a mixing bowl until smooth and creamy. Add the sugar, flour, lemon zest, vanilla and salt and beat until combined. Add the eggs one at a time, beating well after each addition. Spread the cream cheese mixture over the baked layer. Spoon mounds of the lemon curd over the filling and swirl together with the tip of a knife.

Bake, covered with foil, for 30 minutes. Remove the foil and bake for 30 minutes. Re-cover with the foil and bake for 30 minutes longer or until the cheesecake tests done. Cool on a wire rack. Chill, covered, for 8 hours or longer before serving.

cook's note ■ Fill any cracks with additional Lemon Curd.

poached pears with mascarpone cheese

1 (750-milliliter) bottle red
　　wine (cabernet sauvignon,
　　merlot, shiraz)
1 1/2 cups orange juice
1 cup sugar
4 whole cloves
Grated zest of 1 orange

1 cinnamon stick
4 Bartlett pears, peeled and cut
　　lengthwise into halves
1 cup mascarpone cheese
2 tablespoons sugar
1/4 cup chopped pistachios
　　or walnuts

Bring the wine, orange juice, 1 cup sugar, the cloves, orange zest and cinnamon stick
to a boil in a large saucepan over high heat and reduce the heat to low. Add the pears
and poach for 1 hour or until the pears are tender. Remove the pears to a bowl
using a slotted spoon, reserving the poaching liquid. Chill the pears.

Cook the reserved poaching liquid over medium heat until reduced by half and of a
syrupy consistency. Let stand until cool and strain, discarding the solids. Whisk the
cheese and 2 tablespoons sugar in a bowl until blended. Arrange the pear halves cut
side up on a serving platter and spoon some of the cheese mixture in the center of
each pear half. Sprinkle with the pistachios and drizzle with the wine syrup. The pears
may be poached up to 2 days in advance and stored, covered, in the poaching
liquid in the refrigerator.

cook's note ■ The red wine
syrup can be drizzled over ice
cream or cakes, or used as a
marinade for pork, chicken, and
duck. Try this variation using the
wine syrup. For Oranges and
Peaches in Red Wine
Syrup, toss the grated orange
zest of 2 oranges with 1 tablespoon
sugar. Mix 3 chopped peeled
peaches and the chopped sections
of 6 oranges and divide the fruit
mixture evenly among six dessert
bowls. Drizzle with the red wine
syrup and sprinkle with the sugared
orange zest. Serve as is, or spoon
over ice cream.

*For Pears in Vanilla
Cream, preheat the
oven to 400 degrees.
Coat a 9×13-inch
baking dish with butter
and dust with brown
sugar. Peel 4 Bosc
pears or Bartlett pears
and cut lengthwise into
halves. Arrange the
halves cut side down
in the prepared baking
dish. Sprinkle with
1/4 cup packed brown
sugar and dot with
2 tablespoons butter.
Bake for 10 minutes.
Mix 1 cup heavy cream
and 1 teaspoon vanilla
extract in a bowl and
pour over the pears.
Bake for 20 minutes
longer. Serve garnished
with vanilla beans. Easy,
but elegant dessert.*

cherries jubilee

Quick and easy, but impressive.

1 (15-ounce) can black cherries
1 tablespoon cornstarch
1 tablespoon sugar
1/4 teaspoon grated orange zest

Dash of lemon juice
1/2 cup brandy
Vanilla ice cream

Drain the cherries, reserving the juice. Combine the reserved cherry juice, cornstarch, sugar, orange zest and lemon juice in a saucepan and mix well. Cook over low heat for 4 to 5 minutes or until thickened, stirring constantly. Stir in the cherries and remove from the heat.

Add the brandy to the cherry mixture and ignite. Allow the flames to subside. Let stand until cool. Spoon over vanilla ice cream in stemmed dessert goblets. Serve immediately.

peach cobbler in a pinch

[serves 8]

4 peaches, peeled and sliced, or
    1 package frozen sliced
    peaches, thawed
5 slices white bread, crusts removed

1 1/2 cups sugar
1/2 cup (1 stick) butter, melted
2 tablespoons all-purpose flour
1 egg, beaten

Preheat the oven to 350 degrees. Place the peaches in an 8×8-inch baking dish. Cut each bread slice into five strips and arrange the strips over the peaches.

Mix the sugar, butter, flour and egg in a bowl and pour over the prepared layers. Bake for 35 to 45 minutes or until golden brown. Serve warm or at room temperature.

basic fruit crisp

4 to 5 cups sliced peeled fruit (pears,
    peaches, berries, apples or
    a combination)
$1/3$ cup granulated sugar
$1/4$ teaspoon ground cinnamon

1 to 2 tablespoons water (optional)
Butter to taste
1 cup all-purpose flour
$1/2$ cup packed brown sugar
$1/2$ cup (1 stick) butter, softened

Preheat the oven to 350 degrees. Arrange the fruit in a greased soufflé dish and sprinkle with the granulated sugar and cinnamon. Drizzle with the water and stir. Dot with butter to taste. You may prepare in advance to this point and store, covered, in the refrigerator.

Mix the flour, brown sugar and $1/2$ cup butter in a bowl until crumbly. Sprinkle the crumb mixture over the top of the fruit mixture and bake for 1 hour. Serve warm with ice cream or whipped cream.

Photograph for this recipe on page 165.

red hot apple crunch

The red hot cinnamon candies give this dessert a great color.

6 tart apples, peeled and sliced
$1/2$ cup red hot cinnamon candies
1 teaspoon vanilla extract
1 cup all-purpose flour
$3/4$ cup sugar

$1/3$ cup butter
$1/2$ teaspoon ground cinnamon
$1/2$ teaspoon ground nutmeg
$1/4$ teaspoon salt
$1/8$ teaspoon mace

Preheat the oven to 350 degrees. Toss the apples, cinnamon candies and vanilla in a bowl. Spoon the apple mixture into a buttered 9×13-inch baking dish. Combine the flour, sugar, butter, cinnamon, nutmeg, salt and mace in a bowl and mix with a pastry blender until crumbly.

Sprinkle the crumb mixture over the apple mixture and pat lightly. Bake for 30 to 45 minutes or until the apples are tender and the top is brown. Serve warm with ice cream.

dark chocolate
mousse charlotte

[serves 8 to 12]

For Mocha Mousse in a Minute, combine 6 ounces semisweet chocolate chips, 3/4 cup scalded milk, 2 eggs, 2 tablespoons Grand Marnier, dark rum or Cognac and 2 to 3 tablespoons strong coffee in a blender. Process at high speed for 1 1/2 minutes. Pour into four dessert bowls or wine glasses and chill for 2 hours or longer. Serve plain or topped with a dollop of whipped cream and sprinkled with any flavored chips, shavings or candy pieces. If you are concerned about using raw eggs, use eggs pasteurized in their shells, which are sold at some specialty food stores, or use an equivalent amount of pasteurized egg substitute.

1/2 cup sugar
1/2 cup baking cocoa
3/4 cup milk
2 envelopes unflavored gelatin
1/3 cup warm water

2 teaspoons vanilla extract
3 egg whites, at room temperature
1/4 cup sugar
2 packages ladyfingers
Liqueur (optional)

Combine 1/2 cup sugar and the baking cocoa in a saucepan and mix well. Stir in the milk and bring to a boil over medium heat, whisking constantly. Spoon the chocolate mixture into a large heatproof bowl and let stand until cool.

Sprinkle the gelatin over the warm water in a bowl and let stand for 5 minutes or until softened. Add the gelatin mixture and vanilla to the cooled chocolate mixture and mix well.

Beat the egg whites in a mixing bowl at high speed until foamy. Gradually add 1/4 cup sugar to the egg whites, beating constantly until stiff peaks form. Fold 1/4 of the meringue into the chocolate mixture to lighten and then fold the remaining meringue into the chocolate mixture.

Line the bottom and side of a springform pan with opened ladyfingers and lightly drizzle with any liqueur. Spoon the chocolate mixture into the prepared pan and chill, covered, for 8 to 10 hours. If you are concerned about using raw egg whites, use eggs pasteurized in their shells, which are sold at some specialty food stores, or use an equivalent amount of pasteurized liquid egg whites or meringue powder.

cook's note ■ The mousse may be spooned into dessert bowls or stemmed goblets and chilled for 2 hours.

strawberry rhubarb mousse [serves 8 to 10]

A wonderfully versatile dessert that may be served as a traditional mousse or in a cookie crust.
It will make rhubarb lovers out of everyone.

3^1/$_2$ cups (1-inch) pieces rhubarb
    (about 1 pound)
1 cup sugar
^{1}/$_4$ cup water
2 envelopes unflavored gelatin
^{1}/$_2$ cup cold water
2 cups strawberries, mashed

1 tablespoon lemon juice
1 cup heavy whipping cream
2 cups shortbread cookie
    crumbs (optional)
6 tablespoons butter,
    melted (optional)
Strawberries for garnish

Combine the rhubarb, sugar and ^{1}/$_4$ cup water in a saucepan. Bring just to the boiling point over high heat, stirring constantly. Reduce the heat to low and cook for 10 minutes or until the rhubarb is tender, stirring occasionally. Process the rhubarb mixture in a blender or food processor until puréed and return the purée to the saucepan.

Sprinkle the gelatin over the cold water in a bowl and let stand for 2 minutes or until softened; stir. Stir the gelatin mixture, mashed strawberries and lemon juice into the rhubarb purée. Cook over low heat for 3 minutes, stirring occasionally. Pour into a bowl and chill, covered, for 2^1/$_2$ hours or until the mixture begins to firm in soft mounds, stirring occasionally. Beat the whipping cream in a mixing bowl until stiff peaks form. Fold the whipped cream into the rhubarb mixture.

Preheat the oven to 350 degrees. Mix the cookie crumbs and butter in a bowl. Pat the crumb mixture into a deep-dish pie plate and bake for 15 minutes. Cool on a wire rack.

Spoon the mousse into the shortbread crust, a large glass serving bowl or parfait glasses. Chill, covered, for 8 to 10 hours. Garnish with whole or sliced strawberries.

cook's note ■ This recipe must be prepared in advance to allow time to set. Freeze fresh rhubarb for future use.

Photograph for this recipe on page 164.

strawberry cloud

1 egg white	1 quart fresh strawberries, hulled
1/2 teaspoon cream of tartar	1/2 cup strawberry preserves
1/4 cup sugar	3 tablespoons kirsch
1/2 cup heavy whipping cream	3 tablespoons Grand Marnier
1/2 teaspoon vanilla extract	Whipped cream for garnish

Beat the egg white with the cream of tartar in a mixing bowl until frothy. Add the sugar gradually, beating constantly until firm peaks form. Beat 1/2 cup whipping cream in a mixing bowl until stiff peaks form. Fold the whipped cream and vanilla into the meringue.

Spoon the whipped cream mixture evenly into four dessert goblets or dessert bowls. Arrange the strawberries pointed ends up over the tops. Mix the preserves, brandy and liqueur in a bowl and drizzle over the strawberries. Serve garnished with a dollop of whipped cream. If you are concerned about using raw egg whites, use eggs pasteurized in their shells, which are sold at some specialty food stores, or use an equivalent amount of pasteurized liquid egg whites or meringue powder.

a little slice of heaven

Indescribably wonderful with a surprise ingredient.

10 soda crackers, finely crushed	1 cup pecan pieces (optional)
1 teaspoon baking powder	1/2 cup (1 stick) butter, melted
3 egg whites	Whipped cream for garnish
1 cup sugar	Bourbon for garnish
1 teaspoon almond extract	

Preheat the oven to 325 degrees. Mix the cracker crumbs and baking powder in a bowl. Beat the egg whites in a mixing bowl until stiff peaks form. Add the sugar and flavoring and beat until blended. Stir in the pecans.

Stir the cracker crumb mixture into the pecan mixture. Add the butter and mix well. Spoon the meringue mixture into a 9-inch deep-dish pie plate and bake for 20 to 25 minutes. Garnish each serving with whipped cream lightly flavored with bourbon.

cook's note ■ Graham crackers or round butter crackers may be substituted for the soda crackers. If using a shallow pie plate, place on a baking sheet while baking to catch any overflow.

cinnamon bread pudding with [serves 6]
hot buttered rum sauce

bread pudding
5 slices cinnamon raisin bread
5 tablespoons butter, softened
$2^1/2$ cups milk, heated
3 eggs
1 teaspoon vanilla extract
$1/4$ teaspoon salt
$1^1/2$ cups lightly packed
    brown sugar
$1/2$ cup raisins
$1/2$ teaspoon grated fresh nutmeg

hot buttered rum sauce
1 cup sugar
$1/2$ cup (1 stick) butter
1 cup rum

To prepare the pudding, preheat the oven to 350 degrees. Spread both sides of the bread slices with the butter and tear into 1-inch pieces. Whisk the warm milk, eggs, vanilla and salt in a mixing bowl until blended.

Spread the brown sugar over the bottom of a buttered or oiled 8×8-inch baking dish and layer with the bread pieces. Pour the warm milk mixture over the prepared layers and sprinkle with the raisins and nutmeg. Bake for 45 to 50 minutes or until a wooden pick inserted in the center comes out clean.

To prepare the sauce, heat the sugar and butter in a saucepan until the butter melts and the sugar dissolves, stirring frequently. Stir in the rum. Serve warm with the warm bread pudding. Or, serve the bread pudding with half-and-half.

Adamson House

The Adamson House was constructed in 1929 on the Malibu shore for Rhoda Rindge Adamson and Merritt Huntley Adamson. Rhoda Rindge Adamson was the daughter of Frederick Hastings Rindge and May Knight Rindge, the last owners of the Malibu Spanish Land Grant. Most notable for its views and classic Malibu tile, the Adamson house was designed by architect Stiles Clements. It was purchased by the State of California in 1968 and today it is open for public tours.

nancy reagan's persimmon pudding

persimmon pudding

1 cup sugar
1/2 cup (1 stick) butter, melted
1 cup all-purpose flour, sifted
1 teaspoon ground cinnamon
1/4 teaspoon salt
1/4 teaspoon ground nutmeg
2 teaspoons baking soda
2 teaspoons warm water
1 cup puréed persimmon pulp (about
    3 or 4 very ripe persimmons)
3 tablespoons brandy
1 teaspoon vanilla extract

2 eggs, lightly beaten
1 cup seedless raisins
1/2 cup chopped walnuts (optional)
1/4 cup brandy, heated (optional)

brandy sauce

1 egg
1 cup sifted confectioners' sugar
1/3 cup butter, melted
1 tablespoon brandy flavoring
Dash of salt
1 cup whipping cream

To prepare the pudding, mix the sugar and butter in a bowl. Sift the flour, cinnamon, salt and nutmeg into a bowl and mix well. Stir the flour mixture into the butter mixture. Dissolve the baking soda in the warm water in a bowl and stir into the butter mixture. Add the persimmon purée, 3 tablespoons brandy and the vanilla and mix well. Add the eggs and stir just until combined. Fold in the raisins and walnuts.

Spoon the persimmon mixture into a buttered heatproof 5- to 6-cup mold and cover. Place the mold on a rack in a steamer and add enough boiling water to the steamer to reach halfway up the side of the mold. Simmer, covered, for 2 1/2 hours. Let stand for several minutes and invert onto a serving platter. Pour 1/4 cup heated brandy over the pudding and ignite. Allow the flames to subside.

To prepare the sauce, beat the egg in a mixing bowl until light and fluffy. Add the confectioners' sugar, butter, flavoring and salt and beat until blended. Beat the whipping cream in a mixing bowl until stiff peaks form and fold into the egg mixture. Chill, covered, in the refrigerator until serving time. Serve with the pudding. If you are concerned about using raw eggs, use eggs pasteurized in their shells, which are sold at some specialty food stores, or use an equivalent amount of pasteurized egg substitute.

cook's note ■ Reprinted with permission from the Reagan Library, Simi Valley, California.

ozark pudding

An old family recipe from the Ozarks of Missouri and Arkansas.
This was a favorite at the Truman White House.

3/4 cup sugar
2 teaspoons all-purpose flour
1 1/4 teaspoons baking powder
1/8 teaspoon salt
1 egg
1/2 cup chopped apple
1/2 cup chopped dates
1/2 cup chopped pecans
1 teaspoon vanilla extract

Preheat the oven to 350 degrees. Mix the sugar, flour, baking powder and salt in a bowl. Beat the egg in a mixing bowl until smooth. Add the sugar mixture and beat until blended. Fold in the apple, dates and pecans and stir in the vanilla.

Spoon the batter into a greased 9-inch pie plate and bake for 30 minutes or until brown on top. Cool in the pie plate on a wire rack. Cut into wedges and serve with vanilla ice cream or whipped cream flavored with rum.

Entertainment Industry

The entertainment industry is a vibrant part of California's history and identity. The first movie studio was built by Thomas Edison in 1893 in New Jersey, but by the turn of the century, the movie industry was moving west due to the temperate climate and longer days. The twenties brought the mega-production companies, such as Warner Brothers, Fox, MGM, RKO, and Paramount Pictures, that controlled the film industry for many years. Television revolutionized the industry in the 1950s and signaled the end of the golden era of film. Today, Hollywood remains the epicenter of the entertainment business.

pumpkin flan

A wonderfully flavored flan that is a good substitute for pumpkin pie.

2 1/2 cups sugar
1 teaspoon ground cinnamon
Pinch of salt
1 1/2 cups puréed cooked pumpkin or
    canned pumpkin
5 eggs, lightly beaten
1 1/2 cups evaporated milk
1/3 cup water
1 1/2 teaspoons vanilla extract
Whipped cream sweetened with vanilla and sugar
    for garnish

Preheat the oven to 350 degrees. Heat 1 1/2 cups of the sugar in a heavy skillet over low heat until a golden syrup forms, stirring constantly. Immediately pour the caramel into a 1 1/2-quart soufflé dish, tilting the dish to coat the bottom evenly.

Combine the remaining 1 cup sugar, the cinnamon and salt in a bowl and mix well. Add the pumpkin and eggs and stir until blended. Stir in the evaporated milk, water and vanilla. Spoon the pumpkin mixture over the prepared layer. Set the soufflé dish in a large baking pan and add enough hot water to reach halfway up the side of the dish. Bake for 1 1/4 hours or until a knife inserted in the center comes out clean. Cool in the dish on a wire rack. Chill, covered, until serving time.

Run a knife around the side of the dish to loosen the flan and invert onto a serving platter. Cut into wedges and garnish each serving with a dollop of whipped cream.

Photograph for this recipe on page 204.

mocha ice cream

1 cup sugar
1 cup half-and-half
6 egg yolks, lightly beaten
1/2 teaspoon salt
3 ounces unsweetened chocolate, chopped
1/2 cup (or more) cappuccino chips or
    chocolate chips, or to taste
1 tablespoon instant coffee
1 quart (4 cups) heavy cream
1 teaspoon vanilla extract

Combine the sugar, half-and-half, egg yolks and salt in a saucepan. Cook over medium heat just until the mixture comes to a boil, stirring constantly. Remove from the heat. Add the chocolate, cappuccino chips and coffee and stir until the chocolate melts.

Let stand until cool and stir in the cream and vanilla. Chill, covered, in the refrigerator. Pour into an ice cream freezer container and freeze using the manufacturer's directions.

County Fair Fudge Sauce *makes a great holiday or hostess gift. Pour the sauce into a glass jar and tie with a festive ribbon. To prepare, bring 1 cup heavy cream, 1 cup lightly packed brown sugar and 1 cup granulated sugar to a boil in a saucepan over medium-low heat, stirring occasionally. Boil until the sugar dissolves, stirring constantly. Remove from the heat and stir in 2 ounces chopped unsweetened chocolate. Cook over low heat for 15 minutes, stirring occasionally; be careful not to scrape the side of the pan if there appears to be any grainy sugar. Remove from the heat and stir in 1/2 cup sliced butter until blended. If desired, stir in 1 cup chopped nuts. Store in an airtight container in the refrigerator. This sauce tastes like melted fudge from the county fair.*

meyer lemon sherbet

This refreshing sherbet is lighter than ice cream and features Meyer lemons, which are sweeter than other varieties of lemons and are very popular in California gardens.

1 1/2 cups sugar
Juice of 4 Meyer lemons
Grated zest of 1 Meyer lemon
1 quart (4 cups) milk

Combine the sugar, lemon juice and lemon zest in a bowl and mix well. Chill, covered, for 8 to 10 hours. Gradually add the milk, stirring constantly until blended; do not be concerned if the mixture curdles.

Pour into an ice cream freezer container and freeze using the manufacturer's directions. For a stronger lemon flavor, add additional lemon zest.

lemon delight

1 (12-ounce) can evaporated
    milk, chilled
Juice of 3 lemons (6 tablespoons)
2/3 cup sugar
Butter for coating
Vanilla wafer crumbs
Fresh berries

Beat the evaporated milk in a mixing bowl until it almost reaches the top of the bowl. Gradually blend in the lemon juice and then the sugar. Let rest at room temperature while proceeding with recipe.

Coat an 8×8-inch dish with butter and cover heavily with vanilla wafer crumbs. Layer the lemon mixture and vanilla wafer crumbs 1/2 at a time in the prepared dish, ending with the crumbs. Freeze, covered, for several hours. Let stand at room temperature until softened and spoon into dessert bowls. Top each serving with fresh berries.

pomegranate granita

[serves 4 to 6]

Refreshing as either a palate cleanser or dessert.

3/4 cup water
3/4 cup sugar
1 (15-ounce) bottle
    pomegranate juice

1/2 cup mixture of orange, lime and
    lemon juice

Make a simple syrup by heating the water and sugar in a saucepan until the sugar dissolves. Stir in the pomegranate juice and citrus juice mixture. Pour into a 9×13-inch dish and freeze, covered, for 8 to 10 hours. Scrape into glasses to serve.

cook's note ■ Serve in hollowed-out oranges or lemons. Can easily be made into a sorbet by freezing in an ice cream freezer.

german apple cake

[serves 10 to 12]

5 tablespoons sugar
1 tablespoon ground cinnamon
5 or 6 pippin apples, thickly sliced
3 cups all-purpose flour
2 1/3 cups sugar

1/2 teaspoon salt
1 cup vegetable oil
1/3 cup orange juice
4 eggs, lightly beaten
2 teaspoons vanilla extract

Preheat the oven to 350 degrees. Mix 5 tablespoons sugar and the cinnamon in a bowl. Add the apples and toss to coat. Combine the flour, 2 1/3 cups sugar and the salt in a bowl and mix well. Stir in the oil, orange juice, eggs and vanilla.

Spread 1/3 of the batter in a greased bundt pan or tube pan and sprinkle with 1/2 of the apple slices. Layer with half the remaining batter and the remaining apples and their juices. Top with the remaining batter.

Bake for 1 1/2 hours. Cool in the pan for 10 minutes and remove to a wire rack to cool completely. Serve with Nutmeg Sauce (sidebar), if desired.

cook's note ■ To enhance the flavor, allow the cake to rest for 24 hours before serving.

Drizzle Nutmeg Sauce over German Apple Cake, ice cream, bread pudding or pound cake. Combine 1/4 cup sugar and 1 tablespoon cornstarch in a saucepan. Gradually stir in 1 cup apple juice. Add 2 tablespoons butter and cook over medium heat until thickened, stirring constantly. Cook for 2 minutes longer, stirring constantly. Remove from the heat and stir in 1/2 teaspoon vanilla and 1/4 teaspoon freshly ground nutmeg. Serve warm.

most devilish chocolate cake

The name says it all.

chocolate cake

Butter for coating
All-purpose flour for dusting
2 cups cake flour
3/4 tablespoon baking soda
1/2 teaspoon salt
1 cup packed brown sugar
1 cup granulated sugar
1/2 cup baking cocoa
1 cup hot brewed espresso or
    French roast coffee
4 ounces unsweetened chocolate,
    finely chopped
1/2 cup peanut oil
2 eggs, at room temperature
1/2 cup buttermilk
1/2 cup sour cream,
    at room temperature
2 teaspoons vanilla extract

creamy espresso frosting

1 cup heavy whipping cream
1/2 cup (1 stick) butter,
    cut into pieces
1/3 cup sugar
1/4 teaspoon salt
16 ounces (2 2/3 cups) semisweet
    chocolate chips
1/4 cup hot brewed espresso or
    French roast coffee
2 teaspoons vanilla extract

To prepare the cake, preheat the oven to 325 degrees. Coat two 9-inch cake pans with butter and dust with all-purpose flour. Line the bottoms with baking parchment. Sift the cake flour, baking soda and salt together. Mix the brown sugar, granulated sugar and baking cocoa in a bowl and stir into the flour mixture. Pour the hot coffee over the chocolate in a heatproof bowl and stir until the chocolate melts.

Whisk the peanut oil and eggs in a large bowl until blended. Stir in the buttermilk, sour cream, vanilla and coffee mixture. Fold in the dry ingredients 1/3 at a time, mixing well after each addition. Spoon the batter evenly into the prepared pans. Tap the pans on a hard surface to remove any bubbles.

Bake for 30 to 40 minutes or until a wooden pick inserted in the center comes out clean. Cool in the pans on a wire rack for 5 minutes. Run a knife around the edges of the pans to loosen the layers and invert onto the wire rack. Cool completely before removing the baking parchment.

To prepare the frosting, combine the cream, butter, sugar and salt in a heavy saucepan and cook over low heat until the butter melts; do not boil. Stir in the chocolate chips and cook until the chocolate melts and the mixture is smooth, stirring constantly. Remove from the heat and stir in the coffee and vanilla. Let stand until of a spreading consistency, stirring occasionally. Do not chill or force to cool as the frosting will separate.

Place one cake layer bottom side up on a cake plate and frost generously. Arrange the remaining layer bottom side down over the first layer and frost the top and side with the remaining frosting. Let stand for 1 to 2 hours before serving. Store, covered, at room temperature.

cook's note ■ For true decadence, use the best quality chocolate available.

decadent chocolate and tangerine mousse cake

Do not be intimidated by this recipe. It is actually pretty easy to prepare and is well worth the preparation time.

chocolate cake

Butter for coating
All-purpose flour for dusting
1 cup (2 sticks) unsalted butter
12 ounces bittersweet or semisweet
   chocolate, chopped
3/4 cup sugar
5 eggs, lightly beaten
1/2 cup ground toasted hazelnuts
Vegetable oil for coating

tangerine mousse and assembly

3 cups strained fresh tangerine juice
1/3 cup sugar
2 envelopes unflavored gelatin
3 tablespoons fresh lemon juice
12 ounces white chocolate, chopped
1/2 cup sour cream
2 cups whipping cream, chilled
3 ounces white chocolate for garnish
Baking cocoa for garnish
Fresh raspberries, sprigs of
      mint and/or tangerine slices
      for garnish

To prepare the cake, preheat the oven to 350 degrees. Coat a 9-inch springform pan with butter and line the bottom with baking parchment. Dust the pan with flour. Melt 1 cup butter and the chocolate in a saucepan until blended, stirring occasionally. Remove from the heat and whisk in the sugar, eggs and hazelnuts. Pour the batter into the prepared pan and bake for 45 minutes or until a wooden pick inserted in the center comes out with moist crumbs. Cool in the pan on a wire rack.

Remove the side of the pan and invert the cake onto a hard work surface. Remove the baking parchment. Cut off the outer 1/2-inch edge of the cake, creating an 8-inch cake and reserving the cake trimmings. (Remember, this does not have to be perfect.) Rinse the springform pan and reattach the side. Coat the side with oil. Set the cake in the center of the pan and arrange the reserved cake trimmings on the top. The space around the cake will be filled with the mousse. Chill, covered, in the refrigerator.

To prepare the mousse, bring the tangerine juice and sugar to a boil in a heavy saucepan and boil for 30 minutes or until reduced to 11/2 cups. Sprinkle the gelatin over the lemon juice in a small bowl and let stand for 10 minutes or until softened. Add the gelatin mixture to the tangerine juice mixture and stir until dissolved. Stir in 12 ounces white chocolate and cook over low heat just until the chocolate melts, whisking constantly. Whisk in the sour cream. Pour the tangerine juice mixture into a large bowl and chill for 2 to 3 hours or until thickened but not set, whisking occasionally. Beat the cream in a mixing bowl until stiff peaks form. Fold into the tangerine juice mixture just until incorporated. Pour over the chilled cake, covering the top and side completely. Chill, covered, for 8 to 10 hours. Shave 3 ounces white chocolate into thin curls using a vegetable peeler. Run a sharp knife around the side of the pan to loosen the cake. Remove the side of the pan and place the cake on a cake plate. Sprinkle the chocolate curls over the top of the cake and dust the top very lightly with baking cocoa. You may cover and chill at this point for up to 1 day. Garnish with raspberries, sprigs of mint and/or tangerine slices.

cook's note ■ This is a great recipe for any celebration. In the spring, the orange color of the mousse dazzles your table. For the winter holidays, raspberries and mint can be arranged to look like holly sprigs. The cake is delicious served by itself.

Photograph for this recipe on page 165.

gingerbread with lemon curd

This travels well and makes a great gift.

lemon curd
3/4 cup sugar
1 tablespoon grated lemon zest
2 eggs, lightly beaten
2/3 cup lemon juice
2 tablespoons butter

gingerbread
2 1/2 cups all-purpose flour
1 tablespoon baking soda
2 teaspoons ground ginger

1 1/2 teaspoons ground cinnamon
1/2 teaspoon ground cloves
1/2 teaspoon ground nutmeg
1/2 teaspoon baking powder
3/4 cup packed dark brown sugar
3/4 cup molasses
2 eggs
3/4 cup shortening or unsalted
   butter, melted
1 cup boiling water

To prepare the lemon curd, combine the sugar, lemon zest and eggs in a saucepan. Cook over medium heat for 3 minutes or until the sugar dissolves and the mixture is light in color, whisking constantly. Mix in the lemon juice and butter and cook for 5 minutes or until the mixture thinly coats the back of a spoon, stirring constantly. Let stand until cool. Pour into a bowl and chill, covered, in the refrigerator for up to 1 week or freeze for future use. The mixture will thicken as it cools.

To prepare the gingerbread, preheat the oven to 350 degrees. Grease and lightly flour a 5×9-inch loaf pan or an 8×8-inch baking pan. Line the bottom of the 8×8-inch baking pan with waxed paper if turning out. Sift the flour, baking soda, ginger, cinnamon, cloves, nutmeg and baking powder into a bowl and mix well. Beat the brown sugar, molasses and eggs in a heatproof mixing bowl until smooth. Add the shortening and beat until blended. Add the flour mixture 1/3 at a time, mixing well after each addition. Stir in the boiling water.

Spoon the batter into the prepared pan and bake for 30 to 40 minutes or until a wooden pick inserted in the center comes out clean. Serve with the Lemon Curd.

nicaraguan sponge cake with four milks (pastel de cuatro leches)

This version of the traditional South American Three-Milk Cake has four milks. It is very rich and delicious and almost like a bread pudding.

1 teaspoon butter
1 cup all-purpose flour
2 teaspoons baking powder
Dash of ground cinnamon
3 egg whites, at room temperature
1 cup sugar

3 egg yolks, at room temperature
1/4 cup milk
1 cup heavy cream
1 (14-ounce) can sweetened
   condensed milk
1 (12-ounce) can evaporated milk

Preheat the oven to 325 degrees. Coat a 7×11-inch or an 8×10-inch baking dish with the butter. Mix the flour, baking powder and cinnamon together. Beat the egg whites in a mixing bowl at medium speed for 2 to 3 minutes or until soft peaks form. Increase the speed to high and gradually add the sugar, beating constantly until glossy. Add the egg yolks one at a time, beating well after each addition. Stir in the flour mixture 1/4 cup at a time. Add the milk and stir until smooth.

Spoon the batter into the prepared baking dish and bake for 25 to 30 minutes or until the cake pulls from the side of the dish. Let stand until warm and pierce the top of the cake at 1-inch intervals with a wooden pick.

Mix the heavy cream, condensed milk and evaporated milk in a bowl and gradually pour over the warm cake. Let stand until cool. Chill, covered, for 1 to 10 hours. The flavor is enhanced if the cake is allowed to chill overnight.

zucchini cake

A great way to sneak vegetables into your children's diet.

zucchini cake

1 cup all-purpose flour
1 1/2 teaspoons freshly
   ground nutmeg
1 teaspoon salt
1 teaspoon ground cinnamon
1/2 teaspoon baking soda
1/2 cup (1 stick) butter, softened
1 cup sugar
1 egg
2 cups shredded zucchini
1 cup pecans, chopped

brown sugar glaze and assembly

1/4 cup (1/2 stick) butter
1/2 cup heavy cream
1/4 cup granulated sugar
1/4 cup packed dark brown sugar
1/2 teaspoon vanilla extract
Whipped cream for garnish

To prepare the cake, preheat the oven to 350 degrees. Mix the flour, nutmeg, salt, cinnamon and baking soda together. Beat the butter in a mixing bowl at medium to high speed for 30 seconds. Add the sugar and beat until combined. Beat in the egg until blended. Add the flour mixture and mix just until moistened. Fold in the zucchini and pecans.

Spoon the batter into a greased 8×8-inch cake pan. Bake for 40 minutes or until a wooden pick inserted near the center comes out clean.

To prepare the glaze, melt the butter in a saucepan and stir in the heavy cream, granulated sugar and brown sugar. Bring to a boil over medium heat, stirring constantly. Remove from the heat and stir in the vanilla.

Pour the hot glaze over the hot cake and let stand until cool. Garnish each serving with whipped cream.

berry blitz torte

A dreamy custard torte topped with colorful berries.

torte

1 cup all-purpose flour
4 teaspoons baking powder
Pinch of salt
1/2 cup sugar
1/4 cup (1/2 stick) butter, softened
4 egg yolks, beaten
1/4 cup milk
1 teaspoon vanilla extract
4 egg whites
3/4 cup sugar
1/3 cup slivered almonds

custard filling and assembly

1/4 cup sugar
1 tablespoon cornstarch
2 egg yolks, lightly beaten
1 cup milk, scalded
Sweetened whipped cream
Mixed berries (strawberries,
        blueberries, raspberries)

To prepare the torte, preheat the oven to 325 degrees. Mix the flour, baking powder and salt together. Beat 1/2 cup sugar and the butter in a mixing bowl until creamy. Add the egg yolks and beat until blended. Add the flour mixture alternately with the milk, mixing well after each addition. Blend in the vanilla. Spread the batter evenly in two shallow cake pans.

Beat the egg whites in a mixing bowl until soft peaks form. Add 3/4 cup sugar and beat until stiff peaks form. Spread the meringue evenly over the prepared layers. Sprinkle with the almonds and bake for 30 minutes. Cool in the pans for 10 minutes. Remove to a wire rack to cool completely.

To prepare the custard, mix the sugar and cornstarch in a double boiler. Gradually stir in the egg yolks. Mix in the scalded milk and cook until thickened, stirring constantly. Cool slightly.

Arrange one cake layer meringue side up on a cake plate and spread with half the custard. Layer with the remaining cake layer meringue side up and spread with the remaining custard. Top with whipped cream and fresh berries. Chill until serving time.

cook's note ■ For a shortcut, substitute commercially prepared lemon curd for the custard, or try the Lemon Curd found on page 186.

glazed apple and almond torte

[serves 8]

A bountiful harvest of layered flavors.

brown sugar crust

1 cup all-purpose flour
$^1/_3$ cup granulated sugar
3 tablespoons brown sugar
1 teaspoon vanilla extract
$^3/_4$ cup ($1^1/_2$ sticks) butter or
    margarine, chilled and
    cut into pieces

apple filling and assembly

8 ounces cream cheese, softened
$^1/_3$ cup sugar
1 egg
1 teaspoon vanilla extract
2 large apples, peeled and
    thickly sliced
$^1/_3$ cup sugar
1 teaspoon ground cinnamon
Pinch of ground nutmeg
Slivered almonds

To prepare the crust, mix the flour, granulated sugar and brown sugar in a bowl and stir in the vanilla. Cut in the butter until the consistency of coarse meal using a pastry blender. Chill briefly if needed. Pat the crumb mixture over the bottom and 1 inch up the side of a 9-inch springform pan.

To prepare the filling, preheat the oven to 450 degrees. Combine the cream cheese, $^1/_3$ cup sugar, the egg and vanilla in a mixing bowl and beat until blended. Spread the filling in the prepared pan. Toss the apples, $^1/_3$ cup sugar, the cinnamon and nutmeg in a bowl until coated. Spoon the apple mixture over the prepared layers and sprinkle with almonds.

Bake for 10 minutes. Reduce the oven temperature to 425 degrees and bake for 20 minutes. Reduce the oven temperature to 400 degrees and bake for 15 to 20 minutes longer or until a knife inserted in the center comes out clean. Let stand until cool. Chill, covered, for 4 to 10 hours before serving.

chocolate walnut cherries [makes 3 dozen]

What a lovely hostess gift.

1 cup chopped semisweet chocolate
or semisweet chocolate chips
1 cup chopped dark chocolate or
dark chocolate chips

1¹/2 cups dried cherries
1¹/2 cups walnut pieces

Melt the chocolate in a double boiler over boiling water. Stir in the cherries and walnuts. Drop the chocolate mixture by teaspoonfuls onto a baking sheet lined with foil. Let stand until room temperature. Store in an airtight container in the refrigerator or freezer.

cook's note ■ If a double boiler is not available, place a heatproof bowl over a saucepan of boiling water. Do not allow the water to touch the bottom of the bowl.

grandma's yum-yums [makes 6 dozen]

These free-form confections are messy to make but oh so good. Great to make with children and grandchildren.

24 ounces (4 cups) chocolate chips
1 package shredded coconut
1 cup chopped walnuts
1 cup raisins

1 cup chopped candied cherries
1 (14-ounce) can sweetened
condensed milk

Combine the chocolate chips, coconut, walnuts, raisins and cherries in a bowl and mix well. Stir in the condensed milk. Chill, covered, for 3 hours.

Preheat the oven to 275 degrees. Line a cookie sheet with foil and coat with oil. Shape the chocolate mixture into 1-inch balls and arrange the balls in a single layer on the prepared cookie sheet.

Bake for 20 to 25 minutes or until light golden brown. Cool completely on the cookie sheet on a wire rack. The cookies will become a sticky mess if not allowed to cool before removing from the cookie sheet.

Cherry Cordials

make great holiday gifts. Soak 13 drained maraschino cherries with stems in 1/2 cup brandy and drain. Arrange the cherries in a single layer on a baking sheet and freeze until firm. Melt 5 ounces semisweet chocolate in a double boiler over hot water, stirring occasionally. Pat the frozen cherries dry with paper towels. Immediately dip the frozen cherries one at a time into the chocolate, swirling around by the stem until completely covered; the chocolate will harden almost immediately. Store in the refrigerator on a rack lined with waxed paper.

white chocolate crunch

Tie White Chocolate Crunch in colorful bags or place in decorative tins for festive gifts.

24 ounces (4 cups) white chocolate chips	2 cups pretzel sticks
6 cups rice Chex	2 cups cashews
3 cups Cheerios	12 ounces plain "M & M's" Chocolate Candies

Melt the white chocolate chips in a double boiler over hot water or in the microwave. Toss the cereals, pretzels, cashews and chocolate candies in a large bowl. Spread the cereal mixture in a single layer on two baking sheets.

Drizzle the white chocolate over the cereal mixture. Let stand until cool and break into bite-size pieces. Store in airtight containers for up to 30 days.

cook's note ■ Be creative with the combination of ingredients, such as adding peppermint candy for the holidays.

apple brownies

Very moist and a year-round favorite

brownies

2 cups all-purpose flour
2 teaspoons baking soda
2 teaspoons ground cinnamon
1 teaspoon salt
2 cups sugar
1 cup (2 sticks) butter, softened
2 eggs

4 cups grated peeled apples
1 cup walnuts, chopped
1/2 cup dried cranberries or raisins

lemon glaze

2 cups confectioners' sugar
3 tablespoons butter, melted
3 tablespoons lemon juice

To prepare the brownies, preheat the oven to 350 degrees. Mix the flour, baking soda, cinnamon and salt together. Beat the sugar and butter in a mixing bowl until creamy. Add the flour mixture and eggs to the creamed mixture and beat until blended. Stir in the apples, walnuts and cranberries. Coat a 9×13-inch baking dish with oil or spray with nonstick cooking spray. Spread the batter in the prepared baking dish and bake for 45 minutes or until the brownies test done.

To prepare the glaze, mix the confectioners' sugar, butter and lemon juice in a bowl. Pour the glaze over the hot brownies. Let stand until cool and cut into bars. Store in an airtight container.

cook's note ■ For a variation, add 1 tablespoon chopped candied ginger to the glaze.

black-out brownies

[makes 2 dozen brownies]

5 ounces unsweetened
   chocolate, chopped
4 ounces bittersweet or semisweet
   chocolate, chopped
1/2 cup (1 stick) butter
1 1/2 cups granulated sugar

4 eggs
1 teaspoon vanilla extract
1/2 cup all-purpose flour
1/4 teaspoon salt
Confectioners' sugar for
   dusting (optional)

Preheat the oven to 350 degrees. Line a 9×13-inch baking pan with foil, allowing a 2-inch overhang on both short sides. Spray the foil with nonstick cooking spray. Combine the chocolate and butter in a double boiler and heat until blended, stirring occasionally. Let stand until cool. Beat the granulated sugar, eggs and vanilla in a mixing bowl at high speed until thickened and pale yellow. Reduce the speed to low and beat in the flour and salt. Add the chocolate mixture and beat until blended. Spread the batter in the prepared pan and bake for 20 minutes or until a wooden pick inserted in the center comes out with moist crumbs attached. Cool in the pan on a wire rack and dust with confectioners' sugar. Remove the brownies using the foil overhang and cut into bars. Store in an airtight container.

peanut butter brownies

[makes 18 to 24 brownies]

Peanut butter lovers, rejoice.

brownies

1 cup all-purpose flour
1 teaspoon baking powder
Dash of salt
1 1/2 cups packed brown sugar
1 1/4 cups creamy natural
   peanut butter
1/2 cup (1 stick) butter or
   margarine, softened
4 eggs, lightly beaten

peanut butter frosting

3 cups confectioners' sugar
1/2 cup creamy natural peanut butter
1/4 cup (1/2 stick) butter or
   margarine, softened
3 to 5 tablespoons milk
1/2 teaspoon vanilla extract

To prepare the brownies, preheat the oven to 350 degrees. Mix the flour, baking powder and salt together. Combine the brown sugar, peanut butter and butter in a mixing bowl and beat until blended. Add the eggs and beat until combined. Stir in the flour mixture. Spread the batter in a greased 9×13-inch baking pan and bake for 20 to 25 minutes or until the brownies begin to pull from the sides of the pan. Cool in the pan on a wire rack.

To prepare the frosting, combine the confectioners' sugar, peanut butter, butter, 3 tablespoons of the milk and the vanilla in a mixing bowl and beat until smooth. Add the remaining 2 tablespoons milk if needed for a spreading consistency and mix well. Spread the frosting over the cooled brownies. Let stand until set and cut into bars. Store in an airtight container.

cook's note ■ One cup of any flavored chip may be added to the brownie batter before baking. Garnish with peanut butter kisses if desired.

farina squares (basbousah)

A popular Egyptian treat.

farina squares

Tahini for coating
3 cups sugar
2 cups sour cream
4 cups farina (Cream of Wheat)
1 cup shredded coconut
2 teaspoons baking powder

syrup

2 cups sugar
2 cups water
Juice of 1 lemon
1/2 cup (1 stick) butter, cut into
    small pieces
1 pinch of vanilla powder

To prepare the squares, preheat the oven to 350 degrees. Coat a 13×18-inch baking sheet with sides with tahini. Mix the sugar and sour cream in a bowl. Add the farina, coconut and baking powder and mix well. Spread the farina mixture in the prepared baking sheet and bake for 45 minutes or until golden brown.

To prepare the syrup, combine the sugar and water in a saucepan and cook over medium-high heat until the sugar dissolves. Add the lemon juice and bring to a boil, stirring constantly. Reduce the heat to low and simmer for 5 minutes, stirring occasionally. Remove from the heat and mix in the butter and vanilla powder. Cool slightly and pour over the baked layer. Cut into small squares.

cook's note ■ Press almonds into the top of the basbousah before baking, allowing one almond per square.

hula bars

Macadamia nuts and coconut add a touch of the Islands to this flavorful bar cookie.

12 individual Almond Roca®
    Buttercrunch Toffees
2 cups all-purpose flour
1 tablespoon baking powder
1 teaspoon salt
3/4 cup (1 1/2 sticks) butter

1 (16-ounce) package light or dark
    brown sugar
2 eggs, lightly beaten
1 cup macadamia nuts, chopped
1/2 cup sweetened coconut
2 teaspoons vanilla extract
Confectioners' sugar (optional)

Preheat the oven to 350 degrees. Process the candy in a food processor until chopped. Mix the flour, baking powder and salt together. Melt the butter in a saucepan over low heat. Add the brown sugar to the butter and cook for 2 minutes or until the sugar begins to dissolve, stirring constantly. Remove from the heat and let stand until cool. Add the eggs to the brown sugar mixture and mix well. Stir in the flour mixture, macadamia nuts, coconut and vanilla. Spread the macadamia mixture in a buttered 9×13-inch baking pan and bake for 20 minutes or until a wooden pick inserted in the center comes out clean. Cool in the pan on a wire rack. Dust with confectioners' sugar and cut into bars. Store in an airtight container.

cook's note ■ For traditional Caramel Brownies, omit the macadamia nuts and coconut. For gooier, denser bars, decrease the flour by 1/2 cup.

old world raspberry bars [makes 1 dozen bars]

Any fruit preserves can be substituted for the raspberry preserves.

2¹/4 cups all-purpose flour
1 cup sugar
1 cup (2 sticks) butter or margarine,
   softened

1 egg, lightly beaten
1 cup chopped pecans or walnuts
1 (10-ounce) jar raspberry preserves
   (³/4 cup)

Preheat the oven to 350 degrees. Combine the flour, sugar, butter and egg in a bowl and mix well. Stir in the pecans. Reserve 1¹/2 cups of the pecan mixture.

Pat the remaining pecan mixture over the bottom of a greased 8×8-inch baking pan. Spread the preserves over the prepared layer to within ¹/2 inch of the edge. Crumble the reserved pecan mixture over the top and bake for 40 to 50 minutes or until light brown. Cool in the pan on a wire rack and cut into bars. Store in an airtight container.

cook's note ■ For an even richer bar cookie, immediately sprinkle with chocolate chips upon removal from the oven.

philippine food for the gods [makes about 4 dozen bars]

A heavenly treat.

1 cup all-purpose flour
1 teaspoon baking powder
1 cup (2 sticks) butter, softened
1¹/2 cups sugar

2 eggs
1 (8- to 10-ounce) package
   dates, chopped
2 cups walnuts, chopped

Preheat the oven to 350 degrees. Line a 9×12-inch baking dish with foil and coat with nonstick cooking spray. Mix the flour and baking powder together. Beat the butter, sugar and eggs in a mixing bowl until creamy. Add the flour mixture and beat until blended. Stir in the dates and walnuts.

Spread the date mixture in the prepared baking dish and bake for 1¹/4 to 1¹/2 hours or until set. Cool in the pan on a wire rack and cut into bars. Store in an airtight container. Freeze for future use if desired.

Silicon Valley/High-Tech Industry

Silicon Valley is located in the San Francisco Bay area, stretching from the Santa Cruz Mountains to the San Francisco Bay. The industrial area was given the name Silicon Valley because of the amount of silicon chips and high-tech products that were developed and manufactured there. Computer firms and semiconductor companies leased the land after Stanford University made it available in the late 1960s. The high-tech industry thrived in the mid-1990s with the dot-com boom, but the crash of high-tech stocks featured on NASDAQ in early 2000 closed many of these Internet companies. Today, Silicon Valley is home to the top research and development firms that lead the industry in innovation.

walnut dessert bars

A beautiful finish to a luncheon, buffet, or tea.

butter crust
1/3 cup butter, softened
3 tablespoons light brown sugar
1 egg
3/4 cup all-purpose flour
1/4 teaspoon salt
1 teaspoon vanilla extract

walnut filling
2 tablespoons all-purpose flour
3/4 teaspoon baking powder

1/4 teaspoon salt
2 eggs
1 cup packed light brown sugar
1 1/2 cups chopped walnuts
2 teaspoons vanilla extract

confectioners' sugar icing
1 1/2 cups confectioners' sugar
3 to 4 tablespoons cold water

To prepare the crust, preheat the oven to 350 degrees. Beat the butter and brown sugar in a mixing bowl until blended. Add the egg and mix well. Stir in the flour, salt and vanilla. Press the dough over the bottom of a greased and lightly floured 9×13-inch baking pan. Bake for 10 minutes. Maintain the oven temperature.

To prepare the filling, mix the flour, baking powder and salt together. Whisk the eggs in a bowl just until blended and stir in the brown sugar. Add the flour mixture, walnuts and vanilla and mix well. Spread the filling over the baked layer and bake for 15 minutes or until the filling pulls from the sides of the pan.

To prepare the icing, sift the confectioners' sugar into a bowl if lumpy. Add the water 1 tablespoon at a time until of a spreading consistency and mix well. Spread the icing over the warm filling. Cool slightly before cutting into bars. Store in an airtight container.

pizza pan cookie

A kid favorite.

1 cup (2 sticks) margarine or butter, softened
1/2 cup granulated sugar
1/2 cup packed brown sugar
1 egg
2 teaspoons vanilla extract
1 3/4 cups all-purpose flour
1 1/2 cups (9 ounces) semisweet chocolate bits
1/2 cup crisp rice cereal or peanuts
2 cups miniature marshmallows
Red and green maraschino cherries, cut into halves

Preheat the oven to 350 degrees. Beat the margarine, granulated sugar and brown sugar in a mixing bowl until blended. Add the egg and vanilla and beat until smooth. Gradually add the flour, mixing constantly until blended.

Pat the dough onto a greased and floured 12-inch pizza pan. Bake for 20 minutes or until firm in the center and slightly crisp on the edge. Sprinkle the chocolate bits, cereal and marshmallows over the baked layer. Arrange the cherries in a decorative fashion over the top. Bake for 15 minutes longer or until golden brown. Let stand until cool and cut into wedges.

Craftsman Architecture (Green & Green)

Pasadena is known for its architectural tradition and boasts more than six hundred buildings that are registered with the National Register of Historic Places. A major reason for this is the strong presence of the Craftsman-style home. Architects Charles and Henry Green became famous for their Craftsman designs found in the neighborhood just below the Rose Bowl. Among the most famous of their designs, known as Green & Green homes, is the Gamble House. Built in 1908 for David and Mary Gamble of Procter and Gamble, the house remained in the Gamble family until 1966, when it was deeded to the city and the University of Southern California School of Architecture.

orange coconut oatmeal cookies

An intriguing oatmeal cookie.

1 cup all-purpose flour
1 teaspoon baking soda
1/2 teaspoon salt
1 cup (2 sticks) butter, softened
1 cup packed brown sugar
1/2 cup granulated sugar
2 eggs
1 teaspoon vanilla extract
Grated zest of 1 orange

Juice of 1/2 orange
1 teaspoon orange liqueur such as
    Triple Sec or Cointreau
    (optional)
3 cups quick-cooking oats
1 cup dried cranberries
1 cup chopped walnuts
1/2 to 1 cup shredded coconut

Preheat the oven to 350 degrees. Mix the flour, baking soda and salt together. Beat the butter, brown sugar and granulated sugar in a mixing bowl until creamy. Add the eggs and vanilla and beat until blended. Mix in the orange zest, orange juice and liqueur. Add the flour mixture and beat at low speed until the mixture adheres. Stir in the oats, cranberries, walnuts and coconut.

Drop by rounded tablespoonfuls onto an ungreased cookie sheet. Bake for 10 to 12 minutes or until light brown. Cool on the cookie sheet for 1 minute and remove to a wire rack to cool completely. Store in an airtight container. The cookie dough may be stored in the refrigerator for 3 to 4 days, or frozen for future use.

lace cookies

A delicate cookie that is wonderful served with mousses and ice cream.

1 cup old-fashioned oats
1 cup sugar
1 1/2 teaspoons all-purpose flour
1/4 teaspoon salt

1/2 cup (1 stick) butter, melted
    and hot
1 egg, lightly beaten
1/2 teaspoon vanilla extract

Preheat the oven to 325 degrees. Line a cookie sheet with foil or a silicone mat. Mix the oats, sugar, flour and salt in a bowl. Add the hot butter and stir until the sugar dissolves. Stir in the egg and vanilla.

Drop the dough by 1/2 teaspoonfuls 2 inches apart onto the prepared cookie sheet. Bake for 10 to 12 minutes or until golden brown. Cool on the cookie sheet for 2 minutes and carefully remove to a wire rack to cool completely. Store in an airtight container.

cook's note ■ This recipe is easily doubled and freezes beautifully. Reserve any broken cookies and serve sprinkled over ice cream.

pecan lace cookies with lemon ginger filling

The ginger filling makes this an exceptional cookie.

pecan lace cookies

$1/3$ cup sugar

$1/4$ cup ($1/2$ stick) butter

2 tablespoons light corn syrup

$1/3$ cup all-purpose flour

1 teaspoon vanilla extract

1 cup coarsely ground pecans

lemon ginger filling

$1^1/2$ cups confectioners' sugar

$1/4$ cup ($1/2$ stick) butter, at room temperature

1 tablespoon lemon juice

1 tablespoon ginger preserves or marmalade

1 tablespoon minced crystallized ginger

1 teaspoon grated lemon zest

To prepare the cookies, place the oven rack in the center of the oven and preheat the oven to 350 degrees. Line two cookie sheets with baking parchment. Combine the sugar, butter and corn syrup in a heavy saucepan and cook over low heat until blended, stirring frequently. Increase the heat to medium-high and bring to a boil. Remove from the heat and stir in the flour and vanilla. Add the pecans and mix well.

Drop the dough by heaping $1/2$ teaspoonfuls 2 inches apart onto the prepared cookie sheets. Bake the cookies one sheet at a time for 11 minutes or until light brown and bubbly. Cool on the cookie sheet for 10 minutes and remove to a wire rack to cool completely.

To prepare the filling, combine the confectioners' sugar, butter, lemon juice, preserves, ginger and lemon zest in a bowl and mix well. Spread 1 teaspoon of the filling on the bottom of one of the cookies. Top with another cookie bottom side down and press lightly to adhere. Repeat the process with the remaining filling and remaining cookies. The cookies may be prepared up to 2 days in advance. Store between sheets of waxed paper in an airtight container at room temperature.

cook's note ■ Ginger preserves can be hard to locate but worth the effort of special ordering from the grocer or ordering online. Any flavor marmalade may be substituted for the ginger preserves.

raspberry delight cookies

A classic linzer cookie.

$1/2$ cup almonds
10 tablespoons (or more) butter
$11/4$ cups sifted all-purpose flour
$1/2$ cup granulated sugar

$1/2$ teaspoon ground cinnamon
$1/2$ cup raspberry jam or preserves
Confectioners' sugar for dusting

Preheat the oven to 350 degrees. Process the almonds in a food processor until ground. Add the butter, flour, sugar and cinnamon to the food processor and pulse until the dough is smooth and adheres. Add additional butter if the dough is too crumbly. Roll $1/4$ inch thick on a lightly floured surface. Cut into rounds using a $11/2$-inch cutter or any shaped cookie cutter.

Arrange the rounds on a cookie sheet and bake for 15 minutes or until light brown. Cool on the cookie sheet for 2 minutes and remove to a wire rack to cool completely. Spread half the cookies with the jam and top with the remaining cookies. Dust with confectioners' sugar. Store in an airtight container.

cook's note ■ Use different cookie cutter shapes such as hearts, stars, and/or holiday varieties.

white chocolate and pistachio cookies

Pistachios give a nice crunch and a hint of natural green to the blonde cookie.

$21/4$ cups all-purpose flour
1 teaspoon baking soda
$3/4$ teaspoon salt
1 cup (2 sticks) unsalted
   butter, softened
1 cup packed brown sugar

$1/2$ cup granulated sugar
2 eggs, at room temperature
1 teaspoon vanilla extract
12 ounces (2 cups) white
   chocolate chips
1 cup coarsely chopped pistachios

Preheat the oven to 350 degrees. Sift the flour, baking soda and salt together. Beat the butter, brown sugar, granulated sugar, eggs and vanilla in a mixing bowl until creamy. Add the flour mixture and beat until blended. Stir in the white chocolate chips and pistachios.

Drop by rounded spoonfuls 2 inches apart onto a cookie sheet. Bake for 10 to 12 minutes or until light brown. Cool on the cookie sheet for 2 minutes and remove to a wire rack to cool completely. Store in an airtight container.

Photograph for this recipe on page 164.

blueberry pie with cinnamon bourbon sauce

The Cinnamon Bourbon Sauce makes the blueberries pop.

sugar pie crust

1 1/4 cups all-purpose flour
1/2 cup (1 stick) butter, chilled and
    cut into pieces
2 tablespoons sugar
Pinch of salt
1/4 cup ice water

blueberry filling

1 cup sour cream
3/4 cup sugar
1 egg, beaten
2 tablespoons all-purpose flour
2 teaspoons vanilla extract
1/4 teaspoon salt
2 1/2 cups fresh blueberries

pecan topping

6 tablespoons all-purpose flour
1/4 cup (1/2 stick) butter, chilled
1/3 cup pecans or walnuts, chopped
2 tablespoons sugar
1 teaspoon ground cinnamon

cinnamon bourbon sauce

1/2 cup (1 stick) unsalted butter
2/3 cup sugar
2 eggs
1/2 teaspoon ground cinnamon
1 tablespoon hot water
1/2 cup whipping cream
1/2 cup bourbon, whiskey or rum

To prepare the crust, combine the flour, butter, sugar and salt in a food processor and pulse until crumbly. Add the water 1 tablespoon at a time through the feed tube and pulse until the mixture forms a ball. Flatten the dough into a disc and wrap with plastic wrap. Chill for 10 minutes.

Preheat the oven to 400 degrees. Roll the dough on a lightly floured surface and fit the pastry into a 9-inch pie plate. Prick the pastry with a fork and cover with foil. Weight with pie weights, dried beans or rice. Bake for 10 to 12 minutes or until the side is set. Maintain the oven temperature.

To prepare the filling, mix the sour cream, sugar, egg, flour, vanilla and salt in a bowl. Fold in the blueberries and spoon the filling into the baked pie shell. Bake for 25 minutes. Maintain the oven temperature.

To prepare the topping, mix the flour and butter in a bowl until the mixture adheres. Stir in the pecans, sugar and cinnamon. Sprinkle the topping over the pie and bake for 10 to 12 minutes longer or until light brown, covering the crust to prevent overbrowning if necessary. Cool on a wire rack. Chill if desired.

To prepare the sauce, melt the butter in a double boiler over simmering water. Whisk the sugar, eggs and cinnamon in a bowl until blended and add to the butter. Stir in the hot water and cook for 7 minutes or until the mixture coats the back of a spoon. Remove from over the water and cool slightly. Stir in the cream and bourbon. Serve the pie with the sauce and/or vanilla ice cream.

cook's note ■ Other fruits such as apples, peaches, or cherries may be substituted for the blueberries.

southern chess pie

A southern classic which dates back to the Civil War era. The story goes that the name comes from the phrase "It's jus' pie."

Tournament House and Wrigley Gardens
Chewing gum mogul William Wrigley commissioned the construction of his Pasadena residence in 1908. By 1914, construction of the Italian Renaissance–inspired mansion was complete. Used as a winter retreat, the ornate structure is seated on four and one-half acres along Orange Grove Boulevard. Today the mansion is home to the Pasadena Tournament of Roses Association® and is open to the public from February to August. During the annual Rose Parade®, the mansion hosts the Tournament of Roses Queen and her court. The grounds are superbly manicured and feature hundreds of roses, camellias, and other signature Pasadena species.

2 cups sugar
1 1/2 tablespoons all-purpose flour
1/2 teaspoon salt
1/2 cup (1 stick) butter or margarine, softened
3 eggs
1/2 cup evaporated milk
1 tablespoon vanilla extract
1 unbaked (9-inch) pie shell

Preheat the oven to 350 degrees. Mix the sugar, flour and salt in a mixing bowl. Add the butter and beat until crumbly. Add the eggs and beat until the sugar dissolves and the mixture begins to thicken. Stir in the evaporated milk and vanilla until blended using a spatula. Pour the filling into the pie shell and bake for 40 to 45 minutes or until set.

cook's note ■ Try these variations. For Chocolate Chess Pie, add 3 tablespoons baking cocoa to the dry ingredients. For Lemon Chess Pie, add 1/4 cup lemon juice and the grated zest of 1 lemon with the evaporated milk and vanilla.

south african melktert

A South African staple that can be made with or without the crust.

1 unbaked (9-inch) pie shell (optional)
1 cup all-purpose flour
2 teaspoons baking powder
1/4 teaspoon salt
1 cup sugar
1 tablespoon butter, melted
3 egg yolks
4 cups milk
1 teaspoon vanilla extract
3 egg whites
1 tablespoon cinnamon and sugar

Preheat the oven to 375 degrees. Grease a 9-inch pie plate if not using the pie shell. Sift the flour, baking powder and salt together. Combine the sugar and butter in a mixing bowl and beat until smooth. Add the egg yolks and beat until light in color. Stir in the flour mixture. Mix in the milk and vanilla.

Beat the egg whites in a mixing bowl until stiff peaks form. Fold the egg whites into the filling. Spoon the filling into the pie shell or greased pie plate and sprinkle with the cinnamon and sugar. Bake for 25 minutes. Reduce the oven temperature to 325 degrees and bake for 25 to 30 minutes longer or until the center of the pie appears set when lightly jiggled.

Mosaic Canyon

Mosaic Canyon in Death Valley National Park gets its name from a type of rock formation called Mosaic Breccia from the Italian word meaning fragments. These colorful rock fragments have become embedded in the marble walls of the canyon and worn smooth by countless floods. The canyon in western Death Valley is easily accessible by car from nearby Stovepipe Wells. The hike through the lower canyon and the main part of the upper canyon is short and easy enough for novices, and there are numerous side canyons that can be explored by more intrepid hikers.

Clockwise from left to right: Pumpkin Flan (page 180), Baja Tequila Taco Bar (page 140), Verde Chicken Enchiladas (page 126)

party menus

Highland Park Gateway
Teddy Sandoval, 2003
Implemented by Paul Polubinskas

City of Angels — Metro Arts Program

Commuters utilizing Southern California's Metro Rail System enjoy more than a safe and timely ride to their various destinations. In addition to the views of the landmarks dotting the routes and spectacular scenery of the ocean, mountains, and cityscapes alike, riders are treated to the artwork of numerous local artists whose visions, in the form of mosaics, sculptures, metalwork, murals, and paintings, await them at departure or arrival at the stations along the Red, Gold, Blue, and Green lines of the Metro Rail System.

As diverse as the artists themselves, these works of inspiration cover everything from the history of California, including the Indian cultures that dwelled here hundreds of years ago and the pioneering peoples who developed communities with their rich tapestries of culture, to the futuristic views of what may lie ahead for our great state. Even the whimsy and humor of our smallest citizens—our children—is celebrated. Each work is a statement of unity, diversity, community, and beauty.

Established in 1989, the Metro Arts Program was designed to include permanent and temporary artwork by artists selected by a peer review process with community consensus. Each original piece has been commissioned especially for its related site to enhance an engaging and pleasurable journey for the Metro Rail traveler.

Food photography sponsored by Nestlé USA
Mosaic photography sponsored by the 2005–2006 Finance Committee

après ski dinner

Christmas Pepper Jelly

Cream Cheese Biscuits

Fresh Lemon Herb Salad

Après Ski Chili

Cinnamon Bread Pudding with Hot Buttered Rum Sauce

asian evening

Asian Pork Lettuce Wraps

Sesame Salmon with Orange Miso Sauce

Shrimp Egg Rolls with Sweet-and-Sour Peach Sauce

Chinese Stir-Fried Beef

Bangkok Mussels with Red Curry Sauce

Shrimp Fried Rice

Asian Snow Peas

Philippine Food for the Gods

all-american barbecue

Layered Cheese Torta

Ultimate Quick and Easy Munchies

Lemon Basil Bread

Herb-Marinated Watermelon and Feta Cheese Salad

A Californian's Memphis Barbecue

Grilled Brazilian Beer Chicken

Fire-Roasted Artichokes

Texas Spicy Beans

Peach Cobbler in a Pinch

Peanut Butter Brownies

italian dinner

Garlic Pesto Goat Cheese Spread

Tuscan Bread Salad

Osso Buco

Orzo with Prosciutto and Asparagus

Zucchini Cake

california brunch

Bloody Marys (sidebar)

Pancetta Spinach Tart

Sweet-and-Spicy Bacon

Baked Strawberry-Stuffed French Toast

Rolls as You Like Them

Pear and Pomegranate Salad

Berry Blitz Torte

middle eastern celebration

Serve with pita bread.

Feta and Oregano Dip

Falafel with Tahini Dip

Cucumber Grape Salad

Tabbouleh

Easy Cheese Squares (Armenian Boerag)

Armenian Layered Lamb and Cabbage Casserole

Farina Squares

White Chocolate and Pistachio Cookies

Bloody Marys are the perfect opening for a brunch. Combine 2 cups vegetable juice cocktail, 2 cups tomato juice, the juice of 1 large lemon, 1½ tablespoons Worcestershire sauce, 1 heaping tablespoon prepared horseradish, 1½ pressed garlic cloves, 2 teaspoons ground pepper and ¼ teaspoon Tabasco sauce. Chill for 8 to 10 hours to enhance the flavor. For each Bloody Mary, mix one part vodka with three parts Bloody Mary mix. Pour over ice in glasses and garnish with a splash of lemon juice and a celery stalk. Increase the pepper and Tabasco sauce for a spicier beverage.

valentine's dinner for two

Ham and Cheese Crisps

Orange Poppy Seed Salad

French Chicken with Cream and Port

French Beans with Shallots

Sugar-Browned Potatoes

Poached Pears with Mascarpone Cheese

Cherries Jubilee

Pomegranate Granita

new year's cocktail party

Goat Cheese and Dried Apricots

Shrimp Angel Toasts

Spanish Olive and Pecan Dip

Cranberry Brie

Elegant Caviar Romanoff

Broiled Prosciutto-Wrapped Asparagus

Swedish Meatballs

Rosemary and Lemon Lamb Rib Chops

Italian Chicken Bites

Shrimp Cakes with Grilled Pineapple Salsa

Lemon Rosemary Crackers

Chocolate Peanut Butter Cheesecake

Cherry Cordials

White Chocolate Crunch

Walnut Dessert Bars

Lace Cookies

southern sip-and-see luncheon

*The Sip-and-See is a Southern tradition where
friends and family are invited to "sip" tea or maybe something
a little stronger and "see" the new bundle of joy.
It is usually held when the new mother and baby have had time to
recover from the hospital and to adjust to their new schedule.*

Smoked Trout in Endive

Hot Chicken Salad

Cheesy Herb Popovers

Fab Spinach Salad

Zucchini Pancakes

Cheesy Corn Grits

Sherried Macaroons

Pecan Lace Cookies with Lemon Ginger Filling

cinco de mayo

Serve with tortilla chips.

Easy Margaritas (sidebar)

Tortilla Soup

Verde Chicken Enchiladas

Baja Tequila Taco Bar

Pico de Gallo

Tomatillo Salsa Verde

Pineapple Mango Salsa

Pumpkin Flan

*What drink goes best
with Mexican food? Try
these Easy Margaritas.
Combine 1 can frozen
lime juice concentrate,
1/2 lime juice can
tequila, 1/4 lime juice
can Triple Sec and
ice in a blender.
Process to the desired
consistency. Pour into
salt-rimmed margarita
glasses and garnish
with lime wedges.*

surfer's luau

Serve with assorted grilled summer vegetables.

Greek Salsa with Toasted Pita Wedges

Tricolor Tomato Salad

Avocado Gazpacho

Apricot-Glazed Pork Loin with Tropical Salsa

Hawaiian Chicken Kabobs

Stuffed Tomatoes

Hula Bars

tapas buffet

Serve with assorted olives, cheeses, and sausages.

Sangria (sidebar)

Caprese Skewers

Dates Wrapped in Bacon

Greek Tartlets

Slow-Roasted Tomatoes with Chèvre and Arugula

Sea Scallops

Flank Steak Spirals

Lobster Quesadillas with Brie

Green Beans in Prosciutto

Braised Italian Cipollini Onions

oktoberfest

Serve with assorted German sausages, mustard, pickles, and good German beer.

Shrimp Dip

Warm German Potato Salad

Bavarian Beef

Brussels Sprouts with Bacon

Red Cabbage with Apples

Butternut Squash and Mashed Potatoes

Gingerbread with Lemon Curd

To prepare Sangria, combine one 750-milliliter bottle red wine, 1 cup fresh orange juice, 1/4 cup fresh lemon juice and 1 shot of your favorite brandy or Cognac. Add 3/4 cup sugar and stir until the sugar dissolves. Stir in sliced apples, sliced oranges and/ or sliced limes or sliced fresh fruit of your choice. Chill for 24 hours. To serve, mix equal parts of the Sangria and sparkling water and pour over ice in glasses. Do not add the sparkling water until just before serving.

california festivals

Southern California loves any excuse for a festival or celebration, and with the abundance of agriculture and cultural diversity, we have plenty of reasons to do just that. Festivals are not only fun, they provide an opportunity for education as well. Following is just a small sampling of some of our many Food and Cultural Festivals.

January/February

Chinese New Year Food and Cultural Faire, San Diego

Carrot Festival, Holtville

National Date Festival, Indio

March/April

Los Angeles County Irish Fair and Music Festival, Pomona

San Francisco Oyster & Beer Festival, San Francisco

Stockton Asparagus Festival, Stockton

California Poppy Festival, Lancaster

Santa Clarita Cowboy Festival, Newhall

Celebration of the Whales, Oxnard

Southern California Indian Storytelling Festival, Palm Springs

CubaFest, Santa Monica

May/June

Artichoke Festival, Castroville

Holland Festival, Long Beach

California Strawberry Festival, Oxnard

Cairo Carnivale, Glendale

July/August

"Reds, Whites, and Blues" California Wine Festival, Santa Barbara

California Peach Festival, Marysville

Southern California Indian Center Annual Powwow, Los Angeles

Obon Festival, Los Angeles

Persian Art and Cultural Family Festival, Santa Ana

Samoan Tafesilafa'i Festival, Long Beach

Caribbean Seabreeze Festival, Long Beach

Gilroy Garlic Festival, Gilroy

Oxnard Salsa Festival, Oxnard

Old Spanish Days Fiesta, Santa Barbara

Woofstock: A Festival of Dogs and People, Cardiff By the Sea

Tofu Festival, Little Tokyo, Los Angeles

Tomato Festival, Fairfield

July/August

Olive Festival, Paso Robles

African Marketplace and Cultural Faire, Mid-City LA

Sri Lanka Day, Santa Monica

San Gabriel Valley Greek Festival, Covina

September/October

Baja Splash Cultural Festival, Long Beach

Festival of Philippine Arts and Culture, San Pedro

Aloha Days Longboard Surf Contest and Hawaiian Festival, Hermosa Beach

Danish Days, Solvang

Brazilian Street Carnival, Long Beach

Los Angeles Jewish Festival, Woodland Hills

Santa Barbara Sandcastle Festival, Santa Barbara

Precious Cheese Feast of San Gennaro, Hollywood

Harvest and Grape Stomp Festival, Temecula

Ojai Renaissance and Pirate Faire, Ventura

Assyrian Cultural Festival, Ceres

Los Angeles Korean Festival, Mid-City LA

Kern Valley Turkey Vulture Festival, Weldon

Big Bear Lake Troutfest, Big Bear Lake

Old Pasadena Oktoberfest, Pasadena

Little Italy Festa, San Diego

California Avocado Festival, Carpinteria

Wild Wonderful Chocolate Festival, Oakhurst

Seaside Highland Games, Ventura

Calabasas Pumpkin Festival, Calabasas

California Lemon Festival, Goleta

Lobster Festival, Redondo Beach

Pismo Beach Clam Festival, Pismo Beach

Borrega Days Desert Festival, Borrego Springs

Julian Fall Apple Harvest, Julian

Pilgrim Festival, Claremont

Indio International Tamale Festival, Indio

Japanese Garden Festival, Descanso Gardens, La Canada Flintridge

cookbook committee

Cookbook Chair 05–06

Testing and Compilation
Florence "Flo" Friedgen

Cookbook Assistants 05–06

Carol Deeter

Susan Pippert

Chapter Chairs

Jean Shin Douglas

Stella Estevez

Martha Padgett

Susan Pippert

Patricia Plunkett

Kristen Todd

Kimberly Velazco

Barbara Williams

Nonrecipe Text

Martha Padgett

Writers

Teresa Foote, *Non JLP Volunteer*

Florence "Flo" Friedgen

Kristen Todd

Committee Members

Amy McConnell

Janine Sauer

Alma Apodaca, *Tasting Support/ 06–07 Cookbook Marketing*

Gina Calderon, *Active Advisor*

Jennifer Cargill, *President*

Bonnie DeWitt, *Sustaining Advisor*

Dana Jones, *Fundraising Director*

Mara Lague, *President-Elect*

Kathi Martinez, *Tasting Support/Center Stage Chair*

Vickie Reinhardt, *Tasting Support/Office Manager*

Rebecca Shukan, *Graphics Support/ Provisional Chair*

Katy Tafoya, *Tasting Support/ 06–07 Cookbook Marketing*

Provisional Interns

Renee Bischof

Monica Mihaly

Liza Palmer

Marie Plantard de St. Clair

Cookbook Chair 04–05

Recipe Submission and Foundations
Florence "Flo" Friedgen

Cookbook Committee 04–05

Susan Pippert, *Cookbook Assistant*

Page Curtin

Patricia Plunkett

Valerie Russell

Patti Sano

Rema Sarkissian

Kathleen Seguin

Gwinn Volen

Barbara Williams

Allison Withers

Mary Anne Borovicka, *Sustaining Advisor*

Noelle Barmann, *Fundraising Director*

Jennifer Cargill, *President-Elect*

Sarah Horner, *President*

Cookbook Chair 03–04

Theme Development and Foundations
Kimberlee Carlson

Cookbook Committee 03–04

Florence "Flo" Friedgen, *Cookbook Assistant*

Cardin Bradley

Mary Falkenbury

Christine Franke

Maureen Mitchell

Susan Pippert

Tracy Rudolph

Gina Salzman

Patti Sano

Rema Sarkissian

Nicole Von Thaden

Mary Anne Borovicka, *Sustaining Advisor*

Carol Liebau, *Fundraising Director*

Sarah Horner, *President-Elect*

Mary Snider, *President*

underwriters

Sponsors

Mary and John Snider

Donors

Jennifer and Sam Cargill

Bonnie and John DeWitt

Kandis and Jonathan Jaffrey

Susan McDonnell

Nestlè USA

Ginny and Gene Noll

Theresa and Kashif Sheikh

Supporters

Bill and Claire Bogaard

Avery Dennison

Betsy Farhat

Alya Haq

Amy Hotmer

Tiffany Kim

Sarah Rogers Krappman

Mara Lague

Amy and David Lamb

Brenda and Steve O'Neil

Tiffany Pang

Joyce Sakonju

Laura Scarsi

Cathy Woolway

Contributors

Alice Brodhead

Clairbourn School

Jean, Andy and Alexander Douglas

Georgianna B. Erskine

Mr. and Mrs. George C. Good

Sherry Gray

Hahn & Hahn LLP

Jennifer Higginbotham

Dana and Albert Jones

Charlene Liebau

Pam Massar

Julie Mayo

Harriet Plunkett

Mr. and Mrs. Eric Reed

Karie Reynolds

Helen Spitzer

Mary Ulin

Friends

Jo Jeanne Angeloff

Barbara and Dick Baptie

Jennifer and Reed Bender

Cynthia B. Coleman

Diane Parker Coyer

James M. Crabtree, D.D.S.

Wendy Currier

Jane Fall

Brooke Larsen Garlock

Patricia and Wallace Hage

Carol Hoover

Nancy F. Kennedy

Phillip and Lois Matthews

Suzanne McLean

Jeannette M. Muirhead

Ann Murphy

Elizabeth Nesbitt

Jennifer Odermatt

Vickie and Steve Reinhardt

Bettina Wulfing Rosenfeld

Linda J. Roth

Maureen Schimmoller

Eileen Reekie Schoelkopf

Leslie Sharp

Mrs. Robert D. Volk

Kelly Watson

Sally S. Wood

recipe contributors

Salwa Abdel-Aal

Alma Apodaca

Teresa Aubert
and Family

Maria Azuela

Xochilt Baez

Betty Jane Barringer

Ruth Bedevian

Linda Berard

Louise Barbic

Kim Besen

Best Years Preschool,
Staff and Families of

Karen Betson

Michele Biggar

Anita Blauvelt

Carol Blauvelt

Lisa Bogaard

Mayra Bonilla

Cynthia Bradley

Britta Bucholz

Sandra Butler

Gina Calderon

Toni Callahan

Sanaa Canella

Kylie Carbajal

Kimberlee Carlson

Pamela Case-Gustafson

Evan Casey

Michele Ciampa

Beverly Clark

Marie Cleaves

Adrian Brooks Collins

Joanna Crawford

Chrisy Currier

Page Curtin

Amy Dahlberg

Sandy Daniels

Ann Davenport

Vida de Belen

Carol Deeter

Jeff Deeter

Lori Deeter

Karen Delgado

Terry Deluca

Bonnie DeWitt

Cordelia Donnelly

Jean Shin-Douglas

Julie Echols

Carrie Engemann

Stella Estevez

Mary Falkenbury

Jane Fall

Betsy Farhat

Sally Farhat

Doris Ferguson

Ceil and Karen Fisher

Lisa Fishman

Teresa Foote

Amanda Friedgen

Dianne Friedgen

Ellie Friedgen

Elliot Friedgen

Florence Friedgen

Mark Friedgen

Mark Friedgen, Jr.

Rita Gaulding

Linda Genovese

Peggy Geragos

Leigh Gluck

Lynn Goforth

Jacqueline Goodman

Sherry Gray

Evelyn Greathouse

Amanda Guillot

Amie Lu Haake

Kelley Hannafin

Marilyn Henderson

Bryce Hendry

Ellen Hendry

Ian Hendry

Natalie Hendry

Mrs. William Holbrook

Michell Ahnstedt Horn

Maria Horner

Sally Horner

Sarah Horner

Amy Hotmer

Shiao-Wen Huang

Debby Inak

Sara Ingrassia

Alex Isenberg

Jillian Johnson

Rebecca Johnson

Andrea Jones

Patricia Kaminski

Roza Karakashian

Shakeh Karakashian

Elizabeth Karr

Muna Karram

Irene Keipert

Nancy Kennedy

Mara Lague

Susan Leslie

Jason Lewis

Sheridan Link

Christiana Liu

John Luke

Susan Maclean

Suzanne McLean

Simran Malhotra

Kathi Martinez

Mary Mason-Leskowitz

Micki Mass

Valerie McAndrews

Carri McClure-Miller

Darren Miller

Amy McConnell

Tori Mordecai

Didi Mumford

Monty Najera

Bruce Nye

Lynn Nye

Jennifer O'Rafferty

Martha Padgett

Mrs. Gerald Patterson

Samantha Pietsch

Susan Pippert

Harriet and William
Plunkett

Patricia Plunkett

Melanie Polk

Alex Quezada

Joe Quintanilla

Pam Ragus

Karie Reynolds

Ann Rice

Allison Robinson

Anne Rogers

Lainie Rose-Miller

Bettina Rosenfeld

Elisabeth Rosenson

Linda Roth

Carolyn Rowland

Charles Rowland

Michael Rowland

Virginia Rowland

Valerie Russell

Joyce Sakonju

Elizabeth Saldebar

Patti Sano

Janine Sauer

Joanne Scribner

John Scribner

Kathleen Seguin

Kerry Shantz

Martha Shenkenberg

Shepherd of the Valley
Lutheran School,
Staff and Families of

Kim Shirley

Rebecca Shukan

Linda Sly

Smart Post Sound

David Smugar

Anna Walker Stillman

Katy Tafoya

Jessica Theis

Kristen Todd

Theresa Thomas

Flo Uhlhorn

Kimberly Velazco

Gwinn Volen

Anne Wagner

Bill Wesley

Billy Wesley

Debbie Wesley

Kaitlyn Wesley

Ryan Wesley

Beatrice Wier

Ford Wilkinson

Lucy Wilkinson

Barbara Williams

Allison Withers

Mary Brent Wright

Alex Zucco

acknowledgments

Nick Boswell

Nick Boswell has been operating his photography studio in San Marino, California, since the 1990s. His full-service studio photographs children, families, and events, and his impressive list of subjects includes many prominent area families, as well as politicians, international dignitaries, and celebrities. Nick also provides food photography for several prominent area restaurants.

Kevin Isacsson

Kevin Isacsson, CEC, is a Certified Executive Chef by The American Culinary Federation and former president of The Channel Islands Chefs Association. A 1980 alumnus of The Culinary Institute of America, Chef Isacsson has over thirty years of food service experience in hotels, resorts, restaurants, and clubs. Currently, Chef Isacsson is Executive Chef at The Athenaeum, the university club for the California Institute of Technology in Pasadena, California.

Camille Renk

Camille Renk is a Los Angeles-based food stylist who has also worked as a chef in the United States and Europe. Her artistic vision together with her culinary and art training have shaped her unique approach to food styling. She has broad knowledge of world food and works with a mixture of technical challenges for still advertising and packaging with the creative imaginative requirements for editorial and brochures. Camille's portfolio showcases a wide range of skills and culinary knowledge along with her creative, innovative flair and passion for beauty. Her versatility and positive approach make her much in demand. www.camilleskitchen.com.

Derrick D. Spears

Derrick Spears graduated from The Culinary Institute of America, Hyde Park, New York, in 1993. Since that time, Chef Spears has gained extensive food service experience in hotels and restaurants across the United States where he has composed award-winning menus and hosted many featured chef dinners that have allowed him to work closely with many of the leaders of the culinary world. Currently, Chef Spears is Executive Sous-Chef at The Athenaeum, the university club for the California Institute of Technology in Pasadena, California.

recipe index

spreads
chicken chutney spread, 23
cranberry brie, 21
elegant caviar romanoff, 22
garlic pesto goat cheese spread, 20
layered cheese torta, 23
olive tapenade, 14
salmon and pesto pâté, 24
salmon pâté, 24
white bean and basil spread, 20

squash
butternut squash and mashed
potatoes, 156
butternut squash soufflé, 158
panko-coated fried squash
blossoms, 158
squash rice casserole, 157

stews
argentine beef stew in a
pumpkin shell, 96
cabbage patch stew, 95
crab cioppino, 97

strawberry
baked strawberry-stuffed
french toast, 49
strawberry cloud, 176

strawberry grand marnier sauce, 49
strawberry rhubarb mousse, 175

tomatoes
balsamic-marinated lamb with
tomatoes and feta cheese, 47
curried tomato halves, 159
penne with sun-dried tomatoes,
capers and olives, 163
slow-roasted tomatoes with
chèvre and arugula, 27
stuffed tomatoes, 159
sun-dried tomato basil pesto, 24
sun-dried tomato pesto, 12
tricolor tomato salad, 66

trout
lemon dill trout in foil, 132
smoked trout in endive, 15

turkey
armenian layered lamb and
cabbage casserole, 110
turkey burgers with
caramelized onions, 127
turkey cottage pie, 128
turkey matzo ball soup, 90
turkey mole soup, 91
turkey waldorf salad, 72

veal
caribbean balsamic-glazed
veal chops, 109
french-canadian tourtière, 106
osso buco, 108
roasted red pepper and
raisin sauce, 109

vegetables. see also individual kinds
baked heirloom beets with
balsamic vinegar, 149
brussels sprouts with bacon, 150
southern greens, 152
swiss chard with orange
gremolata, 151
traditional slow-cooked greens, 152

zucchini
asian pork lettuce wraps, 29
cuban vegetable chili, 84
sausage and vegetable
frittata, 41
zucchini cake, 188
zucchini pancakes, 159
zucchini stuffed with
italian sausage, 118

mosaic index

appetizers ■ Untitled, Millard Sheets, 1970 (Families enjoying recreational activities at a local beach);
2600 Wilshire Boulevard, Santa Monica, California

breakfast, brunch & breads ■ Los Angeles Child Guidance Mosaic, June Edmonds, 2005;
3031 South Vermont Avenue, Los Angeles, California

salads & dressings ■ Indians and Yuccas Near Indian Hill, Millard Sheets, 1969; 393 West Foothill Boulevard,
Claremont, California

chili, soups & stews ■ The Story of Santa Cruz in 4 Different Mosaics, Carole Choucair Oueijan, 2005;
Harbor Beach Promenade, 2222 East Cliff Drive, Santa Cruz, California

main dishes ■ The Will to Progress (El Deseo de Progresar), Ricardo Mendoza, 2004; Metropolitan Transit Authority
Blue Line: Firestone Station, Los Angeles, California

vegetables & side dishes ■ Untitled, Millard Sheets, 1977 (Scenes from the rural lifestyle of an earlier era);
17107 Ventura Boulevard, Encino, California

desserts ■ Watts Towers, Simon Rodia, 1921 to 1954; 1765 East 107th Street, Los Angeles, California

party menus ■ Highland Park Gateway, Teddy Sandoval, 2003, Implemented by Paul Polubinskas;
Metropolitan Transit Authority Gold Line: Southwest Museum Station, Highland Park, California

cover insert ■ Tribute to Freedom, Annmarie Socash, 2002; Fairplex, Pomona, California; Courtesy of the
Los Angeles County Fair Association

for additional copies of

california MOSAIC

Please contact:
The Junior League of Pasadena, Inc.
149 South Madison Avenue
Pasadena, California 91101
Cookbook Hotline: 626.796.0162
www.jrleaguepasadena.org

$29.95 plus $6.00 postage and handling for the first book
and $1.00 for each additional book. Gift wrap additional $3.00 per book.
California residents add 8.25% tax.

The Junior League of Pasadena, Inc., accepts Visa and MasterCard.
Make personal checks payable to The Junior League of Pasadena, Inc.
Please include your e-mail address if interested in
future communications about the League's cookbooks.